A PLAGUE
UPON
HUMANITY

A PLAGUE UPON HUMANITY

The Secret Genocide of Axis
Japan's Germ Warfare Operation

DANIEL BARENBLATT

HarperCollins*Publishers*

HarperCollins books may be purchased for educational, business, or sales promotional use. For information, please write: Special Markets Department, HarperCollins Publishers Inc., 10 East 53rd Street, New York, NY 10022.

FIRST EDITION

Designed by Joseph Rutt

Photographs courtesy of Li Zhong Yuen; Museum of the Chinese People's Anti-Japan War, Beijing, People's Republic of China

Printed on acid-free paper

Library of Congress Cataloging-in-Publication Data
Barenblatt, Daniel
    A plague upon humanity : the secret genocide of Axis Japan's germ warfare
    operation / by Daniel Barenblatt.—1st ed.
        p.   cm.
    Includes index.
    ISBN 0-06-018625-9
        1. World War, 1939–1945—Biological warfare—Japan. 2. World War,
    1939–1945—Campaigns—China. 3. World War, 1939–1945—Atrocities—Japan.
    4. Human experimentation in medicine—Japan. 5. Genocide—Japan. 6. Japan.
    Rikugun. Kantågun. Butai, Dai 731. 7. World War, 1939–1945—Regimental
    histories—Japan. I. Title.
    D810.B3B37   2003
    940.54'05'0952—dc21   2003051051

04 05 06 07 08 ❖/RRD   10 9 8 7 6 5 4 3 2 1

For the Chinese, Korean, and Russian people

and all other victims of biological warfare,

and for my father and mother

CONTENTS

PREFACE

WHEN, IN THE EARLY AUTUMN OF 1994, I STARTED TO EXPLORE the topic of Japanese biological warfare and human experimentation, it seemed at first that I had delved into one of the most inaccessible, lonely areas of the past that history had to offer. I was moved to begin my research after watching a television news segment about a traveling historical exhibit that had become a sensation in Japan. It chronicled the secret history of Imperial Japan's biological warfare program during the 1930s and 1940s, led by a physician and microbiologist named Shiro Ishii under the aegis of a research facility called Unit 731. Over a period of fourteen years, that unit metastasized into a network of state-sponsored biological terror and mass murder, whose death camp and laboratory locations ranged across the vast expanse of Japan's Asia-Pacific empire. Man-made epidemics were strategically created by some of the top Japanese civilian scientists, university professors and medical doctors among them. Germs were deployed as invisible, untraceable, and silent weapons against unsuspecting human populations.

The exhibit—complete with relics of equipment used by Unit 731 troops and scientists, and appearances by elderly Japanese men and women who confessed to their participation in the secret experiments—was drawing huge crowds as it moved from city to city. At the time, I was a graduate student in experimental cognitive psychology with a strong interest in the history of science. I was curious about this bio-war program, about which I'd heard nothing before, and I decided to try to dig up what I could find on the matter in New York City. Within months, I found myself spending long hours at the library poring over a fragile old tome that I had discovered while searching through the stacks for books about biological and chemical warfare. It bore the less-than-beguiling title of *Materials on the Trial of Former Servicemen of the Japanese Army Charged with Manufacturing and Employing Bacteriological Weapons*. Until I came along in the mid-1990s, the last time someone had checked it out had been in 1979.

Materials on the Trial of Former Servicemen of the Japanese Army Charged with Manufacturing and Employing Bacteriological Weapons is, at 535 pages, a partial transcript of a 1949 Soviet war crimes trial of Japanese scientists and military leaders captured in Manchuria in the closing days of World War II. The trial was held in the city of Khabarovsk, in the Russian Far East, where those in the dock were accused of waging germ warfare and conducting inhuman experiments on their prisoners: men, women, and children. The book's graphic details belied its obscurity and immediately posed a clear contradiction and a series of challenges to me, both morally and intellectually.

The contradiction that I found in its testimony is why the acts exposed in great detail by witnesses, and confessed to by some of the bio-war ringleaders themselves, should remain so unknown to today's educators and the public at large. I searched out other available sources of information. The Japanese atrocities bear a striking resemblance to the well-known experiments of the Nazi doctors in the Holocaust, and were carried out before and then concurrent with those crimes.

Yet unlike the German experiments, the facts of Imperial Japan's biological warfare have remained hidden from public awareness. I decided to do what I could to amend this situation by making readers aware of what happened in the war years and in the postwar cover-up. I wanted also, with this popular history (a strange-sounding phrase, perhaps, to describe the chronicling of heinous acts), to convey to a wide audience the profoundly important scientific knowledge that came of these events and the equally profound evil that this knowledge represents in a world where, unfortunately, the past is often prologue.

As I write this in the spring of 2003, mainstream concern about biological weapons is at unprecedented levels. Back in 1994 I would have described the subject as an esoteric back-alley study in the fields of microbiology, weapons development, and the history of science. Ironically, part of what spurred me in the early stages of my research was a deep concern that such repellent war crimes had languished in obscurity and remained unknown to the world at large. But I also believed, optimistically, that humanity would not allow this story to remain untold. A number of exhibits and academic books on the subject had begun to appear by the mid-1990s, in Japan, China, and the United States.

Hoping to make my own contribution, I traveled across America and to Asia, conducting interviews with American ex-POW survivors of Japanese bio-war experiments, meeting with Chinese survivors of the germ warfare attacks, making contacts around the world, and collecting documents. Over the past nine years I have witnessed signs that this dark piece of history is finally beginning to move into public consciousness. In 1997 a lawsuit was commenced against the government of Japan for restitution to relatives of those who died from infectious microbes spread in Japanese bio-war assaults, or who were killed as prisoners in human experiments. That suit, along with the traveling Unit 731 exhibit and subsequent media attention in Japan and China, has spurred activism and grassroots calls for justice in those countries. As a consequence, an awareness of the destruction wrought by Japan's biological warfare program is beginning to emerge in the United States as well.

At the same time there has in the past decade been a sea change in scholarly understanding of Japan's biological warfare campaigns. For decades the conventional wisdom had held that several thousand prisoners were killed in gruesome studies at secret bases in Manchuria, and that a number of Chinese civilians, perhaps a few hundred or so, were also killed in so-called field tests of germ weapons. It was in these terms and numbers that the Japanese military's germ warfare program was usually explained to an audience—when there was an audience for the subject.

But the latest research, revealed in this book, shows that in two bio-war campaigns alone, those in Yunnan Province in southern China and Shandong Province in the north, more than 400,000 people died of cholera. Special army forces waged germ attacks across China, at countless locations under Imperial Japan's heel of occupation, and even in unoccupied regions that were subject to fly-overs by Japanese planes. Plague literally rained down upon people's heads, sprayed from special bio-war air team planes of the military; cholera, typhoid, dysentery, anthrax, paratyphoid, glanders, and other pestilences infected their food, drinking wells, crops, and livestock.

As of 2002, historical researchers in China had estimated the number of people killed by Japanese germ warfare and human experiments to be approximately 580,000. This is the figure that was presented and mutually agreed upon at the International Symposium on the Crimes of Bacteriological Warfare, a conference on the subject of Japanese bio-war attended by scholars and investigative journalists, held in December 2002 in the city of Changde, Hunan Province. Yet even the total of 580,000, large as it is, must be considered only a preliminary accounting, as it stems from the summing up of mortality totals from places where researchers are still conducting house-to-house interviews with survivors, victims' relatives, and eyewitnesses, in the growing number of investigations that are now taking place throughout China. And each set of interviews continues to bring forth additional cases, incidents, and outbreaks to be reckoned.

The number of physicians and scientists involved in these germ attacks and in the human experiments totaled more than 20,000. Most of them were biomedical professionals in the civilian sector of society, men of healing who were recruited into the secret bio-war projects by Ishii and his colleagues in the military. With their expertise, the Japanese army exterminated large numbers of Asian people through its covert harnessing of the ancient and dreaded scourge of infectious disease. The objective was to depopulate, make miserable, and demoralize the Chinese people through the spreading of vast man-made epidemics in strategic areas. The microbe became an instrument of imperial rule. Comparisons with the genocides of Japan's ally and ideological brother, Nazi Germany, are entirely appropriate. By the standards of today and those of 1948, when the United Nations recognized and codified the term "genocide" as "calculated acts of human extermination resulting in the mass murder of enormous numbers of civilians, targeting a certain population group," the Japanese germ warfare program more than meets the definition.

Yet after the war many of the doctors and scientists who orchestrated Japan's bio-war program returned to their former lives in academia and medicine. Some of them attained great status and wealth. Why it happened underscores the need for disclosure from the Japanese and American governments of the classified data they hold on the matter. How it happened is explained in this book.

Today, as advances in biotechnology and genetic engineering often progress without public scrutiny, Japan's 13-year biological campaign in the period from 1932 to 1945 has left a legacy that is as much part of the fabric of the future as it is of the past. This generation and the next must know of the story of Unit 731, and how such a thing could come to pass, so that it never comes to pass again.

ACKNOWLEDGMENTS

IN THE YEARS SPENT WRITING THIS BOOK, THE MANY FRIENDS I have made and the inspiring people I have encountered along the way have made it all an uplifting and richly rewarding experience. Coming to know these individuals has more than compensated for the heavy impact of gathering such intensely disturbing knowledge. Foremost among them is Sam Chen, who has always been there to assist with organizational details, translations, and other support since we first met when the Unit 731 exhibit came to Lafayette Street in 1998. I don't believe it is too much of a stretch to say that the world owes him a great debt of gratitude for all he has done to help get the truth out on this and other subjects.

For his encouragement and counsel I would like to thank John William Powell, a journalistic pioneer on this topic. I would also like to express my admiration of Mr. Powell, a true hero for the bravery and resoluteness he displayed years ago in the face of McCarthyite government harassment. I also thank Gregory Rodriquez and his father, the late Gregory Rodriquez, Sr., for their interviews and devotion to the cause of prying open the U.S. vaults of secret files on Unit 731 in their efforts to determine exactly what happened to the American prisoners of war.

I shall always fondly remember the late Sheldon H. Harris, author of the important work *Factories of Death* and a pioneering scholar. He was a warm and witty man who was unstinting in his moral support, kind words, and helpful suggestions to me, and I miss him.

For her great assistance in helping me to obtain source material, providing interpretations, and always being there to lend an ear, I extend a special thanks to my friend Wang Xuan. Her remarkable strength and energy would seem to certify her as being something more than a brilliant and sensitive woman; indeed, she may qualify as one of the primal forces of nature.

Others who generously provided help with translations from the Chinese and Japanese languages include Dr. Kevin Chiang, Christine Xue, Jenny Liu, and Fuyuko Nishisato.

I feel quite fortunate to have as my literary agent Susan Rabiner, who did some great work in getting this project off the ground and steering it through to completion. I would also like to thank Tim Duggan, my editor at HarperCollins, for his deft and generous support at key intervals.

Those who made significant contributions in helping me collect source material for both the book and a film project include the members of the New York Alliance in Memory of Victims of the Nanking Massacre (AMVNM), in particular Tzuping Shao, Patricia Loo, and Theresa Wang. I also thank Dr. Ray Ge, Syoji Kondo, Art Campbell, Arthur Christie, Stephen Endicott, Nancy Tong, Christine Choy, David Irving, Ken Bowser, and Sue Edwards.

Finally, I thank the people who assisted with their valuable editorial contributions and insights into the myriad issues involved in this book, or who provided other kinds of support and courtesy to the author: Lisa Chase, Iris Chang, Christian Gough, Jean Fox Tree, Alison Rogers, Lloyd Barenblatt, Li ZongYuan, James Yin, Tong Yuanzhong, Ralph Blumenthal, Rabbi Abraham Cooper, and Yoshimi Yoshida.

INTRODUCTION

In the East Asia of the 1930s, one of humanity's worst fears came true. It materialized in a manner beyond the most alarming visions of science fiction. The history has remained little known for decades afterward, and key facts have been suppressed. Now more information is coming to light, and little by little, as public awareness grows, the full understanding of this history seems likely to have a profound effect on our understanding of the relation between technology and society, and the depths to which human beings can sink.

> Toward the end of August in 1942, the Unit 731 and other biological operations troops disseminated cholera cultures in the central district of Jiangshan and surrounding rural villages. Many different methods were used to scatter bacteria. One was to drop cholera cultures in wells to infect people who drank water from them. Others included injecting cholera bacteria into ripe fruits and distributing cholera-infested rice cakes and other food items.
>
> Cholera-infested food was either directly handed to local residents or mixed in baskets of vegetables, which were left under trees along the roads or in front of farmhouses. In either case, Japanese soldiers were cowardly enough to put on everyday Chinese clothes and disguised themselves as Chinese civilians or soldiers of the People's

Army to execute the biological warfare program. In Jiang-shan, at least 80 people were killed in germ warfare. I also lost one of my nephews and two of my nieces.

These are the words of Peize Xue, himself a victim and sur-vivor of the Imperial Japanese Army's biological warfare within the territory they occupied in Zhejiang Province, East Central China. From 1931 until the nation's surrender in August 1945, Japan's military and its affiliated civilian medical researchers con-ceived, developed, and used biological weapons on a massive scale. They began the first confirmed use of scientifically orga-nized germ warfare in history, and expanded these operations to range across China and other Asian nations to a level that would eventually kill more than half a million civilians.

Mr. Xue is one of the group of 180 Chinese who are relatives of people who died in Japanese biological warfare attacks and secret experiments, and who have filed a high-profile class-action lawsuit against the government of Japan, seeking both compensa-tion and an official government apology, on behalf of themselves, their family members, and the 2,100 people they have docu-mented as having been killed by germ warfare in the plaintiffs' home districts of China. The compensation claimed for suffering was for an amount in yen equal to $83,500 each in damages.

That suit, which commenced in 1997, resulted in court pro-ceedings and a trial that lasted until August 2002, when the Japanese court rendered its verdict rejecting compensation claims or an apology even as the judges admitted that Japan did in fact kill the plaintiffs' family members and enormous numbers of Chi-nese with germ weapons. In the spring of 2003 the Chinese, refusing to accept this verdict, filed an appeal to a higher-level court, as the legal process goes on.

"There were a number of laboratories inside Unit 731 and each focused on producing a different kind of pathogenic germ.

For example, the Ejima team was producing the dysentery bacillus, the Tabei team typhoid, the Setogawa team cholera and so on. My job was to breed the germs as well as to handle the tools used in the process." So reads a confessional statement by Japanese World War II veteran Yoshio Shinozuka, describing the preparations inside a secret laboratory and human experiment prison complex for a 1939 biological warfare mission. In this mission, deadly bacteria were thrown into a river at the border between Russia and the area of northeastern China then occupied by Imperial Japan, and commonly referred to as Manchuria. Shinozuka, 76 years old at the time he wrote this statement, submitted it in 1997 as a "Japanese testifier" for the litigants in the Tokyo civil trial. He is one of the many Japanese veterans who have confessed to acts of biological human experiments and warfare and who have revealed intimate details of the inner workings of Japan's vast and technologically advanced "Secret of Secrets," as its own architect, Shiro Ishii, called it. The secret was the military network that refined disease microbes for their lethality through testing on human guinea-pig prisoners—some of them children and infants—and strategically deployed the germs as disease weapons of mass killing. Many other medical experiments unrelated to germ warfare were conducted on the prisoners—studies involving human dehydration, starvation, frostbite, air pressure, animal-to-human blood transfusions, and a raft of other horrors that used human beings as lab rats.

The prisoners of the Japanese became completely dehumanized in a death camp system of testing for biological and chemical weapons development. Stripped of their identities, they were forced to wear numbered uniforms and cards containing each inmate's biomedical particulars. Tens of thousands of these people disappeared, rounded up by the secret police, without family or friends knowing what had happened to them. Only now are they achieving at least one kind of liberation, as they are emerging from a decades-long prison of invisibility in history's memory. It is my hope that as this book helps spread awareness, their suffering will ultimately have a greater meaning and triumph.

As an author and researcher into these events, I continually find myself asking the obvious question, no matter how many times I go over the material: How is it that this startling information is not common knowledge, as is the Holocaust and the experiments of the Nazi doctors? Why was I not taught about this in high school or college? Why weren't my teachers taught about this? It can't be because there is no stomach for it. The facts and implications of Axis Japan's secret program immediately call to mind the medical experimentation on Jews, Gypsies, and other prisoners of Axis Germany, which have become common knowledge and a reference point for the definition of medical atrocity. Their revelation led to the Nuremberg Code, established in 1947, setting ethical requirements for the use of human subjects in experimentation.

Yet until the 1990s almost nothing at all was written or discussed publicly about the Japanese bio-war crimes. The entire wide-ranging program is now often called simply Unit 731, in shorthand form, after its central headquarters near the city of Harbin in Manchuria. But this designation belies the fact that Unit 731–affiliated stations in the city of Nanking (Unit 1644), or Beijing (Unit 1855), or Changchun (Unit 100), or in any one of a large number of other branch experimental detachments and battalions of the army, wreaked lethal epidemics at many locations across occupied China and other Asian nations. The civilian victims killed in Japan's human experiment prisons included women, children, and even infants. They were largely Chinese, Russian, Mongolian, and Korean. There are also cases of Australian, British, and American POWs being experimented on and killed.

The Japanese military used a variety of methods to disseminate their laboratory-bred microorganisms. Specially fitted airplanes and elite air squadrons were employed to spray insects and jellied bacterial compounds. Plague-infected fleas were raised by the millions and released on unsuspecting villages and cities; so too were disease-carrying rats, dogs, horses, and birds. Bacteria-containing bombs made of fragmenting ceramic and glass were dropped on populated areas, balloons laden with lethal germs were sent aloft, and anthrax-carrying feathers were spread about farms and villages. Tainted vaccine injections were administered to children, and poisoned food was handed out to hungry Chinese people by smiling soldiers and physicians of the occupying power. In these ways and others, Imperial Japan's man-made epidemics caused the suffering and deaths of adults, children, and infants.

The Japanese plague makers were not solely military men; they were also many of the country's best and brightest doctors of the medical and biological research community who coldly violated every ethical precept of the healing profession. Instead they applied their considerable talents to running an enormous network—an assembly line, really—of human experimentation in the pursuit of scientific goals completely untethered to morality. For Imperial Japan, germ warfare was cheap in terms of budget expenditure and the raw materials needed, frightening, and, under the right conditions, extremely effective at killing large numbers of people and causing social disruption. Germ warfare was also, importantly, deniable.

It is in the nature of biological weapons that they function as stealthy and invisible units of murder, as living microscopic creatures that infect human beings, silently and without warning. As such, they are also an application of science that turns life against life in such a way that may be easily blamed by its perpetrators on a "natural outbreak," or merely an "emerging," previously unknown disease.

What the Unit 731 network accomplished remains coveted military information because of this deniability, coupled with the potential of germ warfare epidemics to cause mass death efficiently and inexpensively—a key goal of any expansionist state aiming to conquer other nations and peoples.

In these times, with the rapidly advancing state of biotechnology, concomitant with the crafting of ever more insidious and destructive weaponry, the obvious questions become even more imperative: Exactly what happened? How can we make sure that it never happens again?

That these crimes have occurred is a sordid and dismaying fact of history. That the human experiments and large-scale biological warfare have been denied and marginalized for six decades constitutes a second crime against humanity and a crime against history itself.

In retrospect, it seems this need not have been the case. While Americans acting in the Tokyo war crimes trial of 1946–48 suppressed evidence regarding the atrocities of the Unit 731 system, there *was* a very public war crimes trial, held in the Soviet Union city of Khabarovsk in 1949, at which twelve Japanese bio-war-complicit officials were convicted. The Khabarovsk proceedings constitute neither a mere show trial nor an exercise in false propaganda. Similar and corroborating confessions by surrendered Japanese officers, attesting to biological warfare and atrocious human experiments on prisoners, were also submitted to the Tokyo war crimes trial. And yet the revelations remained buried in the docket, and not one individual was charged with biological or chemical warfare crimes at these hearings in Japan, which the press had dubbed "the Nuremberg Trial of the East."

Meanwhile the Khabarovsk trial results were publicly dismissed as false by the head of Allied occupation forces in Japan, General Douglas MacArthur, and by the government of the United States. General MacArthur knew the truth, of course. He had stated bluntly in a 1946 cable to U.S. Army headquarters in Washington, D.C. (now declassified), that "human prisoners were used in experiments" in Manchuria. On December 27, 1949, however, the *New York Times* reported that MacArthur's headquarters, in its response to press releases from the ongoing Khabarovsk trial of Unit 731 personnel, had affirmed "that the Japanese had done some experimentation with animals but that there was no evidence they ever had used human beings." The subsequent willful amnesia created a decades-long loss of vital history and led to needless suffering by the victims. This postwar complicity of the United States and its Western allies itself also constitutes a crime against humanity.

There is yet a third crime to consider: the success and prosperity of the thousands of biological warfare–perpetrating Japanese doctors. In a just and rational world, one would expect them to serve prison terms or be executed for their genocidal atrocities, as were many of the Nazi war criminals. Yet in the years after 1945 they headed not for a courtroom dock to face their victims, or a jail cell, but instead for plush, influential positions in the dean's offices of major universities or the corporate boardrooms of pharmaceutical companies. Hundreds of those physicians and microbiologists, guilty of the most heinous acts of medical atrocity, filled top positions at postwar Japan's most prestigious universities, hospitals, and medical institutions. Their stained past remained hidden to the general public of Japan but known to many in the establishment.

Ironically, the world is finally waking up to the existence and enormity of the Japanese biological warfare of the 1930s and 1940s just as we find ourselves facing an unprecedented number of newspaper headlines, magazine articles, books, and U.S. government statements on various alleged threats of biological warfare and bio-terrorism. The fatal mailings in September through December 2001 of powdered anthrax-laced letters within the United States—attacks that killed five people, caused eleven to contract pulmonary anthrax through inhalation, and made eleven others contract the skin form of anthrax—gripped the nation in fear and resulted in the mass distribution of antibiotics and the irradiation of mail at postal sites to kill the anthrax bacteria inside envelopes. The perpetrators of these lethal anthrax attacks remain at large and unidentified by the authorities.

Yet even with the anthrax mailings, there has been barely any reference in the media, in all the many news reports and discussion programs, to the historical antecedent of the Japanese germ attacks against Chinese civilians—attacks that included the spreading of anthrax. The survivors of the germ warfare, now elderly and still residing in the same villages bacterially besieged so long ago, in some cases still bear the distinctive skin sores and lesions of the Japanese weapons.

This book attempts both to bring to light what is known about the germ genocide committed by Imperial Japan, and to account for the sources of such intense evil and those factors that allowed this crime to escape justice and worldwide exposure. To this end, one must consider the enabling social and psychological factors behind the complete inversion of medical ethics and the most basic kind of human morality in the pursuit of military advancement, unfettered scientific discovery, and domination over others.

Had the Holocaust remained hidden from public sight and knowledge until now, the reality of the mass death camps, gas chambers, and grotesque medical experiments organized around principles of eugenics and genetic extermination of entire ethnic groups might seem like nightmarish science fiction. Many would doubtless refuse to believe in it. Yet the Nazi campaign aspiring to the extermination of the Jewish people and those belonging to other targeted groups has expanded modern thinking to the point that we recognize that the most rational and brilliant minds, planning and acting in secrecy, without fear of onlookers glimpsing the actions taken on their prisoners, are indeed capable of the most unthinkable and grotesque acts against humanity.

While the Japanese government has acknowledged the existence of the Unit 731 human experiment program only recently, after decades of postwar denial and obfuscation, it continues to refuse to confirm the accounts of the former soldiers, technicians, and doctors who have confessed to their experimentation and germ warfare. To this day, Japanese officials have stonewalled on the issue of admitting the nation's biological war guilt and releasing related archival documents to the public. Nor will they apologize to the many victims of these attacks in China and other nations.

There can be no denial of the Japanese biological warfare conspiracy and its catastrophic consequences, and until Japan is willing to begin an open discussion of its crimes, the final chapter of the story of Unit 731 is still to be written.

A PLAGUE
UPON
HUMANITY

ONE

A DOCTOR'S VISION

Few have the imagination for reality.
—GOETHE

IT BEGAN IN KYOTO IN 1927. DR. SHIRO ISHII HAD HIS DECISIVE revelation while going about his customary routine, thumbing through a stack of scientific research journals, making his usual effort to keep abreast of the latest research literature. At the age of thirty-five, the physician had just received his Ph.D. in microbiology from Kyoto Imperial University, one of the world's top institutions in that field and a school comparable in distinction to an American Ivy League college. Ishii was a rather eccentric young man, but he was even then highly respected among his Japanese peers and professors, with a reputation for brilliance and innovation that caused many of them to overlook his extracurricular activities and tastes.

Browsing through a medical periodical, Ishii came across an article that electrified him. He had discovered a report on the Geneva Convention of 1925, to which Japan had been a signatory. The article, written by a War Ministry delegate to the conference, First Lieutenant Harada, explored why Japan had signed the convention, a treaty organized by the League of Nations that banned the use of chemical weapons. As of 1925, some 1.3 million men in Europe and North America still suffered severe health problems resulting from their exposure to poisonous gas in the battles of World War I. Few in the league wanted to see this calamity repeated, and to the convention was added one more prohibition: It was also forbidden to make weapons from the germs responsible for infectious disease epidemics and pandemics such as bubonic plague, or the Black Death, as it was called, which wiped out 25 million Europeans in a five-year period during the fourteenth century.

Ishii read the text of the Geneva Convention over and over again, with both fascination and a sense of validation, for this was the direction in which he had been heading for some time. Titled the "Protocol for the Prohibition of the Use in War of Asphyxiating, Poisonous or Other Gases, and of Bacteriological Methods of Warfare," the compact states that "the use in war of asphyxiating, poisonous or other gases and of all analogous liquids, materials or devices, has been justly condemned by the general opinion of the civilized world . . . [T]he High Contracting Parties . . . accept this prohibition, agree to extend this prohibition to the use of bacteriological methods of warfare and agree to be bound as between themselves according to the terms of this declaration."

The treaty was signed in Geneva on June 17, 1925, by 128 nations—nearly every country on the planet. The prospect of germ warfare obviously created universal feelings of terror and revulsion among the civilized nations of the world. But Shiro Ishii took a different lesson from the Geneva Convention. If the prospect of germ warfare created such dread, he reasoned, Japan must do everything in its power to *create* the most virulent germ weapons, as well as effective methods for destroying wartime enemies with lethal diseases.

For years Ishii had spoken to colleagues and military officials of the strategic military potential of disease, and now the framers of the Geneva Convention had inadvertently done the Japanese physician a great service. Their fear of germ warfare catalyzed him to new levels of action. He would visit offices of Japan's top military officers, trying once more to persuade them that a program to conduct biological and germ warfare was the key to victory for Imperial Japan in any future wars.

By 1927 the nation had already conquered and occupied Korea and large portions of China, and powerful men in the ruling circles of Japanese society hungered for further expansion. Ishii now saw the way to make real his dream of state-of-the-art laboratories that could produce billions of deadly germs upon a general's request. The bacteriological weapons so reviled by the dignitaries who had traveled to Geneva in 1925 would become Japan's secret weapon. Ishii would be their mastermind.

At nearby Kyoto Army Hospital, to which Ishii had been attached as an active duty officer soon after attaining his doctorate, he proselytized about the military's need to make biological weapons. He took a train to Tokyo to see his old army buddies posted at the Tokyo Army First Hospital, where he had been on staff as a military surgeon five years earlier. There he managed to charm his way into the offices of high-ranking officials. He also got in to see top commanders and tacticians in Japan's War Ministry.

Ishii pleaded with them to begin researching biological weapons, citing the Harada article. He urged them to make tactical plans for the deployment of germ weapons. He also reminded them that most of the nations that had used chemical gas weapons in World War I also had ratified the Hague Convention of 1899, which banned the use of poison gas. One had to expect, he argued, that in the event of war, other countries would again develop banned weapons regardless of whatever international treaties to which they had sworn agreement.

The generals, colonels, and military scientists listened politely to Ishii, and not for the first time. The young doctor's face was well known around staff headquarters. "He always emphasized the role of bacteriological warfare in our tactical planning," wrote

General Saburo Endo in his diary. But Ishii's ideas fell on deaf ears at the War Ministry. The government at the time, under Prime Minister Giichi Tanaka, had stressed a more limited role for the military and a less aggressive foreign policy. The Japanese army and navy commanders went along for the most part with the Tanaka directives, and those heading up Japan's military were unimpressed with the theoretical concepts of biological warfare. They preferred to abide by Japan's moral obligations as outlined broadly in the 1925 Geneva Convention, which Japan had signed, although not ratified.

Japan had ratified the 1899 Hague Convention, which banned chemical weapons. The nation had not used chemical weapons in the First World War even when the firing of poison gas shells became common practice by the major nations on both sides of the conflict. Furthermore, a remarkably high level of concern for and attention to the prisoners' medical well-being was shown by the Japanese military in previous conflicts, including the Sino-Japanese War of 1894–95, the Russo-Japanese War of 1904–05, and World War I. Army doctors saw to it that enemy soldiers' wounds were sterilized and carefully dressed with bandages, and that the prisoners were promptly hospitalized with proper medication if they suffered from chronic conditions. In civilian medicine, Japan had established itself as a leading country in the advancement of disease research and treatment, drug development, and patient care.

Ishii, however, saw war prisoners as subhuman and expendable, and despite the attitudes within the military, he was not about to give up on his ideas. His pleas to top commanders to create a germ warfare research division were consistent with his deep ambitions to move up in rank and further his own status in Japan's military and scientific strata.

He made plans for a trip outside Japan to see what he could discover about biological weapons research. If he found evidence that other nations were secretly pursuing it, he could make his case before the military that Japan had to stay current and compete in the field, for reasons of defense and national security, if nothing else.

What drove Ishii to commit the acts that made him one of the most heinous figures of World War II, a physician who institutionalized a secret system of germ warfare campaigns and macabre biological experiments on living human beings? It is no exaggeration to say that he was personally obsessed with spearheading a sophisticated program of biological warfare, and that such an obsession could only take root in a singular type of mind, one that was at once outrageous and calculating.

He was born on June 25, 1892, to a wealthy family of landed aristocrats in Chiyoda Mura, a farming village near Tokyo. The Ishii family dominated Chiyoda Mura, and for centuries they had received feudal tribute from hundreds of its lower-class residents. Young Shiro grew up waited on by servants, in a stately villa surrounded by groves of bamboo and an orchard. The rarefied atmosphere of entitlement undoubtedly contributed to his strong self-confidence and innate sense of superiority. Under the lingering feudal dictates of Japanese society, families of noble lineage enjoyed the legal, career, and economic privileges born of a rigid class system. This dividing of people into lesser and superior sorts of beings was generally accepted among Japanese at the time, in the name of harmony and order. Such rules against fraternizing with the so-called lower classes, woven into the social fabric of everyday life, must have made a deep impression on Ishii. It made it all the easier for him and the other Japanese perpetrators of lethal human experimentation to descend into a callous disregard for human life.

Another factor in the formation of Ishii's personality was his soaring intelligence, and from the earliest age it was clear that he was an academic star: Shiro was the youngest of four brothers, and even as a young child he had surpassed them all academically. He could memorize entire books virtually overnight, a feat his older siblings could not match. As a consequence, he was treated specially by his teachers as he progressed through his primary education. Growing into adolescence, the talented boy developed an impressive physique to complement his other gifts. At five feet, ten inches, Ishii stood unusually tall for a Japanese person of the early twentieth century. In fact, he towered over most people. His normal speaking voice was unusually big too, coming across as loud and assertive in regular conversations, something of an anomaly in the demure society of Japan.

He received top grades throughout his schooling and was admitted to the exclusive Kyoto Imperial University, where he took up the study of medicine. There too Ishii's professors recognized the young man as a prodigious student and assigned him to research projects well beyond the scope of the topics his classmates were pursuing. Ishii was not popular among his peers, to whom he seemed selfishly driven and one who chose his friends on the basis of how they could help to advance his career and social standing. To his classmates, Ishii appeared supremely detached, as if his childhood of receiving gifts of tribute and being put on a pedestal by his family and teachers had created in him a sense that the world existed to serve him and his desires and that he owed nothing in return.

Professor Ren Kimura, Ishii's Ph.D. adviser, described his former student as "cheeky" and "flamboyant," not words usually associated with Japanese doctoral candidates. "At that time there were thirty to forty research students and they had to be careful to share the laboratory equipment because there wasn't enough to go round," Kimura recalled. Ishii, however, "would come at night to do his work after everyone had left. He would use test tubes and apparatus that other students had washed clean," then leave without bothering to clean up his own mess. "The others," Kimura noted, "would be really annoyed when they came in and found them dirty the next morning."

The home of the Kyoto Imperial University president Torasaburo Araki, an esteemed and powerful man, was close to the laboratory where Ishii conducted his research, and young Ishii began to drop by frequently to converse with him. The audacity shocked Kimura; such a thing simply was not done. The professor was even more shocked when Ishii greatly burnished his status by marrying the beautiful Kyoko Araki, the president's daughter. Ishii now had a key and powerful supporter in his father-in-law, who helped to advance the young doctor's career and social standing significantly.

Ishii was a mass of paradoxes: loud and rude, yet also a skilled social and career climber; an ardent nationalist and a devoted scientist, but a wild partygoer too. On one hand, his intelligence and ability to turn on the charm were earning him entrée to Japan's highest circles. On the other, he had certain debased proclivities. While it wasn't unusual for married men to frequent geisha houses, Ishii would engage in legendary bouts of drinking and whoring through Tokyo and Kyoto, all-night benders during which he would order the brothel madams to bring him girls no older than sixteen. Drawing from his family's wealth, he would spend lavishly on evenings out. Ishii's ability to pass the yen around so freely had his impecunious coworkers and classmates green with envy.

His social skills manifested themselves in increasingly bizarre ways as he grew older. He became infamous for demonstrating the high quality of a filtration device he had invented that solved a persistent health problem: troops drinking contaminated water from puddles, ponds, and rivers. His portable water filter removed germs, eliminating the need to boil water or use chlorine. True to his narcissistic form, Ishii named his invention the Ishii Filter, and in the 1930s he personally promoted it to leaders of both the army and the navy with unusual showmanship: In some instances Ishii startled his audience by actually urinating into the filter and then drinking a glass of the liquid that had been his own piss. One time he put on such a performance for the emperor himself.

Former army major general Chiso Matsumura wrote in his memoirs that Ishii gained a reputation as being the "army's crazed surgeon." Yet he was at the same time perceived as "manful and resolute," noted Matsumura, and highly respected for his scientific acumen, organizational skills, and personal magnetism. Relating another display of urine exhibitionism by "crazed" Ishii, Matsumura recalled a 1937 incident when Ishii burst into army staff headquarters and demanded funds for his biological warfare unit, while "startling" the top generals by making a show of licking salt that he said was made from human urine.

Another Ishii stunt presented a mixture of the homicidal threat and the juvenile tantrum. In the early days of his biological warfare laboratory projects, Ishii sought to greatly expand the scope of his experiments, but he knew that he would have a hard time obtaining funds from the fiscally conservative finance minister, Korekiyo Takahashi. So he paid a personal visit to Takahashi's home, and proceeded to enter the kitchen displaying a large flask of cultured cholera bacteria. Ishii then threatened to pour the cholera culture all over the kitchen if Takahashi did not approve the funding appropriation he was seeking.

But Takahashi held firm and refused. Ishii then abruptly switched tactics and announced he would not leave the house until Takahashi gave him the money. He wound up staging a twenty-four-hour-long sit-in, badgering the finance minister continually and arguing that Japan was lagging behind other nations in the bio-war field. Finally, Takahashi gave in and granted Ishii the appropriation he had been seeking: secret funding in the amount of 100 million yen. Ishii's aggressive impudence had paid off handsomely.

Throughout his life Ishii proved himself prone to corruption and thievery. In the early 1930s he fraudulently obtained 50,000 yen by setting up dummy stockholders to receive illegal company dividends, and years later in 1945 he embezzled 1 million yen from a special army fund entrusted to him. Both times he was seeking to enrich himself personally; he clearly felt entitled to take whatever he wanted. Both times he begged his social and military connections to save him, and they did. Ishii was the archetype of a highly functioning sociopath, playing the dramatic role of the unstable "mad doctor" with flourish.

Shortly after graduating, Ishii worked in army medical research projects. Eschewing the medical school graduate's usual routine of commencing his practice as a civilian medical doctor or researcher, he opted for a career within the military. He enlisted in the army, and in April 1922 received a commission as an army surgeon in Tokyo at the Army First Hospital, with the rank of first lieutenant. Ishii was a sincere patriot, and his nationalistic attitudes contributed to the ease with which he lived and worked in a military environment and to his later enthusiasm for biological weaponry and the wartime advantage it could give Japan.

By all accounts he worked hard at his hospital rounds, impressing his superiors, even as he continued to play hard in spates of after-hours carousing on the town. When he returned to civilian life and Kyoto Imperial University in 1924, he did his doctoral work in the analysis of blood sera, bacteriology, and human pathology. Also in that year he joined a research mission to Shikoku, an island south of the main Japanese island of Honshu, and north of the largest southern island of Kyushu. An outbreak of mosquito-borne encephalitis had occurred there, in the district of Kagawa. The disease was of an especially virulent strain, with a mortality rate of 60 percent. It eventually killed more than 3,500 people, who died due to high fever and acute swelling of the brain.

Ishii made an outstanding contribution to the identification of the virus that caused the Shikoku disease, which became known to researchers as Japanese B encephalitis. He invented an effective filtration device to isolate the pathogenic virus, greatly assisting his peers in their understanding of the disease. This feat would bring the young physician-researcher's talents to the attention of leading figures in the academic community, and would also set him on the path of developing his water filtration devices, as well as antiepidemic public health procedures. Within a decade, Ishii applied his knowledge of both with terrible purpose.

After he had received his Ph.D. in 1927, the army reassigned him to medical corps service, stationing him at Kyoto Army Medical Hospital, where he was promoted to the rank of captain. While at this post, Ishii maintained his links to Kyoto Imperial University through postgraduate research projects. In one of these studies he produced a highly praised journal article on the treatment of gonorrhea patients by artificially inducing fever symptoms, titled "Sedimentation Rate of Artificially Transplanted Malaria Blood Cells and Their Effects."

The paper was coauthored with a childhood friend from the village of Chiyoda Mura, Dr. Tomosada Masuda. One wonders what ideas the study might have given Ishii—the two young doctors deliberately caused fever in patients through transplanted cells, in order to treat the disease of gonorrhea and ultimately heal the patient. It was also during his tenure at Kyoto Army Medical Hospital that Ishii came across the article on the Geneva Convention and began intensively lobbying the Tokyo brass.

The rebuff that Ishii had received from the War Ministry officials in 1927 greatly frustrated him. About what he did next, embarking alone upon a round-the-world trip to study bio-war research in other countries, little documentation exists. What is known is that in April 1928 Ishii left Japan, and that in each port of call along the way he attempted to ask probing questions of the right people—military and university scientists and some scientists in private research foundations—about their biological weapons research. He managed to obtain letters of introduction from the military attachés in Japan's embassies and consulates in various countries.

The long list of nations Ishii visited resembles a geographic hodgepodge: the United States-including New York City, Washington, D.C., Baltimore, Boston, Chicago, and Los Angeles—Canada, France, Italy, Germany, Hungary, Belgium, Singapore, Hawaii (then a U.S. territory), Ceylon, Egypt, Denmark, Sweden, Finland, Switzerland, Turkey, Poland, the United Kingdom, the Soviet Union, Latvia, and Estonia. According to one former associate of Ishii, the military attaché to Japan's embassy in Washington, D.C., reported that he had heard that Ishii had studied bacteriological warfare at the Massachusetts Institute of Technology, though no record of such a visit there is known to exist.

We do know that upon his return to Japan in 1930 Ishii found the political climate much improved for his germ warfare ambitions. The civilian government of Giichi Tanaka, in power when Ishii left on his trip in 1928, was now gone. In 1928 Japanese agents had murdered the Manchurian warlord Chang Tso-Lin and then tried to pin the murder on three innocent Chinese men. The exposure of that assassination conspiracy led to Tanaka's resignation, and new faces greeted Ishii in the reshuffled War Ministry and military high command.

These were younger, more hawkish, and more adventurous military leaders, some of whom pressed for Japan to invade Manchuria, a vast region in China's northeast that was rich in natural resources—coal, iron, oil, and aluminum, as well as abundant cheap labor for Japan's industrial firms to exploit. The militarists referred to poorly defended Manchuria as "Japan's lifeline."

Moreover, an occupied Manchuria could be used as a strategic launching area for further expansion of the Japanese Empire into North China and Mongolia, two more economic-prize regions eyed by Japan. A southern portion of Manchuria, the Liaodong Peninsula, had already been taken from Russia in 1905, and Japan also occupied Korea and Taiwan. Conquering the entirety of Manchuria would also serve to reinforce Japan's hold on these existing colonies. Vehement anticommunism among Japanese leaders gave them further encouragement, as they viewed Manchuria as a perfect staging area from which to launch Japan's military forays against the bordering Soviet Union. Colonel Sheshiro Itagaki, one of the most vociferous militarists, argued in May 1931 that the seizure of Manchuria would give Japan decisive superiority over the Soviets. "Our power will naturally have to extend to the Maritime Province," Itagaki said. In other words, the Russian Far East along the Pacific Coast.

Ishii could not have hoped for a more favorable set of new figures in the War Ministry and army hierarchy. Not only were these leaders aggressive militarists, but their designs for the occupation of Manchuria dovetailed neatly with Ishii's schemes for setting up germ warfare research operations abroad. When he called on these men he claimed that his world tour had confirmed that other nations were secretly developing germ weapons. He also emphasized the small cost of biological weapons, compared to what it cost to develop and manufacture conventional arms, an especially important factor for Japan at this point, as the nation had recently gone into a severe economic slump stemming from the worldwide economic depression that began in 1929. And in a written statement to the military High Command, Ishii again invoked his primary source of inspiration. "Biological warfare must possess distinct possibilities," he wrote, "otherwise it would not have been outlawed by the League of Nations."

This time around, Ishii got a warm and enthusiastic reception. The war minister himself, Sadao Araki (no relation to Ishii's wife), championed the doctor's cause. In addition, Ishii received backing from two of the army's leading hawks, Lieutenant Colonel Yorimichi Suzuki and Colonel Ryuji Kajitsuka. Like Ishii, Kajitsuka was a bacteriologist as well as a military officer. More importantly, he and Ishii had been friends since they'd worked together at the Tokyo Army First Hospital years earlier.

Ishii had the support of two other influential patrons. One was Major General Tetsuan Nagata, an army commander who stressed the need for technological modernization of the Japanese war machine. Some sources have said that Nagata was so impressed with Ishii's germ warfare research plans that he may have arranged for the government to reimburse the expenses that Ishii incurred on his 1928–30 bio-war research tour. General Nagata is also known as one of the collaborators in the infamous incident that served as the false pretext for Japan's invasion of Manchuria in September 1931. Colonel Seishiro Itagaki and Lieutenant Colonel Kenji Ishiwara, two young army officers, masterminded this event, a Japanese self-attack on September 18, 1931. In this incident, officers of the Shimamoto Regiment, which had been assigned to guard the Japanese-owned South Manchurian Railway, arranged for army engineers to secretly set explosive charges along a stretch of its track near the city of Mukden (now known as Shenyang). The Japanese then immediately blamed the explosion upon Chinese soldiers garrisoned nearby, and attacked those troops, most of whom were sleeping in their barracks at the time. Nagata supplied howitzer artillery pieces to Itagaki and Ishiwara for use in that attack. The railway blast became known as the Manchurian Incident or the Mukden

Incident, and was used to justify the invasion and occupation of Manchuria, on the grounds that Japanese interests had to be protected from assaults by the Chinese.

The South Manchurian Railway, then the dominant economic power in Manchuria, had originally been founded and operated by Russians in the region. But with the advent of the Bolshevik Revolution and increasing Japanese influence in Manchuria, control of the railroad network shifted to Japan. The issue of protecting it from bandit attacks had been the excuse for placing Japanese troops in the region a decade earlier.

The other patron who became instrumental in Ishii's success was Colonel Chikahiko Koizumi. Attached to the Tokyo Army Medical College in 1930, Koizumi already had distinguished himself as a military officer, physician, and biochemist. While Japan's military had not used chemical weapons in World War I— Japanese troops fought on the Allied side, mostly in battles in eastern China—it had conducted preliminary research into chemical warfare and gas mask design, beginning in 1915 with poison gas studies. Koizumi, a strident nationalist and militarist, had led this research beginning in May 1918, and almost immediately he was involved in a near-fatal laboratory accident. He was caught, without a mask, in a chlorine gas cloud. He then ordered that a bed be placed in the lab room where he had inhaled the chlorine, so that he could confront the possibility of death from his injury. "Just as it is the duty of soldiers to die on the battlefield," he said, "researchers die in their laboratories." Yet after two months in the lab bed, Koizumi managed to fully recover from the poison. With great enthusiasm and, one guesses, a feeling of invincibility, he resumed the research he had been pursuing on gas mask development.

Koizumi headed up the program for four years after his accident, but despite his death-defying work for the glory of Japan, his superiors at the time relegated chemical warfare research to a low-level, backburner status within the military. When he came across Ishii at Tokyo Army Medical College, Koizumi was taken with the young man's intelligence, his talent for biomedical research as proved through his published scientific papers, and his drive to make Japan the foremost nation in biological warfare, a vision Koizumi shared. Moreover, Koizumi had powerful connections. He counted Hideki Tojo, Japan's future World War II prime minister, among his close friends. Becoming Ishii's university patron, Koizumi acted to gather valuable support for the young doctor's bio-war project from within the scientific circles of academia and hospital research groups. When he began supporting Ishii in 1930 he did so with an eye on his own agenda, which was to increase the stature of his surgeons' corps and to reactivate the dormant chemical weapons program. Koizumi knew that biological and chemical warfare, while distinctly different forms of killing, each involved biological research and testing. He succeeded in his aims, and soon army funding for chemical warfare increased dramatically. By the mid-1930s Japan was manufacturing enormous quantities of poison gas bombs, including shells of chlorine, phosgene, and mustard gas. Not coincidentally, Koizumi's own star was on the rise: In 1933 he was made dean of the Tokyo Army Medical College, in 1934 he became the army surgeon general, and in 1936 he was appointed Japan's minister of health.

Koizumi saw to it that Ishii was promoted to the rank of major, and at the relatively young age of thirty-seven he was appointed chair of the newly created department of immunology at Tokyo Army Medical College. Ishii himself had lobbied the medical college to establish such a department. Immunology lay at the crossroads of microbiology, pathology, and vaccine research, and so it presented a perfect laboratory arena in which to study aspects of biological warfare. Ishii undoubtedly had this in mind when he campaigned to create an academic hub of researchers and biomedical facilities, which he could control and direct.

One year after appointing Ishii to his chair, Koizumi granted him substantial funds to initiate a biological warfare program for the army. Similarly, the status Ishii had gained by receiving a departmental chair lent clout to his requests to create a biological weapons (BW) research program, and to make him its head. Now, in 1931, the army granted Ishii both wishes. His initial experiments began that year, in a laboratory facility of the Tokyo Army Medical College.

A typical schedule for Major Ishii in his early days heading up the BW research program involved lecturing to students and handling administrative matters by day, while covertly researching biological warfare in the evening hours in the lab space of the immunology department that had been allotted to him. Here Ishii and a small team of scientists and laboratory assistants worked to culture lethal bacteria and to develop chemical poisons. They used the same array of equipment—flasks, burners, petri dishes, microscopes, swabs, nutrient media—that had been used in research aimed at preventing and treating contagious disease. Among the organisms studied by Ishii and his team were the flea-transmitted bacterium of bubonic plague, food and water-borne illnesses such as cholera and typhoid, and the anthrax bacterium, known for its ability to withstand cold and cause a highly lethal pulmonary anthrax infection through the inhalation of its spore form.

Those early germ warfare studies conducted in 1931–32 did not involve experiments on human beings. We also know that the research at this time was primarily defensive in nature. For example, Ishii's unit developed vaccines used to protect Japanese troops from disease outbreaks; the doctor and his sympathizers in the scientific community could legitimately argue that what they were doing was not harming anybody. They also could argue that in studying the potential diseases an enemy nation could inflict upon Japan with germ warfare, they might, down the road, save Japanese lives.

Ishii's Tokyo research facilities expanded quickly. In 1932 he was granted a two-story concrete building at the Army Medical College to use entirely for laboratory bio-war studies. Ishii called this building the Epidemic Prevention Laboratory. The growth of Ishii's germ weapon research was greatly aided by the renewal of Japan's chemical warfare unit, a holdover from World War I, directed by Koizumi.

Backed by enthusiasts like Koizumi and Nagata, Ishii was forever the prodigal son of the Japanese scientific and military establishments, and he continued to rise rapidly through the ranks. His phenomenal success may be ascribed to something more than his ability to impress or deploy charm and charisma when needed. He remained a dedicated medical professional who held true to a vision of total military superiority through the study of and experiments in microbiology. Ishii relentlessly urged that he be given more money and resources for his bio-weapon endeavors, and spoke often of the supreme potentials of germ warfare.

He had a speech that he gave frequently to public health officials in the early 1930s. "There are two types of bacteriological warfare research, A and B," he said. "A is assault research, and B is defense research. Vaccine research is of the B type, and this can be done in Japan. However, A type research can be done abroad."

One can easily read between the lines here to understand that those living abroad belonged to population groups whom the Japanese of this era commonly referred to as the "lower races." Japan's educational system indoctrinated its youth in the belief that they were the superior people destined to rule over the lesser nationalities of Asia. The darker one's skin, the lower one's status. Implicit in Ishii's statement was that such "lower races" could be used in types of human research that had hitherto been considered taboo.

Imperial Japan had long been openly racist toward its colonial subjects in Korea and the inhabitants of the regions it already had taken from China: Taiwan, the Pescadores, a portion of Shandong Province (previously occupied by Germany), and what was known as the Kwantung Leased Territory on the southern tip of the Liaodong Peninsula (previously occupied by Russia). Japanese settlers residing in these colonies enjoyed legal and social privileges, while Japanese "advisers" closely supervised the moves of collaborating Chinese administrators and bureaucrats in matters of daily governance, backed up by the ever-alert Japanese military and police forces. Political dissidents and suspected resistance organizers were spied on, arrested, and tortured by Japan's dreaded, Gestapo-like military secret police, the Kempeitai. For its militarism and dictatorial ways, Japan earned the moniker "the Prussia of the East" among Westerners.

The Tokyo militarists courted by Ishii openly laid out their designs for a racially ordered Manchurian society, its ethnically diverse population ruled by the Japanese and run for the benefit of Japanese corporate interests. Lieutenant Colonel Ishiwara, one of the main plotters of the September 18, 1931, Mukden Incident, a violent act that would serve as the rationale for Japan's invasion of Manchuria, had written politically influential tracts in 1929 and 1930 asserting that "the future of Manchuria and Mongolia will only be decided when Japan obtains these areas." Once they came under Japanese rule, Ishiwara wrote, "The four races of Japan, China, Korea and Manchuria will share a common prosperity through a division of responsibilities: Japanese, political leadership and large industry; Chinese, labor and small industry; Koreans, rice; and Manchus, animal husbandry."

Discriminatory policies abroad mirrored age-old, ingrained prejudices against minorities within Japanese society. Ethnic Koreans, natives of Okinawa, *burakumin* (Japanese consigned to a lower caste because their ancestors worked in ritually shunned tannery and butcher positions), and the Ainu, an aboriginal people of the Home Islands, all suffered legal barriers to marriage, employment, and property rights, as well as everyday social ostracism. (Although their legal standing has improved, much bigotry against people in these categories persists to this day in Japan.)

With the Mukden Incident in 1931, Japanese army divisions poured into southern Manchuria from their bases in Korea and in the Kwantung Leased Territory of China's Liaodong Peninsula. By February 1932 this force of about 61,000 troops, called the Kwantung Army or Kanto Army, had subjugated all of Manchuria with its motorized regiments. The Chinese troops guarding Manchuria greatly outnumbered the invading Japanese, but they were too poorly equipped and trained to mount an adequate defense. With its valuable mineral and oil reserves, "Japan's lifeline" was now completely under Tokyo's control. Even though the naked aggression of the Mukden Incident wasn't uncovered until 1945, when one of the September 18 coconspirators confessed, the invasion of Manchuria led to Japan's condemnation in the League of Nations. In response, Japan resigned in 1933 from that international legal body. Four years later it invaded North and Central China, on the road to its attempted military conquest of all East Asia and the United States, commencing on December 7, 1941, when Japan launched simultaneous surprise attacks against Pearl Harbor and targets in Malaysia, the Philippines, and elsewhere in the Pacific. But the invasion of Manchuria is often cited as Japan's most decisive early step on the road toward totalitarian fascism and war.

For Ishii, it meant that a whole new world of germ warfare possibilities was about to open up. The Japanese-controlled state of "Manchukuo" was created, with the former boy emperor of Ching Dynasty China, Henry Pu Yi, installed by Tokyo as its figurehead regent in 1932, then reenthroned as the Manchukuan emperor in 1934. Seeing that his golden opportunity had arrived, Ishii prepared to expand his research facilities into Manchuria and begin his "A type" investigations into biological assault.

"Due to your great help we have already achieved a great deal in our bacteria research," Ishii wrote in a plea to top commanders as 1931 drew to a close. "It is time we start to experiment. We appeal to be sent to Manchuria to develop new weapons." His request was soon approved. And from the beginning of Ishii's human experiments in Manchuria—those tests that he had in Tokyo described in veiled and vague language—he received no official objection from the military officers or civilian scientists who knew of the suffering of his non-Japanese test subjects.

TWO

FORTRESS OF FEAR

FOR THE MILLIONS OF SETTLERS ALREADY THERE, MANCHURIA was China's great frontier: a place to flee to and homestead, a place to start over in one of the region's countless agricultural settlements or prosperous young cities. Its constituent districts were the four northeastern provinces of China—the provinces known today as Heilongjiang, Jilin, Liaoning, and part of Inner Mongolia, and a 1935 census estimated its population at about 30 million. It had a thriving industrial economy, and the South Manchurian Railway maintained five lines running across 700 miles of track.

But its total landmass—an area more than twice the size of California—ensured that outside the big cities, Manchuria remained underpopulated. The region is bounded by the snow-capped Great Khingan Mountains to the west, and on the north by the Amur River, the border with the Soviet Union. Its terrain includes a desert area on the edge of the Mongolian Gobi, thick evergreen forests, cultivated swaths of farmland for wheat and other grains, and broad plains of fertile grasslands. Manchuria also had a well-deserved reputation as a lawless and untamed region, its roads and towns stalked by bandit gangs on horseback. In many ways, Manchuria of the 1920s and early 1930s resembled the Wild West of nineteenth-century America.

When the occupation of Manchuria had been completed in

the beginning of 1932, the Kwantung Army provided Major Ishii with the generous sum of 200,000 yen to set up a biological warfare research facility—the Epidemic Prevention Unit, as he called it—in the city of Harbin. A large, multiethnic provincial capital on the banks of the Sungari River, Harbin was inhabited by 240,000 Han Chinese, 81,000 Russians, and 4,700 Japanese settlers, as well as Gypsies, Mongolians, Manchus, and a Jewish community of about 6,000. A number of West European expatriates had also come to Harbin, and English, French, and German could be heard in the parks and shops. Russian-language newspapers circulated, and the streets of Harbin's city center and suburbs were lined with beautiful exemplars of the nineteenth- and early twentieth-century Russian architectural styles, as well as a Russian Orthodox cathedral, Catholic and Protestant churches, synagogues, mosques, and Buddhist temples. Harbin had world-class universities in the sciences, engineering, and the fine arts, and numerous theaters showcasing plays and operas. The city boasted many excellent cafés and bistros, which hummed day and night with talk of art and politics, and was called the "Paris of the East." Its residential and shopping districts expanded around the city's dynamic industrial factories and its train station, which served as a key hub of both passenger and freight lines for Manchuria's railroad network.

The army had established Ishii's station in an abandoned sake distillery in Harbin's industrial Nan Gang District, along with a block of commandeered shops adjacent to the distillery, with the initial understanding that the work conducted there would include only defensive biological warfare research, such as the development and production of vaccines for soldiers. For that purpose, Ishii, the military, and a group of scientists immediately began refitting the conduits and machine works of the distillery and renovating the shops. But from the beginning Harbin posed problems for Ishii. For one thing, it was a heavily populated area, making secrecy and security difficult. Another concern was that the sake distillery building was too small to allow for what Ishii had in mind in terms of human experiments. He needed a complex large enough to hold a sizable prison within.

Thus, no sooner had the Harbin construction started, with 300 military and scientific personnel (about 50 of them physicians) assigned to research duties there, than Ishii asked to open yet another BW facility—this one in a remote, secluded Manchurian location. The High Command granted Ishii's request for new facilities outside Harbin, and by late summer 1932 construction began adjacent to a small village on the railway line to Harbin, far enough away for secrecy purposes, yet conveniently just a short train trip from that hub city. The place was Beiyinhe, a village located approximately 100 kilometers southeast of Harbin, in Wuchang County, Heilongjiang Province.

Ishii's maneuvering to establish an expanded germ warfare complex was closely linked to Japanese military plans to threaten the Soviet borders of Manchuria and move northward against the Russians, even as they were advancing against the Chinese in the south. "Togo," the code name Ishii chose for his Epidemic Prevention Unit, reflects his anti-Russian and anticommunist orientation. Heihachiro Togo was the admiral, greatly admired by Ishii, who won the 1905 Russo-Japanese War through clever naval strategies. Ishii had aligned himself with the *hokushin*, "northern advance" fascist-leaning faction of the Japanese military High Command, which advocated war with the Soviet Union to occupy Siberia and to weaken communism. The generals of the Kwantung Army, who were funding Ishii in Harbin, tended toward this northern advance position.

Imperial Japan's relations with the Soviet Union were continually tense, and Manchuria was seen as the frontline area where war with the Russians would initially break out, were it to occur. The Japanese had invaded Russia on April 5, 1918, sending troops to the Pacific port city of Vladivostok to intervene, alongside Western nations, in the Soviet Civil War, on the side of the White Russians. Japan withdrew its forces, totaling 75,000 soldiers, in October 1922, after they had occupied large areas of the Russian Far East and suffered approximately 1,500 casualties to Bolshevik defenders. Thousands of White Russian soldiers and collaborators, facing defeat, fled to neighboring Manchuria and settled there. Some would join with the Japanese occupation forces of Manchuria following the 1931 invasion, in military or anti-Soviet espionage capacities. However, Tokyo and the Soviet leaders refrained from declaring war against each other—that was a conflict neither wanted—and they maintained a Japanese-Soviet neutrality treaty even as Japan formed its alliance with the Third Reich and fascist Italy in 1940.

The northern advance advocates were stymied in their ambitions by those within the High Command who preferred to focus on the war with China to the south, and later on the war with the United States. Thus in the 1930s the Kwantung Army found itself in an almost Cold War–like situation with a Soviet opponent that was certainly more organized, better equipped, and more militarily advanced than the Chinese forces, or any previous resistance the Japanese had encountered. For all the bluster to attack the Russians and take their eastern land, the northern advance faction knew they would be in for a tough fight. They looked to the boastful Major Ishii and his BW machine for the promise and strategic advantage of germ super-weapons.

The Kwantung Army officer charged with overseeing Ishii and the Togo Unit was Lieutenant Colonel Ishiwara, the Mukden Incident coconspirator who had written the influential tracts calling for a Manchurian society based on a racial hierarchy, with the

Japanese on top. To make way for Ishii's new facility in Beiyinhe, the military seized and burned to the ground more than 300 homes and shops within an area of 500 square meters, and a large field adjacent to the south was cordoned off to construct a military airport for ferrying supplies and personnel into the secret facility by plane. The Japanese army forced all the inhabitants of one neighborhood in the village to leave within three days of the official pronouncement of appropriation.

The central edifice in the camp, called the Zhong Ma Fortress by the local Chinese, resembled a medieval Japanese castle. The building was surrounded by a wall nine feet high, barbed wire, and electrified fencing. A military guard detachment was posted beside a huge iron door that released a drawbridge for vehicles carrying supplies and specimens in and out. Additional security was provided by guard units, which constantly patrolled outside the camp, threatening anyone coming near with arrest or worse. Tall guard towers and swiveling searchlight beams further protected against infiltration or prisoner escape. To the Chinese villagers living nearby, the mysterious area became known as the Zhong Ma Prison Camp, and the Japanese stationed within the walled perimeter and the adjacent airport as the Zhong Ma Troop.

Evidence suggests that Ishii's medical personnel began systematically conducting lethal experiments on human prisoners in late 1932. These tests were done in absolute secrecy, but the residents of Beiyinhe did notice that bizarre, secret things were going on behind the walls and barbed wire. Trains traveling a track nearly a kilometer from the site were ordered to draw all window shades while passing. Reports leaked out of agonizing screams emanating from the Fortress; according to one story, a boy was killed when he peered into the fenced-in site.

Sometimes Chinese laborers were used to carry material in and out of the area within the camp that was devoted to laboratory research for human testing, and germ and chemical warfare development. These men had to cover themselves with large willow baskets, and carrying their loads beneath these baskets like man-sized cocoons, they were led to the sensitive scientific spaces by Japanese guards. The guards then led the covered Chinese workers outside the secret area, where they removed the baskets.

Those Chinese laborers were the lucky ones. Hundreds of others, who were enlisted by the Japanese army to construct the inner, medical experiment–prison part of the bio-war prison camp—what was called the Fortress—were executed after construction was completed to ensure secrecy. One Chinese, who resided near Beiyinhe and had worked on the outer portion of the camp, said, "When construction started, there were about forty houses in our village, and a lot of people were driven out. About one person from each home was taken to work on the construction. People were gathered from villages from all around here, maybe a thousand people in all. The only things we worked on were the surrounding wall and the earthen walls. The Chinese that worked on the buildings were brought in from somewhere, but we didn't know where. After everything was finished, those people were killed."

Within a year of breaking ground at Beiyinhe, Ishii had ordered the construction of approximately one hundred buildings within the camp's walls. The Chinese laborers brought in by the Japanese military to build the buildings were worked to exhaustion to satisfy Ishii's schedule. They constructed barracks and dormitory-type housing for military personnel and for the medical and scientific researchers who lived on site to engage in the biological and chemical warfare experimentation. There were also administrative offices; laboratory facilities equipped for the study of microorganisms, chemical agents, and human tissues; and veterinary housing for animals that were being tested for their potential as biological warfare vectors. Possibly in a nod to his northern advance sponsors in the army, Ishii made sure that Beiyinhe had a special lab devoted solely to the study of the anthrax bacterium. Unlike most germs, anthrax can survive cold temperatures; the objective in experimenting with it was to have germ weapons employable in a wintry environment such as the Russian border, or for longer-term disease seeding of the Russian soil and animal life. Methods to keep some less hardy species of microbes alive in frigid conditions were studied at Beiyinhe as well.

Beiyinhe marks a terrible departure in the annals of medicine and scientific inquiry—it was unlike anything that came before it. The compound was part prison, part hospital (of a sort), and part microbial and chemical research lab, using people in a method that the world scientific community had previously reserved for monkeys, rats, cats, and other lab animals. The unfortunates shipped to the Zhong Ma Fortress were primarily political prisoners and guerrillas detained for anti-Japanese resistance activity. Sometimes they were merely common criminals and members of the thieving bandit groups that roamed the countryside. Armed partisan resistance groups fought the Kwantung Army throughout the duration of Japan's occupation of Manchuria. These political guerrilla organizations included, among others, the highly active noncommunist Chinese "Red Spears"; Chinese communists associated with Mao's People's Army, which tied up Japanese forces in the southern districts; and Korean communist partisans who were based in eastern Manchuria, led by Kim Il Sung, the future leader of North Korea, who during this time had become an underground folk hero to the Koreans and a major irritant to the Japanese military. Some were intellectuals or relatives of dissidents, who had been netted by the dreaded Japanese Kempeitai on the grounds of being "suspicious" and therefore potentially subversive.

Inside the Fortress, blocks of prison cells housed approximately 500 to 600 human guinea-pig prisoners. They were shackled at the ankles and wrists, yet were also fed well-balanced meals at a nutritional level above that of the average Chinese or Japanese person in the outside world. Their diet included frequent servings of meat and fish. Prisoners were also given time to exercise in a special exercise room.

The only goal of such treatment was to keep the subjects healthy in all respects other than the diseases they contracted when lethal bacteria and viruses were injected into them. In this way the effects of malnutrition, muscular atrophy, obesity, and other problems on the experiments could be eliminated. Ishii also preferred younger-than-middle-aged prisoners for subject material, just as research scientists generally prefer their lab animals to be as young and healthy as possible at the outset, in order to achieve optimum experimental controls and the most accurate results.

Evidence suggests that Ishii's early specimens were all men and almost always under forty, as specified by the biological unit's orders to the Kempeitai stations. There, officers would decide which prisoners would be transferred to the Togo Unit on the basis of the doctors' specifications. This was to ensure that, as Ishii put it, scientists could have "best body" types on which to test the strength of various germs and poisons they were developing. The prisoners would be brought into the laboratories by guards, to be experimented on. Among the diseases tested upon them were glanders, the bacterial disease of horses and humans that the Germans had been accused of deploying in World War I (an allegation that had helped to inspire the League of Nations to draft the 1925 Geneva Convention), as well as anthrax, typhoid, smallpox, dysentery, and bubonic plague.

Major Tomio Karasawa, a biological warfare veteran who had been captured by the Soviets in the closing days of World War II, said, "Ishii told me that he had experimented on cholera and plague on the mounted bandits of Manchuria during the winter of 1933–34 and discovered that plague was effective." One document uncovered by the Chinese after World War II describes a Beiyinhe study performed on three prisoners who had been communist guerrillas. Ishii ordered that mice be captured from northern Manchuria, where bubonic plague naturally occurred. Fleas found to carry the plague bacteria were taken off the mice; the bacteria were then isolated from the fleas and cultured in a Fortress laboratory and injected into the prisoners. A coldly precise observation of the prisoners' physiological state was recorded by Ishii's team of doctors, as the victims died in agony from the disease.

Regardless of the diet provided to the prisoners at Beiyinhe, scholars believe that the life expectancy for prisoners was no more than thirty days. Most had large amounts of blood drawn by medical technicians—in far greater quantities than would be considered safe for patients in a real hospital. The routine mandated the taking a minimum of about 500 cubic centimeters of blood, sampled every two or three days. This produced the effect of a progressive wasting disorder, and the prisoners became weak and listless to the point of incapacitation. Some experiments were simply based on scientific curiosity, as doctors had the opportunity to work on human subjects who were physically expendable; for example, one experiment involved seeing how deeply a person could be drained of his blood before he reached the point of death from low circulation or cellular deprivation.

Later, when scientists wanted to study the effects of their grotesque medical studies on various organs, the prisoners would be dissected, their blood sera and organs collected and studied, often without benefit of anesthesia—for fear that the anesthetic would affect the condition of blood and organs and therefore taint the results of the experiment. The method of murder for some experiment subjects was a strike to the head with an axe, so that the brain could be immediately removed for examination. But most prisoners died of the particular microbial disease or chemical toxin that the doctors had inflicted upon them, or from some medical study such as blood-letting or electrocution experiments, or finally, from a lethal injection if they had survived all else. A crematorium was attached to the lab unit, and each day the remaining flesh and bones of the eviscerated victims were turned to billowing chimney smoke and ash. Beinyinhe was an Auschwitz before there was Auschwitz.

The staff regularly shipped body tissue samples to the Tokyo Army Medical College for further analysis, and once the organs began arriving in Tokyo, it was not long before Japanese scientists there figured out what was going on in Beiyinhe. According to Kanagawa University professor Kei-ichi Tsuneishi, a leading scholar of Japanese germ warfare history, it soon became common knowledge among the military and public health leaders back in Tokyo that Ishii's Togo Unit was conducting human "A type" research. However, there is no record of any higher-up in Tokyo speaking out against the practice of killing—or in the language of the Togo Unit scientists, "sacrificing"—human beings.

Ishii was in fact eager to inform Japanese military higher-ups of his activities. In 1933 he invited Lieutenant General Saburo Endo to inspect his projects at the Fortress. Endo kept a record in his diary of what he saw, a secret world of scientists and physicians set free to test hypotheses and entertain their curiosity without the slightest regard for ethical constraints. In his entry of November 16, 1933, Endo described chemical weapons and electrocution tests: "With Colonel Ando and Lieutenant Tachihara I visited the Transportation Company Experimental Station [one of the code names for the Beiyinhe camp] and observed experiments . . . The Second Squad was responsible for poison gas, liquid poison; the First Squad electrical experiments. Two bandits were used. 1. Phosgene gas [a chemical warfare agent]—5 minute injection of gas into a brick-lined room; the subject was still alive one day after inhalation of gas; critically ill with pneumonia . . . 2. Potassium Cyanide—the subject was injected with 15 mg. of it; lost consciousness approximately 20 minutes later. 3. 20,000 volts—several jolts of that voltage not enough to kill the subject; injection required to kill the subject. 4. 5,000 volts—several jolts not enough; after several minutes of continuous currents, was burned to death. Left at 1:30 P.M."

Another Endo entry for that day read, "[U]sed two communists for the experiment. Victims of experiment were locked up in tight railings and given injections of a variety of germs."

He continued, "At night, talked with Colonel Tsukada till 1:30 A.M., but could not fall asleep, nor did I sleep soundly."

This was Endo's first direct exposure to biological warfare testing on humans, but he was not exactly a neophyte when it came to the implications of germ warfare, having been an assistant to Japan's chief army delegate at the Geneva Convention meeting of 1925 banning germ warfare. An entry in Endo's diary made only three weeks after the November 16 notation indicates his comfort level with Ishii's work. Endo wrote that he found the "germ warfare research facility" to be "superb . . . Operating cost of 200,000 yen may not be unreasonable." He remarked admiringly on the vast laboratory space available at Beiyinhe, estimating it at a stunning "600 meters square. A huge compound." This man, who had been in the diplomatic group that so publicly and high-mindedly signed the treaty against chemical and biological weapons, had in three weeks' time come to accept and even praise the most heinous violations of that accord.

Endo, operating in his new capacity as one of Ishii's military overseers, put the crowning touch of validation to Ishii's twisted thesis that the Geneva treaty had defined what his nation pragmatically should do, by outlining what morally it should not do. Ishii continually sought to gather Japan's most powerful men inside and outside the military for his personal exhibitions of the BW unit's progress on the new secret weapon of disease microbes. The human experiments were filmed, and from 1935 onward movies of the experiments were being shown to senior officers of the Kwantung Army on a regular basis. Among his viewers were Hideki Tojo himself, the prime minister of Japan during World War II and cocommander of the Pacific theater operations against the United States. In the 1930s Tojo served first in the Manchurian Kempeitai as head of the Police Affairs Section, then as chief of staff of the Kwantung Army, and he received multiple screenings of the Beinyinhe prisoner experiment films. The reels showed the agony of the dying prisoners in scientific chambers as methodical Japanese medics in white coats looked on. After several years of watching Ishii's version of home movies, however, even Tojo is said to have begun to find them unpleasant.

The scope of these films later expanded as Japan's biological and chemical warfare moved into the realm of open-air germ attacks on Chinese populations. In July 1940 Ishii ordered that a film be made of Japanese planes loading germ bombs for bubonic plague dissemination over the coastal Chinese city of Ningbo. He also stationed cameramen in the plane to film the bombs as they were unloaded in the air. He then gave a special screening of the film for an audience of "distinguished visitors," including some of Japan's top scientists, generals, and imperial family members, among them Prince Takeda, Emperor Hirohito's cousin, and Prince Mikasa, Hirohito's youngest brother. Mikasa himself, in his memoirs, wrote that he was shown "films where large numbers of Chinese prisoners of war brought by cargo trains were made to march on the Manchurian plain for poison gas experimentation on live subjects."

*   *   *

In late 1932, as Ishii was swiftly launching the world's first bio-war death camp, Hitler and Dr. Joseph Mengele were not yet in power, and the democratic Weimar republic still ruled in Germany. In the United States, New York governor Franklin Delano Roosevelt had just been elected president, and breadlines and soup kitchens dotted the landscape in Depression-devastated towns and cities. One could catch a showing of the Marx Brothers in *Animal Crackers* at the town cinema, or listen to comedian Jack Benny and crooner Bing Crosby entertaining on the radio.

In England that year, Aldous Huxley published his chilling novel *Brave New World*, foretelling life in a dehumanized, totalitarian biological dystopia 600 years in the future. The novel describes future bio-war in which "the explosion of the anthrax bombs is hardly louder than the popping of a paper bag," and a "technique for infecting water supplies" is said to be "particularly ingenious." These events would be realized within ten years' time when Japanese military squadrons released anthrax over China, and poisoned many Chinese water sources with lethal, infectious microbes. *Brave New World* also unveils a society where humans are conceived and born artificially into predestined castes, with many deliberately starved of oxygen in their embryo lab tanks, so that they would develop into a docile population of mentally retarded menial laborers. While the Japanese, unlike the Nazis, did not work toward eugenically breeding and segregating genetic lines of so-called superior and inferior persons, they conducted experiments involving infants and pregnant women in the prison labs that reduced mother and baby to subhuman objects of biological manipulation in a manner reminiscent of Huxley's nightmarish vision. And as in the novel, young people were systematically desensitized to death and human suffering. By the early 1940s, teams of "boy troops," some as young as thirteen, were being sent from Japan to Ishii's secret complex in Manchuria, where in addition to receiving a top-notch scientific education, they were made to assist in gruesome experiments on prisoners and even to participate in dissections of living human subjects. In *Brave New World*, children receive a "death conditioning" at the "Slough Crematorium" in which, explains the character Dr. Gaffney, "every tot spends two mornings a week in a Hospital for the Dying. All the best toys are kept there, and they get chocolate cream on death days. They learn to take dying as a matter of course." In 1932 Huxley's prophetic vision had already begun to come true in Ishii's nascent Togo Unit program at Harbin and Beiyinhe.

A year later the popular movie *The Island of Lost Souls* was released. It told the story of an evil scientist who biologically splices together humans and farm animals to create hybrid beings, experimental subjects, who asked bitterly, "Are we not men?" The film was based on the novel *The Island of Dr. Moreau*, written by H. G. Wells decades earlier in 1896, but it ran in theaters in America and Europe just as Japan's early lethal human experiments were secretly getting under way in Manchuria, and later some of these real-life experiments would indeed involve the transfer of animal blood to human prisoners, people who were being used like laboratory animals.

In 1932 and 1933 something was in the air that both mirrored and portended creeping real terrors in the post–World War I period, as technological advancements multiplied alongside the rising fascism and the remilitarization of the world's major nations.

One wonders how the medical atrocities of Beiyinhe could go on without some form of protest from the Chinese, a call for an investigation, and then a reaction from the rest of the world. Part of the answer lies in the nature of the societal conditions under Japanese occupation. The people who lived near the Fortress and who were drafted to build it were part of an impoverished, repressed community, effectively isolated from any press reports the Japanese did not control in Manchuria. As for Beiyinhe's prisoners, none survived to tell their story—with the exception of one group.

One night in 1934 many of the guards at Beiyinhe were either intoxicated or off-duty at parties related to the Japanese Mid-Autumn Festival, an occasion for heavy drinking. That night, a prisoner named Li managed to knock a guard over the head through his cell bars and grab the keys. Li unlocked his leg irons, opened his cell door, and proceeded to open all the other cells on his block. Most of the prisoners could not even leave their opened cells because they were too weak from their doctor-induced illnesses and repeated blood draining, but those who were physically able ran to the compound's outer wall, where by an amazing stroke of luck, a rainstorm had short-circuited the camp's security system, deactivating the electrified fencing and searchlights.

Li organized a human chain up and over the wall. Finally alerted to what was going on under their noses, the guards began shooting into the mass of escaping prisoners. There were thirty in this group. Li, who had placed himself at the bottom of the chain for others to climb upon, was killed, along with ten others. Twenty men made it over the wall; eight were gunned down outside or soon recaptured. The remaining dozen, however, managed to avoid recapture.

Wu Zemin, a Chinese villager who aided the escapees, recalled in a 1984 interview: "That night I heard footsteps behind the house, then someone banging on the door. Outside there were seven men wearing leg shackles . . . we took the men to a cave on the east side of the house, and we started breaking off the shackles. We were still working on them when the Japanese came to the edge of the village tracking down the escapees."

These seven men, freed of the shackles, managed to leave the village safely, elude the Japanese trackers, and link up with the five other escaped prisoners. Three days after the breakout, the twelve men met an elderly Chinese who took them to a group of partisan guerrillas living in a forest encampment. They told the guerrillas of their ordeal at Beiyinhe, and joined them in the anti-Japanese resistance. One of those men who made it out safely, Wang Ziyang, conveyed the words of Li, who had led the escape and, in an act of self-sacrifice, formed the base of the human ladder over the Fortress wall: Li desired that he tell the world that he was a loyal Communist Party member, and that he had done his best to help the party.

Rumors soon spread throughout the population of Manchuria and the anti-Japanese underground that the mysterious Beiyinhe complex was killing people in cruel and bizarre scientific experiments. However, the Kuomintang government of China did not seem to recognize what was happening in the neighboring Japanese puppet state of Manchuria, and the ex-prisoners' information was not processed through official channels.

Still, for the Japanese, the event had enormous consequences. Ishii responded by pressing the army chiefs in Tokyo for an even larger and more remote research station, where more biological warfare research could be conducted and from whose walls no one could possibly escape. That place was called Pingfan.

THREE

THE END OF HUMANITY

By THE MIDDLE OF 1935 THE BEIYINHE COMPLEX HAD BEEN razed to the ground; nearly all traces of the Zhong Ma prison, labs, barracks, and security wall eliminated. In its place, across the empire that Tokyo called the Greater East Asian Co-Prosperity Sphere, emerged an expanded and even more sophisticated version of Japan's cutting-edge biomedical death camp. An order by Emperor Hirohito himself in 1936 authorized the expansion of the Togo Unit and its formal integration into the Kwantung Army, participating in military BW training and operations. Soon Beiyinhe-inspired BW units were springing up in major cities and remote locations in Japanese-occupied Asian and Pacific territories. The network ultimately included secret bases along the Russian border in northern Manchuria, southern China, Thailand, Burma, Singapore, the Philippines, and New Guinea. Each of these "antiepidemic" stations employed between 120 and 500 persons, commanded by a major or a lieutenant colonel.

The headquarters of this new germ warfare empire was Pingfan, a Manchurian village about twenty-six kilometers southwest of Harbin. Like Beiyinhe, Pingfan was secluded yet conveniently located near the South Manchurian Railway line to Harbin. Ishii quietly contracted with a Tokyo corporation, the Nihon Tokoshu-Kogyo Company Ltd., to build the site. An airport rose on the grounds, causing a continual stream of air traffic in a part of

Manchuria that hitherto had seen few overflights. Planes flew to and from Pingfan and locations in Japan and in occupied China. The entire complex, six kilometers square, was surrounded by a dry moat, electrified fencing, and guardhouses, creating a security perimeter. The airspace over Pingfan became restricted territory as well, with no civilian aircraft allowed to fly over. No Chinese were permitted to reside within a certain radius of the top-secret compound, and, as at Beiyinhe, the military's construction of the new, secret installation forced the displacement of hundreds of poor local families, most of whom had lived there for generations. These families were made to sell their houses and land for a terribly small amount of money and then ordered to evacuate before they had time to harvest their crops, depriving many of them of the food they needed to make it through the harsh Manchurian winter.

Overseers from Nihon Tokoshu-Kogyo hired local Chinese workers at low wages and made them work feverishly, sometimes through the night, to raise the new BW headquarters. Even so, it took three years to complete the facility at Pingfan, though this did not stop experiments on prisoners, the breeding of lethal bacteria, and the testing of germ bombs from occurring while the construction proceeded.

Yue Zhen Fu, who worked as a coolie laborer at Pingfan, recalled seeing soldiers driving from the site to the Japanese consulate in Harbin every other day, then returning with eight or more prisoners. He noted that on Saturday afternoons, special vehicles brought in victims from other holding places in Harbin. In a chilling similarity to the infamous cattle cars used to carry Jews and Gypsies into Auschwitz and other death camps and experiment wards of the Nazis, a rail spur off the main line from Harbin transported prisoners directly into Pingfan in a sealed train car. The stretch of track into Pingfan was officially secret—the South Manchurian Railway did not acknowledge its existence—

and it served no other purpose than to ferry victims and supplies into Pingfan. The use of secret trains by both the Germans and the Japanese reflects the basic practicalities of this method: There is no more speedy and efficient way to clandestinely transport numbers of human victims than by rail. One former laborer told an American TV interviewer in 1995, "In our hearts, we knew what was going on, but we had to keep our mouths shut, otherwise we'd be killed." The man drew his arm across his neck, in a beheading motion.

Another Pingfan worker, Fang Zhen Yue, remembers a day in November 1943 when a "special train" arrived at the complex. He peeked out of a window in the building where he was laboring, knowing he would be executed if he were caught looking by the ever-present Japanese guards. Fang described several Japanese technicians in white coats coming out from Pingfan's huge prison building, pulling flatbed carts up to the doors of the train. At this point packages wrapped in straw were carefully handed off to the technicians from the train. Fang could not believe his eyes: Inside each of the straw bundles were two live human prisoners bound together, head to foot.

Not surprisingly, the Japanese army's treatment of the Chinese workers was abominable. Wages were just enough to keep a laborer's family from starvation; sometimes the Chinese were compensated with heroin-laced cigarettes instead of money. Heroin and opium had been legalized for public consumption in Manchuria by the Japanese authorities, and their military was notoriously involved in drug trafficking and the cultivation of poppy fields in Manchuria and Korea for production of the narcotics. Wage payment in heroin to Chinese workers became common practice in Manchuria, and later in occupied China.

To pacify the villagers living nearby, the Japanese stuck to an increasingly unbelievable story that Pingfan was being developed as a lumber mill. Therefore, they said, locals should not concern themselves with all the construction work. Nor should they worry about the late-night trains rolling into the restricted zone. Although windowless black Dodge vans regularly drove into the Pingfan parking lot, the Chinese neighbors were warned by the Japanese military to also ignore these vehicles. The Japanese referred to them as "special transport" and told the locals that they were to move out of viewing distance of the vans whenever police sirens sounded. Any disobedience of these instructions would lead to severe punishment.

Clearly, the escape of prisoners from Beiyinhe had moved Ishii to redouble his efforts to create in Pingfan a more secure human experiment center. Yet even before the escape, Ishii had been planning a move to a larger central facility, with ambitions to expand BW research efforts and BW lab stations throughout Manchuria. The official titles of this biological and chemical warfare unit, the "Epidemic Prevention and Water Supply Unit of the Kwantung Army," and the "Epidemic Prevention and Water Purification Corps," were themselves shameless acts of deception. Informally, it was known as the Ishii Unit. Its Division 2 was devoted to legitimate water purification and hygiene research, located in the converted sake distillery in Harbin. Divisions 1, 3, and 4 operated in the secret Pingfan installation and executed the unit's main purpose: planning for germ warfare attacks and carrying out human experiments and the mass production of BW germs. Another BW installation, Unit 100, was established at this time at Changchun, the capital city of the Japanese Manchukuo puppet state; this station, smaller than Pingfan, was also known as the Wakamatsu Unit, after its director, Major General Yujiro Wakamatsu, and it specialized in veterinary diseases. Doctors there also lethally experimented on thousands of human prisoners.

In 1941 the Pingfan station received the designation "Unit 731" from the Kwantung Army command, and this became the name by which Japanese military and civilian researchers commonly identified the unit. Among historians of the war, the name Unit 731 generally is used to refer to Pingfan throughout the unit's existence, from 1936 through 1945.

Regardless of the various names Ishii's unit went by, Emperor Hirohito probably knew, from the beginning, that the doctor had been conducting unorthodox human experiments. The military hierarchy of the Manchuria occupation certainly knew, so it is unlikely that the emperor would be out of the loop and believe that he was simply ordering the expansion of a military hygiene division. It is also worth noting that Hirohito was a trained biologist who spent many hours of his life examining slides under the microscope. He took a special interest in sea slugs, and authored peer-reviewed scientific papers on their life cycle and physiology. It would be strange if a man of his scientific enthusiasms was not kept well informed about the largest, most sensational, and most militarily sensitive biological project happening under his rule.

According to the Khabarovsk war crimes trial testimony of Lieutenant General Ryuji Kajitsuka, one of Ishii's earliest military supporters, the Ishii Unit (or Epidemic Prevention and Water Supply Unit, as the expanded Togo Unit had become formally known) was "formed by command of the Emperor of Japan Hirohito. Issued in 1936." Kajitsuka, who had served as chief of medical administration of the Kwantung Army, noted: "The Emperor's command was printed and copies of it were sent to all units of the Japanese Army for the information of all the officers. I myself was shown this command and the detachment's personnel list accompanying it, and certified the fact with my private seal."

Kajitsuka had examined a list of proposed senior officers to be attached to the Ishii Unit, which had been submitted to him by the Ministry of War, and he had helped to recruit junior officers to the unit. "The detachment's location [at Pingfan] was determined by the Kwantung Army headquarters," he recalled. Not

only did the army relocate the detachment to Pingfan, it authorized an increase in the number of scientific personnel under
Ishii's command, from roughly 300 in Beiyinhe to more than
1,000, including many prominent medical researchers from Japan's
best universities. A new stage in the evolution of the military's
involvement with human experimentation and biological warfare
had begun, as Ishii's way of thinking was proliferating throughout
the ranks of army and civilian academic professionals alike.

In the autumn of 1936 Major Ishii delivered a rousing inaugural
address to more than sixty assembled personnel at Pingfan. Speaking in a newly constructed conference room in the large administration building, he exhorted his colleagues in medicine and
biology to be enthusiastic scientific pioneers and to use the lavish
resources and unique freedoms of human experimentation at their
disposal. Standing before them in the spare and elegant space, a
pot of blooming chrysanthemums on a square floor mat the
room's only adornment, Ishii told the unit members, "Our God-
given mission as doctors is to challenge all varieties of disease-
causing micro-organisms; to block all roads of intrusion into the
human body; to annihilate all foreign matter resident in our bodies and to devise the most expedient treatment possible. However, the research work upon which we are now to embark is the
complete opposite of those principles, and may cause us some
anguish as doctors."

   This speech appeared in a January 1952 article in the Sunday
magazine section of the Tokyo newspaper *Mainichi*. The piece,
written under the pseudonym "(ex-)Colonel Sakaki Ryohei," was
the work of a conscience-stricken BW veteran who to this day
remains unidentified. The author called Ishii "Nishikawa," as he
was well aware that Ishii and other Unit 731 leaders were alive

and residing in Japan in 1952. Most scholars of Japan's BW program agree that the article's reconstruction of the scene is probably accurate, and it provides a critical glimpse into the mindset of some of Japan's top physicians and biomedical researchers as they prepared to greatly expand the military's human experiment and germ warfare program.

Ishii's calculated words, acknowledging that these brilliant doctors and scientists might experience some "anguish" for betraying the ethical codes of medicine and science, appear designed to persuade them that jumping into this awful abyss was justifiable, even glorious, in the defense of Japan. "Nevertheless I beseech you to pursue this research," he told the professionals in that room, "based on the dual thrill of One: as a scientist to exert efforts to probe for the truth in natural science and research into, and discovery of, the unknown world and Two: as a military person, to successfully build a powerful military weapon against the enemy."

After all, the twisted research of Unit 731 had the blessings of the army and, it seemed, the emperor himself. Then there was the prominence of Dr. Shiro Ishii, a highly respected army surgeon and microbiologist.

For all of the time that Ishii supervised human experiments and germ warfare operations, he held on to his academic post at the Tokyo Army Medical College, which he had retained since 1931. Ishii also lectured at Tokyo Imperial University; at his alma mater, Kyoto Imperial University; and at other prestigious universities, army medical colleges, and public health institutes. At Pingfan he quickly established a routine in which he spent three months of the year back home in Japan doing bio-weapons research at universities there, and lecturing and recruiting many of the top Japanese scientists and physicians for work at Pingfan and other secret bases of germ warfare and human medical experimentation. Some of Ishii's classroom lectures baldly revealed the unethical work being done in Manchuria, and potential recruits—

medical students and microbiologists—were shown eight-millimeter films of biological warfare research processes. The films displayed not only the production of germs and microscope examinations, but also the infection and dissection of the human subjects. (Pingfan's two pathology sections handled the surgical examinations of the prisoners, and an enormous number of illustrated research reports on the vivisections were issued within Unit 731 and its satellite stations.) Photographs and sample microscope slides were also presented to his classes.

The lure of such unfettered, secret medical research proved to be quite strong for the thousands of civilian scientists who traveled from Japan to Manchuria and occupied China to work for Unit 731 and its affiliated installations. A number of physicians even made special excursions to Pingfan to take advantage of the rare opportunity to witness a human vivisection. That surgical procedure was an unparalleled biomedical opportunity afforded the doctors and scientists by the Japanese BW units. It gave researchers the ability to study the organs of a living person as a disease progressed through the body.

"The results of the effects of infection cannot be obtained accurately once the person dies because putrefactive bacteria set in," one former Unit 731 member remarked. "Putrefactive bacteria are stronger than plague germs. So for obtaining accurate results, it is important whether the subject is alive or not." Anesthesia on the vivisected human beings was optional and frequently not used because of the effects of the anesthetic chemicals upon the body and the sedated state of the body, which create an interference effect upon the particular disease being studied. A live, unanesthetized body produced the purest experimental results.

The vivisections in Manchuria allowed doctors to induce diseases and examine their effects on organs in the first stages. Researchers worked with interpreters to ask about emerging symptoms, and took subjects out of cells at what they judged to be the optimum time for symptoms and effects. "As soon as the symptoms were observed," a Pingfan veteran recalled, "the prisoner was taken from his cell and into the dissecting room. He was stripped and placed on the table screaming, trying to fight back. He was strapped down, still screaming frightfully. One of the doctors stuffed a towel into his mouth, then with one quick slice of the scalpel he was opened up."

The victim tied to the vivisection table did not die immediately after being cut open; frequently, she or he must have been conscious as the doctors and their assistants busily examined the heart, liver, intestines, and other organs. Eventually, the human subject would die from the steady loss of body tissues and blood.

For any doctors listening to Ishii in the Pingfan conference room that day who might still have had misgivings, the major provided an additional incentive. "Compared with the research laboratories with which you are familiar in the universities in the large cities," he said, Pingfan "is inferior to none, and we can be rather proud of the fact that we have several times the equipment. How can anyone, other than those of you assembled here, imagine in his wildest dreams that there exists such a splendid cultural research laboratory in the middle of these expansive wilds? On top of this, we have no worry whatsoever about the availability of research funds."

It was true; Ishii now had the military support, the facilities, and the money to lure a greatly increased talent pool of professionals. Several surviving photos of the Pingfan complex taken from an airplane provide vistas on the stupendous expanse of the facility—more than 150 buildings on a site that measured six kilometers square around its perimeter. It can perhaps best be described as a secret city devoted to human experimentation and the waging of biological warfare. Pingfan's facilities included world-class microbiology laboratories, a pathology lab, factories for the mass production of lethal bacteria, and breeding houses for thousands of rats and millions of insects, with the finest medical equipment and pharmaceuticals available in this, the most technologically advanced of biological and medical research centers. There were veterinary buildings that held monkey cages, stables for horses, and large pens for rabbits, sheep, goats, camels, and cattle. These assembly lines of biological genocide stood adjacent to comfortable dormitory-style housing for the Japanese scientists and military officers whose wives and children sometimes visited and lived with them. The medical and health facilities for the Japanese living and working at Pingfan were the best that Japan had to offer. In fact, the complex lacked for none of the amenities of upper-class Japanese life, boasting a Shinto temple, restaurants, a fully stocked bar, a school for the children of Unit 731 employees with primary- and secondary-level classes, an enormous auditorium that served as a movie theater, storage units for vegetables and fish, a swimming pool, gardens, a library, athletic and recreational fields—even an on-site geisha house. It was like a resort spa enveloped in a biomedical death camp, a shocking expression of human inequality.

The programs at Pingfan and other secret BW bases grew steadily from 1936 onward, and Chinese and Japanese scholars currently believe that at its height, just before the war's end in August 1945, Imperial Japan's BW and human experiment network of death camps and research laboratories employed more than 20,000 civilian physicians, surgeons, nurses, biologists, microbiologists, chemists, veterinarians, entomologists, plant pathologists, and other scientists and technicians, all of them plunging the integrity and legacy of Japan's leading health institutions into a shameful darkness.

In a 1946 postwar interview with an American military investigator, Dr. Ryochi Naito, one of the leading Unit 731 experimenters, testified that so many civilian doctors worked for the BW program that knowledge of the human experiments and use of germ warfare became widespread within Japan's medical and scientific research communities. Naito was himself a top university professor who had been director of the Unit 731 branch unit in Singapore, a civilian cohort of Ishii, with special expertise in the analysis of human blood. It now seems possible, given the steady airplane flights between Tokyo, Harbin, and Pingfan bearing Unit 731 research scientists and specimens, that Naito and other physicians conducted lethal human experiments at the Army Medical College in Tokyo. In 1989 construction workers digging on the former site of the medical college (it was destroyed during the war) found human skeletons buried in the bustling Shinjuku District of Tokyo. The remains were on the former site of the medical college, the bones and skulls bearing the marks of bullets, drill holes, and surgical knife incisions. "Most microbiologists in Japan were in some way or other connected with Ishii's work," Naito said, and it quickly became "common knowledge throughout Japan . . . that humans were used for experimentation at the Harbin installation."

Yet for the fourteen years his units functioned, Ishii referred with pride to the BW program as the "Secret of Secrets." For this reason he trusted only a core group with the most intimate details of Pingfan. They included military officers and scientists who had served in the old Togo Unit in Harbin, and men hailing from his hometown of Chiyoda Mura. These were Ishii's family members, former business venture cronies, and longtime friends, all deeply loyal to him. To be absolutely sure that the prison's security would not be compromised, Ishii appointed his brother Takeo as the director of security for Pingfan's central prison—where the cells holding Pingfan's experimental "precious human material," as Shiro Ishii called the victims, were located. Another brother, Mitsuo, he made the head of Pingfan's animal breeding facilities.

The prison blocks were in a three-story edifice that was in turn surrounded by the Ro building, a five-story structure that housed bacteria-production facilities and infectious-disease research laboratories. The building's name came from the shape of the Japanese *katakana* character "ro," which is square, and the Ro building formed a quadrangle around the prison structures and was purposely built two stories taller than the prison within, so as to hide the prison from the view of those on the Pingfan grounds. The prison compound was the most heavily guarded part of this elaborately defended base. The Ro building was located next to the administration building housing the offices and meeting rooms of Unit 731's directors and researchers, which meant that men, women, and children prisoners suffered in agony and despair just yards from chatting doctors, secretaries, and officers excitedly discussing their research and dreaming up new BW experiments in their stately paneled rooms.

Pingfan's prison held up to 400 inmates at any one time. Victims came to the Number 7 and 8 prison blocks by way of a secret tunnel leading from the administration building to the prison, and there were other tunnels down there too. One ran from the prison to the experimental laboratories, which included a chamber for human poison-gas studies and human vivisection rooms, and another led from the lab area to the crematorium.

The Number 7 block was reserved for adult male inmates only. The Number 8 block imprisoned men, women, and children. Each cell was separated from the next by a soundproof wall of concrete over one foot in width. On the floor of the cell lay bedding materials and blankets, and a flush toilet built into the floor surface. The interiors of these rooms were heated in the winter and air-conditioned in the summer so that environmental temperature could be controlled and did not distort the results of a human experiment one way or the other.

Sometimes prisoners were placed in these cells individually and in isolation from the other human "logs of wood," and at other times they would be grouped together in wider cells that could accommodate up to ten people. It depended upon the doctors' orders for the particular experimental controls of the tests for which each prisoner became a subject. The door to each cell had an opening through which prisoners could extend their arms for mandatory blood drawings or hypodermic injections. If a prisoner was too weak or ill to do this, or refused to put his or her arm through the opening, guards would enter the cell and forcibly hold him or her down to receive the needle.

Prison cells and corridors were kept clean and hygienic by Unit 731 personnel so as to prevent common germs (such as those causing colds and flu) from affecting prisoners' health, and to keep the germs of prisoners who'd been experimented on from traveling throughout the prison and contaminating other "specimens." All these efforts and precautions to keep the prisoners healthy—as at Beiyinhe, prisoners were given balanced meals and encouraged to exercise—were in the service of keeping the specimens, the methodology, and the experiment results as pristine as possible, which really was all that the doctors and researchers cared about.

From the Japanese official line that Pingfan was a lumber mill came a sick joke. If Pingfan was a lumber mill, one researcher commented, the people inside were the logs. The quip caught on, and from that point on the Japanese word for "log," *maruta*, was the term the physicians, nurses, scientists, and military personnel used to describe their victims. Like so many pieces of wood, the inmates were slated by their medical jailers to be carved up and incinerated in the large crematorium. Technician Yoshio Shinozuka, who participated in several vivisections, remembered a refrain among the other doctors and technicians:

" 'How many logs did you down today?'

" 'At my place, we downed two!' "

By the time Pingfan was in full gear in 1939 and Ishii had

been promoted to the rank of colonel, the tall crematorium smokestack spewed the ashes of these human "logs" day and night into the Manchurian sky.

Each prisoner suffered a scientific reductionism of his or her body into its constituent organs, blood, and cellular subsets; each captive was literally harvested for whatever experimental value he or she possessed and then, if the doctors in charge called for it, dissected alive. It appears from the copious testimony, recovered documents, and ongoing confessions of those in charge that this was usually the fate of prisoners at Pingfan. The sophisticated laboratories there maintained a standard daily routine for years. Technicians in the lab would check a bulletin board on the wall to see the status of the prisoner *maruta*, followed by their identification numbers, with respect to the number of injections or germ dosages each had been administered. Notes were made by the physicians and scientists with instructions to the technicians, indicating, for example, which inmates were to be removed from their cells and dragged into the labs; or requesting a certain number of brains, hearts, or livers required for a study. The technicians followed orders to ready the laboratory space in various ways for the next experiment, and to take the victims from Ro buildings 7 and 8 through the tunnels over to that particular lab room.

There was virtually no difference in the way a human subject was experimented on and the way a lab animal or plant would be treated, right down to the vivisection and scooping out of organs for further weighing, probing, and examination of samples under the pathologist's microscope. The utter dehumanization of the victims and the dehumanizing effect on the perpetrators were official policy, and if a Japanese professional acknowledged that the prisoners were human beings, he or she would be looked on with contempt and suspicion by colleagues.

Technicians who assisted the pathologists in vivisections received extra pay, known as the Chemical Weapons Allowance.

In 1997 the former technician Yoshio Shinozuka wrote of the vivisection of a Chinese man. The victim was dissected alive after the biological warfare experiment to which he had been subjected had run its course and he had begun exhibiting severe symptoms:

> I still remember clearly the first vivisection I participated in. I knew the Chinese individual we dissected . . . because I had taken his blood once for testing. At the vivisection I could not meet his eyes because of the hate he had in his glare at me. This intelligent-looking man was systematically infected with plague germs. As the disease took its toll, his face and body became totally black. Still alive, he was brought on a stretcher by the special security forces to the autopsy room. Transferred to the autopsy table, the chief pathologist ordered us to wash his body. I used a rubber hose and a deck brush to wash him. Since this was my first vivisection, I think I was somewhat sloppy in washing him. I remember feeling somewhat hesitant in using the brush on his face. Watching me, the chief pathologist, with scalpel in hand, impatiently signaled me to hurry up. I closed my eyes and forced myself to scrub the man's face with the deck brush. The chief pathologist listened to the man's heartbeat with his stethoscope and then the procedure started.
>
> The man's organs were methodically excised one by one and I did as I was ordered to. I put them in a culturing can we had already prepared.

Whenever the victim died before a live dissection could be performed, the body would be put on a gurney and wheeled into the autopsy room as soon as possible after death, where pathologists performed an autopsy, making a Y-shaped incision upon the person's torso. Often specific organs would be removed and stored for further analysis—the heart and other organs frequently would still be beating and pulsing as they were dropped into formalin-filled glass specimen jars. The corpses would then be carted to the incineration rooms. "The bodies always burned up fast," explained one Japanese veteran who assisted in the burning of the prisoners' bodies after vivisections. "Because all the organs were gone; the bodies were empty."

Japanese veterans who had spent time at Pingfan speak of having visited rooms with large display cases with glass containers holding grotesque specimens: a baby who had died of smallpox; bodies of children; severed heads floating; disembodied organs, arms, legs. The body of a Russian man, suspended in a six-foot-tall glass case of formalin liquid, was split open lengthwise from head to feet.

One Unit 731 veteran, interviewed on condition of anonymity, said: "I saw samples with labels saying 'American,' 'English' and 'Frenchman,' but most were Chinese, Koreans and Mongolians. Those labeled as American were just body parts, like hands or feet, and some were sent in by other military units."

On average, an individual inmate would usually last several weeks before dying of the experiment procedures to which that person had been subjected. If a prisoner had managed to survive the doctors' designs, that person would eventually be dispatched with a lethal injection. Once a prisoner was sent to a Japanese BW prison, the system mandated that he or she would not emerge alive. Unit 731 veterans say that the longest-lived *maruta* would generally survive for four to six months, although there are reports of Pingfan victims surviving longer; in some of these cases the inmates were women and children.

In December 1984 two British television documentary makers

conducted an interview with Unit 731 veteran Naokata Ishibashi, a civilian who had worked as a medical orderly and physician's assistant in a section that conducted checkups on new prisoners. Nine years after that interview, Ishibashi made personal appearances at the educational exhibit of Unit 731 human experiment and biological warfare crimes, which traveled throughout Japan from July 1993 to December 1994. The exhibit caused a sensation in Japan and resulted in a flood of magazine articles, books, and television programs on the subject in a media phenomenon that became known as the "Unit 731 Boom." He presented speeches in person and on videotape that further elaborated on his experiences with Unit 731. "Someone asked me whether I had seen any women *maruta*," Ishibashi recalled. "Personally, I saw only two, in the Number 8 prison block. One was a twenty-one-year-old married Chinese woman; the other was an unmarried Soviet girl of nineteen. I asked her where she came from and she said the Ukraine, very far away. Those women were not used in any experiments during the time that I was there. They said they had not seen their faces in a mirror since the time they were captured, and they begged me to get them one. I sneaked them a mirror and told them to be careful the Kempeitai or the jail guards didn't see it."

Ishibashi's 1984 interview provides further details on these two Number 8 block biological prisoners. Speaking of the young Chinese woman, he said, "It was written on her card that she was not a virgin. She had helped anti-Japanese elements by giving them overnight stays and things. The Russian girl . . . came from Kiev. Our section tried to keep them alive after they recovered from each test. . . . I think the Chinese girl survived for about two years. A friend of mine told me the Russian girl was poisoned in the end. I was very sad. We did terrible things."

Rumiko Nishino, a Japanese author and journalist, has tenaciously pursued the long-suppressed details of Unit 731 venereal disease experiments and the abuse of women within the Japanese bio-war prisons. In investigating Unit 731 medical crimes against female inmates, Nishino has underscored the particular abuse that they suffered at the hands of Imperial Japan and linked it to other crimes of Japanese wartime violence against Asian women, such as mass rape and forced prostitution.

In December 1994 Nishino delivered a disturbing lecture presenting the confession of an unnamed former Pingfan human experiment researcher whom she had tracked down. This former researcher recalled to her that one day at Pingfan, with some free time on his hands before the next scheduled experiment, he and another man took the keys to the cells where women were imprisoned. In one cell, one of the men raped a Chinese woman, while the other Unit 731 member unlocked the door to a separate cell to find another Chinese woman, who had been used as a subject in a frostbite experiment. Nishino describes the scene: "She had several fingers missing and her bones were black, with gangrene set in. He was about to rape her anyway, when he saw that her sex organ was festering, with pus oozing to the surface. He gave up the idea, left, and locked the door."

One Russian woman was pregnant at the time she was brought to the Number 8 prison block of Pingfan. There she gave birth to her child, and both she and the child lived there for two years. During this time, the two were tortured repeatedly by the physicians of Unit 731. Kiyoshi Kawashima, a physician and major general of the medical service, had at different times led both the Unit 731 Division 4, in charge of producing germs, and its Division 1, the grouping of professionals that ran the human experiments. Kawashima testified after the war, at the Soviet war crimes trial in Khabarovsk, that he had seen this Russian woman "with a baby in arms" at Pingfan, and in response to the question of whether "this woman too was not destined to leave the prison alive?" answered, "Such was the rule when I served in the detachment, and that is what happened to this woman too."

Unit 731 used women intensively in its studies of sexually transmitted diseases. Under the direction of Pingfan's Dr. Hideo Futaki, the same research group that worked on tuberculosis experiments were also assigned to syphilis tests, perhaps because both bacterial diseases manifest in victims as slow, chronic illnesses. Unit 731's research into such illness indicates an interest in spreading contagion that would cause long-term hardship to civilian communities. Tuberculosis and venereal diseases served no battlefield-attack or short-term military strategic purposes, but syphilis had become a vexing problem for the Japanese army in Manchuria, as thousands of troops had developed serious infections. It is clear from the nature of the Unit 731 experiments that the research went beyond ascertaining how the Japanese could better protect soldiers from venereal disease. Some of these studies involved pregnant women and the passage of syphilis bacteria from mother to infant.

An anonymous veteran of Unit 731 who had served as Ishii's driver and personal assistant told Nishino: "At first we infected women with syphilis by injection. But this method did not produce real research results. Syphilis is normally transmitted through direct contact. Investigating the course of this disease can offer no useful results unless it is acquired this way. And so we followed a system of direct infection through sexual contact." Nishino learned that "direct infection" of the kind mentioned by the researcher was accomplished through forced sex acts between men and women prisoners. The forcing of involuntary sexual contact between people has occurred at many other times and places in history, for example, by Japanese soldiers during the Rape of Nanking, which raged from December 1937 until February 1938.

From her interviews, Nishino learned that "four or five unit members, dressed in white laboratory clothing completely covering the mouth and eyes, handled the tests. A male and female, one infected with syphilis, would be brought together in a cell and forced into sex with each other. It was made clear that anyone resisting would be shot. Once the healthy partner was infected, the progress of the disease would be observed closely to determine for example how far it advanced the first week, the second week, and so forth. Instead of merely looking at external signs, such as the condition of the sexual organs, the researchers were able to employ live dissection to investigate how different internal organs are affected at different stages of the disease."

Some of the women subjected to the forced sex acts became pregnant, and their babies were born into the hell of the Unit 731 prison laboratories, delivered by the Ishii Unit's doctors and nurses. Those infants, like their mothers, were killed and dissected in experiments. So too were babies born to women who were already pregnant at the time they entered the prison. Several Unit 731 veterans have attested to the fact that one of the babies born in Pingfan was half Japanese. A Unit 731 technician had raped the infant's mother, a "log of wood" prisoner, and the baby was the result. This infant too was subject to experimentation and dissection. Older children, boys and girls of six, seven, or eight years, were also used in germ and chemical tests. No child prisoner ever left Pingfan alive.

Unit 731 scientists, speaking to investigators of the U.S. military after the war, described experiments in which their "logs" committed suicide. One can imagine that a prime motivation for the prisoners, besides seeking to avoid terribly painful deaths by medical atrocity, was to sabotage the experiments and the doctors' research goals. In describing an experiment, one in a series of tests in which prisoners were made to consume milk and sugar water tainted with strains of typhoid bacteria, Unit 731 researcher Dr. Kanau Tabei said that in addition to two deaths from typhoid, three of the prisoner subjects "committed suicide." In a set of thirty-five reports made to the American investigators by dozens of Japanese bio-war scientists, 801 people were recorded as dying in the course of experiments or being "sacrificed," as the Unit 731 professionals euphemistically termed the killing of prisoners at some point in the experiment. According to those reports, an additional thirty prisoner deaths in these tests were the result of suicides.

Tabei had also served as chief of Unit 731's "First Division," which managed the Pingfan prison. He confessed that he had worked on typhoid experiments from 1938 until 1943, when he left Pingfan. Yoshio Furuichi, a medical orderly at Pingfan and witness at the Khabarovsk trial, remembered participating in one of Tabei's experiments in early 1943: "I prepared one liter of sweetened water, which I infected with typhoid germs. This liter I then mixed with more water, and this was administered to about 50 imprisoned Chinese, war prisoners, if I remember rightly, only some of whom had been inoculated against typhoid." During these years he subjected perhaps several hundred victims to infection. In another experiment, Tabei told his American interviewer, "one subject was exposed to a bomb burst containing buckshot mixed with 10 mg bacilli and 10 gm of clay. The buckshot had grooves, which were impregnated with the bacteria-clay mixture. . . . He developed symptoms of typhoid fever with positive laboratory signs."

The interview also revealed incidents of the experimenters themselves becoming ill, an occupational hazard of biological warfare work that claimed lives in Japan's BW program. According to Tabei, the doctors of Pingfan took advantage of their accidents to assess ethnic differences in the inherent immunity of Japanese persons versus that of native Manchurians. Noted Tabei's interviewer: "Laboratory infections occurred in two Japanese investigators [accidentally infected in the course of their research] who seemed to be much sicker than Manchurians although none died. It was the impression of Dr. Tabei that Manchurians had more natural resistance than Japanese." This kind of biological friendly fire sometimes also extended to the battlefield, as when thousands of Japanese troops fighting the Zhejiang Province campaign of summer 1942 became ill with cholera, dysentery, and other diseases that had been disseminated by Ishii's men. Scientists at the BW unit based in Nanking, affiliated with Unit 731, kept statistics on the number of Japanese soldiers that they estimated had been felled by germs intended to target the Chinese. By the end of 1942 they found that 1,700 men had died of BW infections when they entered a contaminated region, and some 10,000 soldiers had become sick enough to be incapacitated. As late as the summer of 1943 the Japanese isolation wards at Hangzhou Army Hospital were filled with thousands of soldiers recovering from the illnesses caused by their own side's BW assaults.

The population of Manchuria was mostly of Han Chinese ethnicity, and these people made up the majority of the inmates at Pingfan. But among the prisoners were also ethnic Russian residents from Harbin and some from Harbin's sizable Russian Jewish community. The prisoners also included Soviet POWs who had been captured in the brutal Nomonhan battles in the summer of 1939 and other border skirmishes, people of the Manchu ethnic group, Koreans, Mongolians, and Europeans of various nationalities. Most were accused of an assortment of crimes, including spying. The case of Colonel Takeo Tachibana is one typical example of the role played by the Kwantung Army's Kempeitai in rounding up human fodder for Unit 731 experiments. At the 1949 Khabarovsk war crimes trial, Tachibana, formerly of the Kempeitai, stated that "special consignments" (Tokui-Atsukai)—people shipped to Pingfan—consisted of broad political- and subversive-dissident classifications.

"The people sent," Tachibana testified, "were of the following categories: persons accused of espionage on behalf of foreign states, or suspected of being implicated in foreign espionage, and also so-called *hunghutzu*, that is, Chinese partisans; then came the category of anti-Japanese elements, incorrigible criminal elements—recidivists. . . . [M]y administration sent to Detachment 731 no less than six people, who never returned from there and perished as a result of experiments."

A top-secret document of the Kempeitai's "Kwantung Gendarmerie Headquarters Exceptionally Important Affairs Division," obtained by the Soviets, details the categories of the people to be sent as Tokui-Atsukai to the Ishii Unit. It is obvious from the instructions to Kempeitai officers contained in this 1943 document that a person even suspected of dissent against the Japanese regime or harboring subversive thoughts became a candidate for shipment to the experiment chambers of Unit 731.

Colonel Tadashi Tamura, chief of the personnel division for General Otozoo Yamada, a commander-in-chief of the Kwantung Army, inspected Unit 731 in June 1945 and reported his observations to General Yamada. Colonel Tamura, a war crimes trial witness, recounted this visit to a Soviet interviewer in 1945. He recalled being "taken to an inner building where, in special cells, each of which had a window on the door, living people were kept in chains, who, as Ishii himself told me, were used for experiments in infection with deadly diseases.

"Among these experimentees I saw Chinese, Europeans, and a woman. As General Ishii himself informed me, this woman and the Europeans were of Russian nationality who had been sent to the detachment by the Japanese Gendarmerie and Military Missions in Manchuria from among those who, in the opinion of the Japanese penal authorities, were to be exterminated. . . . I myself saw that the people in these cells were lying on the bare floor and were in a very sick and helpless condition."

Often times, if a shortfall in the number of people needed for an experiment occurred, or a particular body type, sex, or age was called for, the gendarmerie would, citing Unit 731 directives, snatch Manchurian citizens going about their daily business and ship them off to the laboratories of Pingfan. The General Affairs Section at Pingfan would mandate the secret pickups of unsuspecting people without even the quasi-judicial formalities of police arrest and detention as described by Colonel Tachibana. They simply kidnapped people from the streets and fields, and even pulled them from their homes in sudden raids. Scientists would specify what kind of *maruta*—male or female, child or adult—was needed in the labs, depending on the requirements of their experiments.

The sinister-looking dark Dodge vans observed by the villagers living near Pingfan could also be seen cruising through the busy streets of Harbin, day or night. They even acquired a nickname, *voronki*, the Russian word for "raven," among the Russian-speaking inhabitants of Harbin. In one method of abduction in Harbin, Japanese authorities would advertise jobs. When people naively appeared at certain city offices to inquire about the positions, they were thrown into the *voronki*. The prisoners' cries for help and pounding on the walls of the vans were clearly audible as they drove through the city.

Rumors spread, and the residents of Harbin, like those people living in the districts around Beiyinhe and Pingfan, spoke in whispers to one another of the stories of these terrible secret installations. The Soviet consulate employees naturally realized that something extremely odd and sinister was going on. In addition to the conspicuous vans moving around Harbin, they couldn't help but observe road crews of Chinese under the command of Japanese bosses building a paved road to the obscure place called Pingfan. Soon the traffic on this road included large numbers of cars carrying Japanese military officers. In an effort to figure out what the Japanese were up to, they secretly flew a transparent, small plastic balloon with a spy camera attached, and photographed all of Ishii's large Pingfan installation from high above.

Unit 731 definitely caught the attention of the Russians while it was functioning, but exactly how much they knew of its experiments and germ warfare activities remains an open question. It is likely that further research into this aspect of Unit 731 history by journalists, and the opening of more Soviet files, will reveal more information in the future.

Miou Yutaka was a former member of the Kempeitai "Special Handling Forces" in Dairen, which was responsible for rounding up prisoners to be used in Unit 731 experiments. "We tied them with ropes around their waist, and their hands behind their backs. They couldn't move. We took them by train in a closed car, then the Unit 731 truck would meet us at the station. It was a strange truck—black with no windows. A strange-looking vehicle," he said. "We knew the prisoners would be used in experiments and not come back."

Before being shipped to Pingfan, they were detained in the basement of the same elegant Japanese consulate where suspected spies and political prisoners were held before being sent off by the Kempeitai in shackles. Captives were tortured by the Kempeitai in the basement, then transported to Pingfan or to Unit 100, its satellite Manchurian experiment/BW installation near the Manchurian capital city of Changchun.

Outside Harbin, residents of the villages near Pingfan were also vulnerable to abduction. Mostly poor and struggling, these villagers lived in constant fear of being "disappeared" by the Japanese for the rumored murderous experiments. "My father, who ran a photography studio in Dairen, was arrested by the Japanese military police for 'underground activities' in Tianjin," said Wang Ibing, who was a plaintiff in the class-action civil suit filed in 1997 against the Japanese, seeking compensation for relatives lost to

BW experiments. "I heard from my uncle that my father had been sent to a biological weapons plant, but that was the last we saw of him. With my uncle's support I was finally able to graduate from elementary school. My mother and sisters were still in the farming village, but because my father was no longer around, they supported themselves with money from relatives and by selling farmland. Ultimately they even turned to begging. Because my father had been taken away, our family was subjected to dreadful poverty."

In 2001 a seventy-six-year-old lifelong neighbor of Pingfan named Zhang Guanghui remembered: "They would catch people surreptitiously and bring them to their laboratory. Local residents were afraid every day that they might be kidnapped by the Japanese. Before going outside, I had to stop and think: Are there Japanese around?"

Zhang himself was drafted by the Japanese to work in the area as a slave laborer, and as he left the house each day to go to his labor duties, he warned his family that he might not return to them.

As for those victims sent to the experiment laboratories who had been taken with the judicial formalities of legal charges and arrest, according to a Gendarmerie Headquarters document, the categories of arrest candidates were wide enough in scope to include, under the general heading of "SPIES (saboteurs)":

- Character of crime gives grounds for assuming that if legal proceedings are taken the person will be acquitted or sentenced to a short prison term and will soon leave the prison.

- If he is a vagrant, no permanent residence, no relatives. Opium smokers.

- Persons of like mind with those who come under the category of "special consignments." Also including those people: if notwithstanding the minor character of the crime, their release is undesirable.

Takeo Tachibana admitted that while stationed in the Manchukuo capital city of Changchun, he authorized the transfer of more than a hundred people to Pingfan and that in these cases a "special order" overrode the usual procedure of first requiring a trial before the military tribunal. Once a person was designated "special consignments," he was dispatched immediately to Pingfan. Likewise, suspects who were arrested but could not be put on trial due to lack of evidence were summarily handed over to the biological warfare scientists to serve as research fodder. Instructions specified that "pro-Soviet- and anti-Japanese-minded" people and those falling under the category of "Ideological Criminals Connected with the National and Communist Movements" could be sent to Unit 731 for extermination, along with those suspected of being hostile to the government in thought or actions, even "when the nature of the offense gives grounds for the assumption that, if sent for trial, the person will be acquitted or given a light sentence."

Unit 731 veteran Ishibashi recalled the procedure for processing the newly arrived inmates. Relating a perverse variation on the kind of routine medical testing done at a hospital, Ishibashi said, "We took details of their type of blood, its pulse and pressure and so on. . . . Although, when they arrived, they had cards each with their name, birthplace, reason for arrest and age, we simply gave them a number. A *maruta* was just a number, a piece of experimental material. . . . They seemed to know their fate."

Many Pingfan prisoners tried to resist the orders of the experiment doctors, and there were a number of escape attempts. But each time the rebellious inmates were put down by gas or bullets. No Pingfan prisoner survived to tell his or her story.

FOUR

SCIENCE SET FREE

IT HAS BECOME COMMON TO TYPIFY THE PERSONALITIES OF MEN who perform acts of great evil and inhumanity by the somewhat murky phrase "the banality of evil," a term coined by Holocaust scholar Hannah Arendt and applied to such infamous Nazis as Adolf Eichmann, hanged in Jerusalem in 1962 for his leading role in the Holocaust.

By this, Arendt meant that the perpetrators of Nazi genocide could be described as ordinary people with mundane middle-class lives: wives, children, pets, and hobbies; people who did not especially stand out as odd or antagonistic in their everyday existence, apart from their ghastly day jobs.

But "banality" is the last term one would apply to Dr. Shiro Ishii. The portrait of Ishii that emerges, gathered from all who became associated with him in various ways, is one of a brash and flamboyantly corrupt man who considered himself a visionary.

Simultaneously a military commander, surgeon, and biomedical professor, Shiro Ishii was astounding in his versatility and the scope of his ambitions. He led Japan's biological warfare program, operating under the official title of Boeki Kyusui Bu, or Water Purification and Epidemic Prevention, from 1936 right up until Imperial Japan surrendered in August 1945. (Ishii did fall temporarily out of favor between August 1942 and March 1945, when he lost control of his empire and was transferred to the BW and human experiment station at Nanking. But in the last five months of the war he was reinstated.)

Ishii became a veritable one-man biological weapons barn-stormer. He mastered the skills of flying and personally piloted the planes from Pingfan's airfield to the various Unit 731–satellite bases in Manchuria and China. On the ground, Ishii would conduct personal inspections of the germ and chemical warfare facilities and personnel, giving morale-boosting speeches to the thousands of physicians, scientists, and military men under his watch. He is known to have flown on disease-spreading missions in China near the central city of Changde in 1940 and 1941, and over Zhejiang Province in 1942, and he regularly piloted planes with loads of human prisoners to the Anda open-air proving grounds, 146 kilometers northwest of Harbin. There, in a vast field, the prisoners would be tied to posts, with both arms bound behind their backs or stretched out, crucifixion-style, while germs or poison gas were disseminated upon them through various delivery methods.

In Japan's traditionally conservative medical and bureaucratic worlds, Ishii stood out as a bold eccentric. At times his antics seemed to test the very limits of sanity. His demonstrations of the Ishii Filter—his biggest claim to fame, after his notoriety as the founder of the BW program—in which he urinated on stage, poured his own liquid waste through his filter, and then drank it, vividly illustrate his antisocial tendencies. Yet Ishii's ways appear to have made him few opponents within the overlapping circles of medicine, microbiology, and military hierarchy in which he traveled. Part P.T. Barnum, part con artist, Ishii got away with a lot, including the embezzlement of money allocated for his units and extended drinking bouts at the bars of Harbin. He was free of every moral care, one might say, save perhaps for his professed patriotism to his nation and the war effort, and he would often summon top personnel to impromptu meetings at two or three in the morning when a new idea for an experiment or biological warfare scheme struck him, all with the unyielding support of his staff. As the years progressed and the men under Ishii's command began committing germ warfare crimes on an ever increasing scale, the use of germ weapons and human experimentation became an open secret to those in the intelligentsia. This drama began with Shiro Ishii, but as it unfolded over the years, many of Japan's best and brightest medical minds were transformed into some of the world's most dangerous people, mirrors of Ishii himself.

They idolized their BW leader for his dedication to his germ warfare projects. Ishii's charisma embodied both a scientific brilliance and a zesty enthusiasm for Japan's true scientific innovation—the pioneering and scientifically priceless ability to use living humans as if they were expendable lab animals.

"Ishii was like a god to us, and we thought that what he was doing was necessary for our country to win the war," said Ken Yuasa, a remorseful former army doctor who tried to explain the spell Ishii cast on his staffers. As a military field doctor in occupied China, Yuasa had performed human vivisections on Chinese victims.

Another Unit 731 veteran, a former hygiene specialist, echoed this sentiment in a July 1994 public talk: "Ishii, the unit leader, was an exalted man—he was higher than the emperor. I thought that he was a great man because of the water filtration system he had invented. I almost cried from appreciation."

His living autopsies and deliberate infections of human test subjects appeared to cause no moral qualms in the overwhelming majority of military men and health officials involved in, or aware of, the BW program. On the contrary, the "precious human material," as the Unit 731 doctors called their victims, were the source of his value to the military and scientific community, and thus to Ishii's own standing and to the continuing expansion of the Unit

731 BW network. In terms of advancing biological weapons research, Ishii and his associates definitely made huge gains.

The doctors of Unit 731 and its affiliated units scattered across Asia and the Pacific tested many different pathogenic disease microbes upon their *maruta* human inmates. Their aims differed with respect to the goals of each particular experiment. One such project involved the culturing of germs such as bubonic plague bacteria by injecting them into the human prisoners, then observing which people had the strongest affliction from each laboratory batch. From those victims' organs and blood, doctors cultured the bacteria, breeding ever more virulent strains. Only by experimenting on humans, rather than lab animals, could the Japanese have perfected their biological weaponry.

Chinese doctors fighting plague outbreaks caused by BW attacks in 1942 in Zhejiang Province noted that the strain of plague seemed to be stronger and to have a higher mortality rate than that which had been previously observed in outbreaks of the disease.

The diseases being studied, cultured, and used as agents of germ warfare at Pingfan and elsewhere in the BW network included both bacterial and viral afflictions. While the true variety of pathogens investigated in the labs and disseminated during outside biological warfare missions may never be known, those we know about include anthrax; bubonic plague; typhoid; paratyphoid; tetanus; cholera; gas gangrene (a toxic infection of open wounds caused by clostridia bacteria); diphtheria; pertussis or "whooping cough," a disease especially dangerous to children and infants; tularemia (caused by a germ related to the plague, although somewhat milder in its effects); dysentery; salmonella; streptococcus A "scarlet fever"; bacterial meningitis; tuberculosis; tick-borne encephalitis; and syphilis.

The virus-caused diseases that were developed included yellow fever, viral meningitis, viral pneumonia, Songo (today known variously as epidemic hemorrhagic fever, Korean hemorrhagic fever, hantavirus disease, or Hantaan virus), smallpox, hepatitis A, and hepatitis B.

Another class of infectious microbial organisms, known as rickettsias, were tested on the prisoners of Unit 731, including the rickettsia responsible for typhus. Carried by lice, typhus causes high fever and is the disease that in March 1945 killed Anne Frank; her older sister, Margot; and many other children in the disease-fostering conditions of starvation, filth, and overcrowding at the Nazi concentration camp at Bergen Belsen, Germany.

There were other foci of research and development activity at the BW bases. Unit 731 scientists labored in factory facilities for the production of enormous amounts of germs, to be used in biological assaults across Asia. To deliver the pathogens to the intended targets, usually civilian populations, various means of dissemination were devised and manufactured, and production teams developed bombs that cracked open to release carrier insects. Researchers also bred millions of fleas to be infected with plague bacteria.

A broad division into two types of scientific activity was made at Pingfan: defensive research and offensive research. The defensive studies generally involved the research and manufacture of vaccines. At least 20 million doses of vaccines were produced there annually. Other BW stations in Manchuria also created millions of doses. These Unit 731 sub-units were located at Dalian (called Dairen by the Japanese), Hailar, Mudanjiang, Linkow, and Sunyu (called Songo). The doses were made in liquid units, which were then refrigerated and also freeze-dried in a powdery form. The powder preparations also proved useful for the preparation of offensive microbe emulsions used as biological weapons, indicating the high degree of overlap between the defensive and offensive divisions of vaccine research and germ warfare. Ishii's personnel created vaccines for eighteen diseases, which could be used to protect the soldiers of the Japanese military, an important task for the medical division of any army, and to protect civilians. They could therefore be prepared and sold by Japanese pharmaceutical companies for general use, a bonus to the top civilian researchers of the biological warfare units.

Inmates were the fodder for the development of these vaccines, at the hands of the Unit 731 vaccine squad, which was called the "A Team." In a Pingfan cholera vaccine-development experiment, conducted in May and June 1940, twenty inmates were put into three groups. Eight subjects received a vaccine made by new ultrasonic devices, eight received the standard vaccine then available, and four did not get any vaccine. After a period of twenty days, all twenty subjects were ordered to drink large amounts of cholera-tainted milk.

The four prisoners who got no vaccine contracted cholera and died, some of those who received the standard vaccine came down with the disease and died, and none of those who received the ultrasonically prepared vaccine became ill. (Those who lived were ultimately killed in other experiments.) When a comparable study with bubonic plague vaccine also produced results showing the effectiveness of the ultrasonic preparation method, Ishii ordered the A Team to use only this method going forward.

One may wonder about the career ambitions of the scientists who performed these experiments, knowing that their results were valuable in terms of medical advances and scientific discovery, yet were necessarily conducted under extreme secrecy due to their gross inhumanity. How could they gain fame and share their results with the outside world? The solution was to publish their results in esteemed, peer-reviewed journals—more than a hundred such articles were published or read aloud in lecture halls—but with the subjects described as monkeys, rather than people.

It was not hard to discern the truth. Experiments that did truly use monkeys as subjects provided the proper species name of the monkey, such as "long-tailed monkey"; when humans were used, the subjects were written up simply as "monkeys" or "Manchurian monkeys."

The number of people who realized that they were actually reading about human subjects must have been fairly high. The name Shiro Ishii or Ryochi Naito at the top of a paper, for example, would tip off many readers to the nature of the experiment—as Naito himself said, many in Japan knew about Ishii's program. The discerning reader knew to read between the lines.

For those who did not know about Unit 731, however, there were plenty of other tip-offs, facts, and statistics that just wouldn't make sense to the careful doctor or scientist. Monkeys and men, while both primates, have distinct physiological markers. One case written by Dr. Masaji Kitano and Dr. Shiro Kasahara in a 1944 edition of the *Japan Journal of Physiology*, a top medical periodical in Japan, described a lab monkey with a temperature of 40.2 degrees Celsius during a fever episode. No species of monkey could spike a temperature that high. But a human could.

That same year Kitano—then the chief commander of Unit 731 Pingfan headquarters and of Imperial Japan's network of human experiment compounds and germ warfare campaigns, having replaced Ishii in this capacity in the summer of 1942—wrote an article in another scientific journal, stating that tissue damage caused by hemorrhaging could be seen in the kidneys of the subjects. In a 1985 interview with British researchers, the former Unit 731 scientist and Kitano coauthor Shiro Kasahara admitted that such kidney effects did not occur in monkeys. At the time of his secret research on the prisoners of Pingfan, Kasahara also held a leading academic position at the Kitasato Research University in Japan, and was one of the nation's top civilian microbiologists. Kasahara made it clear that the kind of tissue damage related in the peer-reviewed journal could be observed only in human beings with the Songo hemorrhagic fever.

Yet so brazen were Kitano and the other Unit 731 scientists that they would just as soon let the contradiction stand in the published data of this very important finding. The *Japan Journal of Physiology* article was quite important because it presented the viral-isolation methods Kitano used to find the cause of Songo hemorrhagic fever, a disease that is endemic to Manchuria and is carried by ticks that attach themselves to mice and rats. The disease, which usually has a 10 percent mortality rate in its outbreaks, was first recognized and named by Japanese researchers in May 1938 when they treated Japanese soldiers who came down with the illness while working on a railway near the Soviet border, beside the northern Manchurian town of Songo (also called Sunyu), where Unit 731 had a branch detachment called Unit 673. Kitano and his researchers discovered both the carriers of the infectious agent—the ticks—and the agent itself—a virus that resides inside the tick and is transmitted when the tick jumps from its rodent host to a human. This was a major achievement and something of a surprise to the scientific community, which had generally suspected the causative organism to be a species of rickettsia rather than a virus. Songo Fever was also known at the time of Kitano's research as Epidemic Hemorrhagic Fever (EHF) and is today often referred to as Hantaan virus.

Kitano successfully isolated the causative virus in 1941; the April 2, 1943, edition of *Asahi Shimbun*, one of Japan's leading newspapers, carried a story with the headline "Another Shout for Military Medicine: Pathogen for terrible hemorrhagic fever is discovered." The article reads, "The army exerted itself to identify this pathogen for the purpose of disease prevention within the army and to advance sanitation within Manchuria."

In Pingfan's offensive research sections, many types of germs were investigated and tested on the inmates. Prisoners would be given tainted tools, utensils, and cloth material to handle, so that the researchers could see if those items could infect a person when they had been contaminated with certain germ preparations. Much work was done with tainted drinks—prisoners given water, milk, and coffee, even beer or sake, dosed with some type of organism under study—and bacterially poisoned food, and inmates were made to ingest typhoid-filled melons, cookies tainted with bubonic plague, and chocolates injected with anthrax. Lethal anthrax sweets were also distributed to the population outside Pingfan on at least one occasion, when Japanese soldiers gave them out free to Chinese children. Ishii was curious to test how well his dissemination technique would work in a real-world population of children.

One practical problem was simply growing enough bacteria, viruses, and rickettsias to have a sufficient amount on hand for the creation of epidemics. So large areas at the secret complex were reserved for the incubation of bacteria in rows of specially designed ovens. Each oven measured approximately 14 by 9.85 by 21 inches and weighed 241 pounds, and held fifteen trays for growing colonies of bacteria. Each contained 6.78 pounds of gelatinous agar-agar nutrient medium, upon which the bacteria fed.

The bacteria were scraped off each tray at intervals, the harvesting period depending on the species of bacterium. For example, aerobic bacteria, those that grow better in the presence of oxygen, such as anthrax, glanders, and plague, as well as cholera, typhoid, and paratyphoid organisms, could be collected from the ovens every twenty-four to forty-eight hours. Anaerobic bacteria such as those for tetanus and gas gangrene were more difficult to raise and required a week of growing before they could be gathered.

Kiyoshi Kawashima, the former Chief of Division 4 of Unit 731 at Pingfan, a section in charge of breeding and cultivating germs and producing immunity serums and vaccines, estimated that at peak production the division could produce, per month, about one ton of cholera bacteria, 500 to 700 kilograms of anthrax bacteria, 300 kilograms of bubonic plague bacteria, and 700 to 800 kilograms of typhoid bacteria. The germs were continually collected from their cultivating ovens, put in sealed bottles, then stored for later deployment in the outside world as germ warfare.

For just one bacterial bomb designed for use by artillery, it took 900 ovens to produce enough of the germs to start an outbreak of disease. Thus it became necessary to cultivate germs around the clock in thousands of ovens located in the various units scattered across Manchuria and occupied China. From the inception of Japan's BW program, complex methods of microbial dissemination were invented and experimented with. Initially, gas-containing bombs and metallic shells of the type used in artillery explosive bombs were tested. One such explosive shell was seventy-five millimeters in diameter with a liquid suspension of bacteria placed in the part of the bomb where the charge that sparks the explosion would ordinarily go. The whole Pingfan community got involved, it seems, in the preparation of these bombs. In 1994 a Unit 731 veteran described a scene in 1941 at the barracks of the "education officers," who trained civilian and military personnel in the various tasks of the Unit 731 experiment mill. Next door to the barracks was the Pingfan crematorium building with its towering smokestack, out of which frequently poured the ashes of inmates' bodies. "One day I walked by there," the veteran remembered. "The wives of the officers were polishing brass objects that looked like trophies. Someone told me, 'Those are bombs.'"

A Pingfan civilian researcher told him: "The bacteria that you fellows made were loaded into those and dropped for dispersal. Maybe in Chongqing, or Shanghai."

Metal shells, however, often proved unfeasible as germ delivery systems—the explosion of the bomb or the force of its impact usually killed the organisms, rendering them harmless. So Pingfan researchers turned from modifying shells for bio-war use to designing and building BW bombs created for the sole purpose of disseminating germs. One such shell, called the HA bomb, was designed to disperse from a high altitude anthrax bacteria, dried and powdery, in its hardened cellular or spore form. The HA bomb was bullet-shaped and made of thin-walled steel. It was designed to disperse the germs widely, suspended in 500 cubic centimeters of anthrax bacterial emulsion, upon detonation.

Another type of steel bomb was called the Uji, created to carry virtually any kind of organism, and its "Uji type 50" variant was designed to be dropped from aircraft. Field tests of the HA, Uji, and Uji type 50 bombs were conducted at the Pingfan airfield and Anda test sites on hundreds, perhaps thousands of *maruta* human subjects. From 1939 to 1945 more than 2,000 Uji type 50 bombs exploded in these human field studies. Many more Uji type 50 bombs were dropped by airplane, flying at different altitudes, to determine the usefulness of such aerial methods. And as in the bomb category of modified explosive and gas shells, it was determined that these steel-casing bombs were ineffective at disseminating germs under any conditions, because the explosions necessary to break apart the steel walls of the shells also killed the organisms. To solve this problem, Unit 731 developed ceramic-walled models of the Uji bombs, so that the shells simply cracked open to release their contents upon impact, eliminating the problem of the blast's antiseptic effects. One such Uji bomb was constructed of porcelain and designed to break open to release 10.5 quarts of fluid; it measured 27.5 inches in length and 7 inches in diameter. A modification of this bomb used tailfins made of celluloid on its sides to make for a better-targeted descent from aerial dropping.

Pingfan had an on-site factory that specialized in the manufacture of such ceramic bombs. On the assembly lines, clay and water were mixed to the correct consistency and poured into plaster molds shaped like bombshells. The shells were dried in specially built kilns. Testifying as a witness at the Khabarovsk trial, a former Unit 731 lab assistant, Sub-Lieutenant Kenichi Segoshi, described the unique design of the bombs whose clay composition he tested while working in the Fourth Section of the Unit 731 Materials Division: "These bombs were from 70 to 80 centimeters long and 20 centimeters in diameter. At the bottom was a screw-threaded aperture. The interiors of the bombs were hollow. A time fuse was inserted into the screw-threaded aperture. Zigzag grooves were cut on the outer surface of these bodies. On the upper part of the bombs there were attachments for stabilizer. Explosives were fastened into the grooves for the purpose of exploding the bombs. Dropped from aircraft, these bombs were supposed to explode above the ground."

Small porcelain bulbs were placed inside these ceramic bombs, each bulb containing plague-infected fleas bred in Pingfan facilities. The plague bacteria living within the body of each flea had been tested in Pingfan laboratories for their lethal virulence upon the *maruta* of the Ro prison. The ceramic walls of the bombs described by Segoshi were so thin that only a small amount of explosives, placed in the wall grooves, was needed to shatter them. The walls and bulbs broke open, and the lack of a high temperature or high explosive force spared the lives of the fleas, enabling them to travel and infect people with their plague-transmitting bites.

Ishii applied his active imagination to experimenting with other germ-dispersal methods. He conducted dozens of tests of aerially sprayed BW germs that formed bacteria-containing clouds. The objective was to contaminate and infect people (or animals and crops) with the microbe-filled aerosol haze drifting down: The pathogens would be inhaled by their victims and the germs would also settle on their bodies, clothing, food; in their water supply and the general environment.

Even though specialized airplane equipment was designed to

enable the fliers to control aerosol spraying, this method of germ dispersal was deemed too inefficient by the Japanese; the germs were too fragile to survive the process of pressurized spraying and subsequent exposure to temperature variations, sunlight, wind, and other environmental factors.

Another experiment, more complex than even the cloud-spraying, was Unit 731's "Mother and Daughters" bomb system, in which a "Mother" bomb controlled the detonation of a cluster of the "Daughter" bombs by remote control, through a signal from its built-in radio transmitter. The Daughter bombs contained the bacteria; the goal appears to have been the scattering of germs, in slurries or other preparations, just above the ground, but dropped from planes flying at high altitudes. One Unit 731 veteran explained, "The Mother bomb was dropped first, followed by the Daughters. The Daughter bombs were designed to explode when the Mother bomb struck the ground due to the cessation of the radio signal." Despite its intriguing design, this system, like the other bombs, often failed, and it had the additional drawback of being exceptionally expensive.

The primary purpose of the Uji type and Mother and Daughter bombs was to contaminate the ground with bacteria, rather than targeting humans directly with infection or bacteria-infected shrapnel wounds. In contrast, the HA bomb was made to directly infect people by causing wounds with its shell fragments, and then infection of those wounds with anthrax since the shrapnel would be coated with the bomb's fluid anthrax preparation. Contamination of the land with anthrax was feasible because the organism, *Bacillus anthracis*, is naturally found in the soil, and it could theoretically persist and thrive in this habitat for years, once disseminated there. Ishii and his fellow scientists hoped that permanent zones of infestation and infection could be created with such bombs, sickening and killing all those who lived in the geographical areas or crossed through them. Artificially seeded, ground-residing anthrax had the added benefit of being able to survive the frigid winter temperatures that beset potential target areas in partisan-held territory of Manchuria and the Russian Far East.

In the end, ceramic-walled bombs proved most effective, and they became the delivery systems of choice when Unit 731 conducted germ warfare against Chinese populations. The massive toll on innocent human lives by the bacteria released from these devices is appalling; the enormous May 1942 cholera epidemic created in Yunnan Province, which killed over 200,000 people, is one striking example. Three months later, another 200,000 perished from cholera biological warfare in Shandong Province.

In addition to all those who died in the epidemics of strategic bio-war throughout China, Chinese and Japanese scholars have suggested that altogether as many as 20,000 victims were killed within the confines of human experiment prisons. This estimate does not include the innocent civilians killed in outside "field tests" of lab-cultured organisms, performed stealthily at countless villages and hamlets across Manchuria and occupied China.

The number of people killed at Pingfan may be estimated from the figure stated at the 1949 Khabarovsk war crimes trial by Major General Kawashima, who had for a time directed the mass breeding of germs at the Pingfan labs, participated in the "sacrificing," as Unit 731 termed it, of inmates in lethal experiments, and helped organize military germ warfare assaults in central China. Kawashima testified that "no less than about 600 per annum" prisoners "died from the effects of experiments in infecting them with severe infectious diseases."

Because Pingfan was in full swing from 1940 to August 1945, one may extrapolate from the 600 figure that at least 3,000 prisoners were killed over the period of about five years that the medical-scientific death camp was functioning. However, some prisoners were already being held and vivisected at Pingfan even before construction of the large complex had been completed, so this unknown number of victims in 1938 and 1939 must be taken into account as well. The number of human guinea pigs killed in similar experimental conditions at Ishii's branch units in Changchun, Nanking, Peking, Jinan, Canton, Dairen, Songo, Hailar, Linkow, Mudanjiang, and other places, covering a period from 1939 through 1945, plus those killed inside the Beiyinhe compound from 1932 to 1936, raises the total figure of those killed in experiments much higher. In addition, thousands of prisoners were summarily executed by gassing, shooting, and lethal injections the week that Ishii's Manchurian units hastily retreated from the August 1945 Soviet advance into Manchuria, so that they would not appear and publicly attest to the fact that the Japanese doctors had been conducting exactly the same atrocities as those of the Nazi doctors that had shocked the world.

Even in the context of the shock and horror that was Pingfan, there were experiments conducted by Unit 731 that make the mind reel at the level of inhumanity—experiments that simply seemed to involve scientific curiosity, along the lines of a doctor asking, "What would happen if we did this to a person?" In one such experiment, a victim had his hands sawn off and surgically reattached so that his right hand was sewn onto his left arm and his left hand sewn onto his right arm. Prisoners were hanged upside down in a laboratory to find out how long it would take for a person to choke to death. Others were boiled alive. A giant spinning centrifuge killed test subjects torturously. Lethal radiation exposure testing was performed on prisoners—an ironic harbinger of the massive number of Japanese civilian deaths from radiation at Hiroshima and Nagasaki, and future postwar secret radiation experiments performed by the U.S. military. In one experiment at Pingfan, the prisoners' livers were destroyed by targeted X-ray emissions. Other studies called for the injection of horse urine into human kidneys. Horse blood plasma was also injected into people to see if it could act as a substitute for human blood; it has properties that led the researchers to suspect this might be possible. This would surely be a breakthrough discovery that would eliminate the need for blood banks. But it was not a viable substitute, the doctors found, as the subjects died in agony, the horse blood poisoning their every organ. Horse blood was also employed to transfer microbes to and from the human prisoners to determine if either species could act as an incubator for the other.

"Professional people, too, like to play," explained one Osaka University professor, who in 1945, while a medical student at Kyoto Imperial University, had secretly been shown films of Unit 731 human experiments. He was accounting for the rationale of such experiments. Beyond the awful curiosity factor, experimental surgeries of the switching-hands type had a scientific value that would be impossible to achieve under normal ethical protocols of human medical experimentation. Doctors knew that the immune system usually rejects organs and limbs transplanted from one individual to another, but such transplantation from different parts of the same individual might be possible. This type of immoral surgical experiment would appear to be the only course for directly exploring this biomedical unknown. How many scientists have secretly pondered the discovery potential of such experimentation, of being in a situation where it is possible to disregard all moral considerations in pursuit of scientific achievement?

Gruesomely illustrating this point was the pursuit at Pingfan of treatments to heal frostbite. This was on the minds of many in the Kwantung Army, since frostbite had afflicted many Japanese soldiers in the initial conquest of Manchuria in late 1931 and continued to plague occupation troops fighting partisans in the winter. It would also be a factor in the anticipated Japanese invasion of the Soviet Union, when troops would cross the border northward into Siberia. Ishii went back to Kyoto Imperial University and recruited one of the top civilian physiologists, Dr. Hisato Yoshimura, to conduct experiments at Pingfan investigating the onset, treatment, and prevention of frostbite, urging him to take advantage of the unparalleled and strictly hush-hush opportunity to use involuntary human subjects.

Yoshimura's frostbite experiments on the inmates of Pingfan were described at the Khabarovsk trial by Lieutenant Colonel Toshihide Nishi, who led Branch 673 of Unit 731 at Sunyu (also known as Songo), near the Soviet border. Nishi testified that while at Pingfan, Yoshimura told him: "At times of great frost, with temperatures below −20 degrees [Celsius], people were brought out from the detachment's prison into the open. Their arms were bared and made to freeze with the help of an artificial current of air. This was done until their frozen arms, when struck with a short stick, emitted a sound resembling a board being struck. I also read his account of the experiments."

Other Unit 731 veterans recall that sometimes technicians poured water over the arms and hands of the subjects tied up outside in the freezing cold. As ice formed over the person's skin it would be chipped off with a chipping tool, and then more icy water would be poured over the limbs as the process was repeated to the point that when the tissue was struck it was hard, like wood, indicating that the tissue was sufficiently frozen through.

Yoshimura received funds to construct his own two-story building at Pingfan, containing an indoor human freezing laboratory. Thus he could conduct and refine his frostbite experiments during the spring, summer, and autumn months, no longer dependent on the frigid outside temperatures of the Manchurian winter.

Inside Yoshimura's freeze lab, Unit 731 doctors could work with special apparatuses that allowed them to control the temperature at which the victims' limbs could be exposed; with such machinery it was possible to subject the prisoners to the ultra-cold temperature of −70 degrees Celsius.

Guards ushered the inmates used in Yoshimura's lab back to their cells after the excruciating freezing process. Some of them later had their limbs amputated, but were kept alive minus their arms or legs so that they could be reused in another Unit 731 experiment. Others were left to die of the gangrene infection that affected their frostbitten body parts and poisoned their blood-stream. The nature of such gangrene infection could then also be studied. After trying out various methods of reviving the frozen arms, legs, and hands, the Unit 731 doctors determined that thawing the exposed body part in warm, running water was the best way to bring the frozen tissue back to a healthy state. Their results flew in the face of the prevailing medical assumption of the time, that vigorously massaging a frozen limb was the best treatment. The optimum temperature of the water was found to be slightly higher than 100 degrees Fahrenheit. If the tempera-ture topped 122 degrees, however, the water lost its healing effect. Those men and women who had recovered from the doctor-induced frostbite through amputation or the experimental warm water therapy would inevitably be recycled for and killed in another experiment or live dissection.

Equally cruel were the experiments to study the effects of dehydration and malnutrition. In dehydration experiments, pris-oners would for a period of days be given food to eat, but no water. In other tests, inmates were killed by exposure to intense dry heat using fans. The loss of body water through sweat trans-formed their physiology into that of mummies, and their lifeless bodies shrank down to one-fifth their original weight.

Former medical orderly Naokato Ishibashi described what he observed at one of many malnutrition experiments performed at Pingfan: "The purpose . . . was to find out how long a human being could survive just with water and biscuits. Two *maruta* were used for this experiment. They continuously circled a prescribed course within the grounds of the Unit carrying, approximately, a 20-kilogram sandbag on their backs. . . . The duration of the experiment was about two months. They received only Army biscuits to eat, and water to drink, so they would not have been able to survive for very long. They weren't allowed a lot of sleep either . . . one succumbed before the other."

The degree of contrition expressed by those implicated in the Japanese experiments and biological warfare varies widely. Some scientists received army orders to participate in the program and were more or less forced to do so; other civilian professionals answered appeals from Ishii and those already involved. Some doctors and scientists, to be sure, simply had no ethics and without a second thought enjoyed the benefits of the BW program funding: promotion in status and the opportunity to conduct pure human research unfettered by ethical restraints. Such a rare and ordinarily unthinkable opportunity obviously proved quite tempting for the hundreds, even thousands, of ambitious biological scientists in Japan during the war. Thus the unthinkable becomes thinkable and results in the most disgusting acts of evil.

Some who were at Pingfan have been haunted by their complicity in Unit 731. The former commander of the military police in the Manchurian county of Andong returned to the scene of his crimes, arriving in Pingfan in 1978 with a Japanese "Returning to China Liaison Committee" delegation, part of a reconciliation effort between China and Japan occurring at the time. Communist China and Japan normalized relations in 1972, despite many outstanding issues from the war and Japanese occupation that have yet to be fully resolved between the two. This officer was moved to confess that in 1944 he permitted twenty Chinese to be sent to Pingfan for human experiments. "I killed them," he said. "Thus I have been feeling uneasy for more than thirty years. Now, I have come to Pingfan to apologize."

Yet in 1995 another army veteran, seventy-three-year-old former military bio-war training leader Toshimi Mizobuchi, told NBC reporter Sara James that he did not feel any shame at all at being employed at Unit 731—even as he recalled how "the doctors would check how the virus brought on symptoms at one hour, two hours, or four hours after the injection. Then they would cut open the body for further inspection" to track the progress of the lab-cultured lethal germs through the victim's organs. In this way the Japanese researchers could study how germs could be used to invade people and destroy them. "I am proud to have been a part of this unit," Mizobuchi told James. "This was the world's first unit to use biology in combat."

With a look of disbelief, James replied, "You don't feel any regret at what you did at Unit 731, at all, do you?"

"No, I don't," Mizobuchi said. "It was war."

This justification is a standard refrain among unrepentant Japanese BW veterans. It underscores the tendency of war to bring with it the destruction of man's basic ethical values, indeed the elimination of feelings and emotions, save perhaps for the most hateful and sadistic ones.

In the mid-1990s the Japanese journalist Rumiko Nishino managed to locate a second anonymous member of Unit 731's venereal disease research team, an octogenarian who testified to her of the team's activity while lying ill on a hospital bed in Nagano Prefecture. "He had performed vivisections on six living women," Nishino told a crowded Japanese lecture hall. "The one experience he did not want to speak of was that concerning a Chinese woman. This particular Chinese woman, he told me, was put under chloroform but regained consciousness on the table.

She started getting up, screaming, 'Go ahead and kill me, but please don't kill my child!'" The veteran described to Nishino his team's reaction to the mother's anguished plea: "There were four or five of us working on the vivisection. We held her down, applied more anesthesia, and continued."

Nishino said that this veteran had initially refused to respond to her questions, but that this confession came as he displayed a sudden change of heart. "Last night I thought about our talk," he told her. "I had decided to take this with me to hell, but I thought it over, and now I want to leave it in this world."

Former army field doctor Ken Yuasa, who has publically confessed on numerous occasions to vivisecting Chinese civilians and POWs, has expressed feelings of anguish not just for his horrific acts, but for the soul-numbing effect of those acts, which has remained with him even into his old age. In a 1995 interview, he said, "Sometimes I look at my hands and I remember what I have done with these hands. What's really scary is, I don't have any nightmares of what I've done."

FIVE

WORLDS COLLIDE

FOR A NATION STATE TO USE MICROBES AS A WEAPON TO INFLICT disease outbreaks, certain social factors must be in place. On the scientific level, the intellectual talent necessary to pull it off—to cultivate certain germs and disseminate them—must exist. On political and military levels, the nation's policymakers must be capable of the immoral, of what has been condemned in the world by the Geneva Convention as an unacceptably cruel form of warfare. But biological warfare, which can be waged secretly, often invisibly, and cheaply (relative to the costs of war), against military and civilian populations alike, proved too seductive for some regimes to resist.

Imperial Japan was the first modern country to engage in sci-entifically planned biological warfare. The use of germ warfare and lethal human experimentation also emerged with the flower-ing of the science of microbiology, and the concurrent rise of twentieth-century fascism. Biological weapons became a tool of a militarized, technological state bent upon the invasion and exploitation of foreign peoples. Even considering Shiro Ishii's importance as the man behind the man-made plagues, one sees clearly how the confluence of science, industry, and imperial expansionism made World War II–era Japan a likely place for bio-logical warfare to take root.

One reason that the use of microbes as a weapon of war

wasn't considered seriously before the twentieth century is that
the germ theory of disease did not become widely accepted until
the 1890s. It was then that biologists began to clearly infer a relationship between the tiny microorganisms visible only under a
microscope lens and the onset of human illness. Yet there were
attempts to create epidemics in wars before science had reached
this understanding. Thus one may reach the depressing conclusion that humanity was spared from the specter of intentional
man-made epidemics only because infectious disease itself was
not properly understood. The knowledge was lacking, but not
the willingness and desire.

Wielding disease as a weapon dates back to ancient times. The
Book of Exodus describes biological calamities sent to weaken
nations, such as the ten plagues of Pharaoh's Egypt, which, as we
all learned from a young age, brought on boils, lice, flies, snakes,
frogs, and the death of every firstborn male Egyptian child. The
ancient Greek myth of Oedipus Rex pivots on the dilemma of a
mysterious plague besetting the city of Thebes, killing people,
animals, and crops. The plague is explained away by the Delphic
Oracle as punishment for a sin that must be rectified, the murder
of Theban King Laius, years earlier. Oedipus, the current king of
Thebes, sets out to discover the identity of the murderer to lift the
plague from his people. An intentionally induced epidemic (sent
as retribution, it turns out, for the tragic Oedipus' own unwitting
crimes) thereby sets in motion the events of the tragedy, which in
addition to becoming a key reference of Freudian psychology has
become a universal allegory for the process of unraveling myster-
ies in the pursuit of justice and truth.

The rulers of the Roman Empire seem to have officially
frowned on the use of toxins in warfare, one military admonition
against well poisoning being *Armis bella non venenis geri*: "War is
waged with armaments, not with poisons." Despite this, accounts
exist of Roman soldiers fouling their opponents' wells with animal

carrion. The expressed Roman distaste for toxic weapons also apparently did not extend to political intrigues, as the assassination of opponents by poison is thought to have been a feature of the imperial court. The most famous instance of this is the assassination of Emperor Claudius I in A.D. 54. Claudius was initially sickened by toxic mushrooms fed to him by his wife Agrippina, and when this dose failed to have a lethal effect, he was poisoned to the point of death by his physician, who, conspiring with Agrippina, administered a poison-tipped feather to Claudius, sticking it down his throat in the guise of providing a purgative treatment for his poison.

Poison, it should be noted, usually falls under the rubric of chemical and not biological warfare, primitive examples being the toxin found in the amanita species of mushrooms used by Agrippina, or the poison-tipped darts used by some indigenous peoples of South America. Weapons that consist of harmful living organisms, as opposed to nonliving chemical material, are called biological weapons. Another term, biochemical weapons, is sometimes used—incorrectly, it should be noted—to lump together biological and chemical weapons. "Biochemical" in fact refers only to a subset of chemical weapons, specifically those chemical weapons derived from a living organism; for example, the toxic extract of a certain species of shellfish, the lethal botulinum toxin made by the *Clostridium botulinum* bacteria, or the ricin chemical found in the castor bean, as opposed to synthesized chemicals, such as those that comprise the military agents phosgene and sarin. However, such chemical extracts of living organisms are also sometimes referred to as biological weapons.

Various nonscientific (though intuitively obvious) means of spreading biological poison to an enemy army—methods that did not require an understanding of microbes, such as the contamination of wells and rivers with sewage and carrion—have been practiced in wars throughout history, from the battles for the

Roman Empire to those of the American Civil War, in which Confederate soldiers dropped the bodies of dead horses into wells to pollute the water supply for approaching Union forces.

Bubonic plague and smallpox are two diseases that had been wreaking havoc for centuries, as well. Smallpox has been eradicated today, its elimination the result of extensive worldwide human vaccination campaigns that saw the last natural cases among rural Ethiopians in 1979. The only remaining reserves of the virus currently exist in refrigerated chambers in specially guarded laboratories of the United States and Russia—or so the world hopes.

The plague is still definitely with us. Cases of the disease continue to occur in plague-endemic regions of the world, including the southwestern United States, although it is now curable with penicillin and other antibiotic drugs. As far as epidemiologists know, bubonic plague outbreaks have always started with the appearance of fleas carrying the causative bacterium, then moving to their rodent (usually rats or mice) hosts. The broad epidemics associated with the Black Death period suggest the sustained appearance of the carrier fleas, supporting the generally accepted hypothesis that the plague had its origins in Eurasian trade routes along which the fleas traveled with their rodent and human hosts. One instance of medieval biological warfare has been tentatively associated by scholars with the onset of the infamous bubonic plague epidemic in fourteenth-century Europe. In 1346 an army of Crimean Tartars besieged the Genoese fortress-outpost at Caffa, in the Crimea near the Black Sea, situated along key trade routes leading into Italy from the East. The Tartars catapulted the bodies of their people who had died of the plague over the wall at Caffa, into the Genoese's midst. This was most likely a premeditated attempt by the Tartars to start an epidemic in the opposing army, so that they would become similarly afflicted; a leveling of the playing field, as it were. Sure enough, the Genoese inhabitants were forced to retreat back to Italy as an epidemic took hold within Caffa, and soon after they'd arrived in Genoa, the Black Death, so named because of the black lesions (known as buboes) it caused, was ravaging Genoa and Italy, and then Europe, from Constantinople to England. This was, of course, part of the plague epidemic that wiped out one-third of the population of Europe, though the Tartars can't be entirely blamed, as the disease also appears to have spread westward from Asia along a number of different routes at this time.

The first recorded instance of a planned effort to wipe out enemy forces in warfare with infectious disease occurred in colonial America during the French and Indian Wars; the plan included as its goal the extermination of entire civilian populations of Indians. The instigator was Sir Jeffrey Amherst, governor-general of the North American colonies and general and commander-in-chief of the North American British Forces. In June 1763 Amherst ordered Colonel Henry Bouquet to disseminate smallpox to Native American tribes in the Ohio-Pennsylvania region whom Bouquet's troops were fighting. In a letter to Bouquet, Amherst wrote: "Could it not be contrived to send the Small Pox among those disaffected tribes of Indians? We must on this occasion use every stratagem in our power to reduce them."

Smallpox cases existed at Fort Pitt, which was under Bouquet's command (located in what is today Pittsburgh), and Bouquet wrote back with an offer to transfer infected blankets from Fort Pitt to the tribes. He replied to Amherst on July 13, "I will try to inoculate the Indians with some blankets that may fall into their hands, and take care not to get the disease myself." He also stated that a militarily well-regarded Swiss mercenary, Captain Simeon Ecuyer of Fort Pitt, had on June 24 transferred contaminated items directly to two Indian chiefs: "Out of regard for them, we gave them two blankets and a handkerchief out of the small-pox hospital. I hope it will have the desired effect."

It seems likely that this act of germ warfare did indeed have the "desired effect." Within months, smallpox outbreaks were killing Native Americans in the region who had been waging a guerrilla war against the troops of Fort Pitt. These peoples included the Delaware, Huron, Ottawa, Seneca, and Shawnee nations. In his exchange with Colonel Bouquet, Amherst bluntly expressed his desire that smallpox be employed as a means to wipe out the native peoples entirely, to "serve to extirpate this execrable race."

There can be little doubt that Amherst intended racial genocide by smallpox, a communicable viral disease that causes extensive pustule eruptions across the face and body, and severe fever, nausea, and aches. In fact he went down in history as a great man, a leader who made possible the British victory in the French and Indian Wars, enabling Britain to wrest control of Canada from the French. He was knighted and made an English lord, attaining the title of baron. The town of Amherst, in western Massachusetts, is named after him, and the prestigious Amherst College is named after the town (a fact that many residents of Amherst are not happy about these days).

As Ishii and others in the Kwantung Army saw Chinese, Koreans, and the other peoples of Asia, so the eighteenth- and nineteenth-century British and Americans viewed the Native Americans too as subhuman, barbarous, "execrable," worthy only of subjugation or extermination. Therefore, the British and Americans reasoned, the Christian moral code did not apply when it came to eliminating the savages. While the causative agent of smallpox, the variola virus, was not known to science in the days of Amherst's smallpox assaults (viruses are too small be seen by the microscopes used in the eighteenth century, and in any event, the fact that microbes cause infectious disease was not yet understood), the British recognized that objects such as blankets and handkerchiefs that had been in contact with smallpox-afflicted people were in some way contaminated with the disease and would likely spread it to other people. Certainly it was well known to the British colonialists that the native peoples of the continent had little natural immunity and a marked susceptibility to smallpox, a European-imported disease previously unknown in the Western Hemisphere. In addition, by the eighteenth century European doctors understood that inoculating a healthy individual with the pus taken from a smallpox-afflicted person's pustule would provide the inoculated person's body with a permanent defense against coming down with smallpox. This practice, originally referred to by the British as "variolation," had been performed in Africa and was taught to the Reverend Cottton Mather, a prominent scholar and physician in Boston, by one of Mather's slaves, an African named Ansemius. Mather detailed the procedure in a letter to the English physician Dr. John Woodward in 1716. The 1721–22 epidemic of smallpox in Boston inspired Mather to organize the first mass smallpox inoculations in the New World.

These inoculations became common in white pioneer settlements, but the health practice was never shared with Native Americans. Consequently, vast numbers of innocent people died needlessly from this long-term and strategic withholding of medical knowledge and care. Between the fifteenth and twentieth centuries, smallpox is thought to have killed millions of Native Americans in North, Central, and South America and the Caribbean islands. Other imported diseases such as tuberculosis, typhoid, influenza, and diphtheria took their toll as well.

Smallpox may have been used as a weapon again in North America a few years later, during the American War of Independence. The colonists accused the British army of employing smallpox against them, claiming that the British had sent their recently inoculated soldiers into Boston neighborhoods with smallpox-contaminated items, so as to spread the disease among the city's

civilian population shortly before they retreated from Boston altogether. George Washington warned his troops not to enter Boston
as the British evacuated; Washington declared: "the enemy, with a
malicious assiduity, have spread the infection of smallpox through
all parts of the town."

This claim was used repeatedly as wartime propaganda,
though it remains unsubstantiated. Whatever the truth, beginning
in 1765, exceptionally severe, naturally occurring smallpox epidemics had begun afflicting colonial America, and General Washington had ordered an extensive series of vaccinations for his
Continental Army soldiers to protect them from outbreaks. At the
same time, the British charged that the Americans were using the
vaccinated soldiers as carriers of the disease, dispatched here and
there to spark smallpox outbreaks. In the next century strong
anecdotal evidence suggests that in the period of westward expansion, the U.S. Army and white settlers made a practice of sending
smallpox-contaminated blankets to the Native Americans of the
Plains. One tribe, the Mandan nation of the Northern Plains, was
estimated to have lost seven-eighths of its people to smallpox.

In 1796 Edward Jenner in England produced an effective
smallpox inoculation for people made from cows infected with the
disease of cowpox, the serum of which worked just as well as the
human smallpox variolation method, and these injections are considered the first modern immunization methods. The term "vaccine" itself comes from the Latin *vaccinus*, "from cows," referring to
Jenner's cowpox injections. Still, even with this clever, more efficient method, the fact that microorganisms caused smallpox, or
any other disease, remained unrecognized by scientists.

Microbiology's crucial breakthrough came in France during
the 1860s, when a scientifically inclined brewer named Louis Pasteur observed that organisms only visible under a microscope
(yeast cells) caused the fermentation of sugar to alcohol. Other
kinds of microorganisms that he placed in his containers pro-

duced different compounds. In this way Pasteur demonstrated the effect of microbes on organic chemical processes. The method by which unfavorable microbes could be eliminated in wine, beer, and dairy production was termed "pasteurization," and its inventor went on to prove that a particular species of bacteria caused the poultry disease of chicken cholera, and then that the bacterium *Bacillus anthracis* was the agent responsible for the livestock and human disease of anthrax (a disease that would later become notoriously prominent in the annals of germ warfare research), and developed immunizations against both diseases.

The German physician Robert Koch built significantly on Pasteur's discoveries. Among his contributions, Koch isolated anthrax bacteria in its hardened "spore" form outside an animal, and found in 1882 that the *Mycobacterium tuberculosis* caused the pulmonary wasting disease of tuberculosis. Throughout the 1880s and 1890s a flurry of discoveries by various European scientists identified the bacterial and protozoan microorganisms responsible for typhoid fever, gonorrhea, sleeping sickness, malaria, and tick-borne illnesses.

By the 1890s it had finally become accepted in medical and scientific circles that the germ theory of disease was a proven fact, and that humans now had it within their power to prevent disease epidemics by mass immunizations, improved sanitation methods, and quarantines. Within the early decades of the twentieth century, antibacterial drugs, first the sulfonamide compounds (sulfa drugs) and later the much more effective penicillin and penicillinlike classes of antibiotics, would provide the cures for all the ancient scourges of bacteria-caused infectious disease.

Unfortunately, the sulfa drugs only proved effective against a limited number of diseases. Penicillin, discovered in 1928 by British bacteriologist Sir Alexander Fleming, became the first cure-all "wonder drug" for bacterial infections, but methods for mass-producing it did not exist until 1940 when they were developed in the United States. A second, similarly powerful antibiotic called streptomycin was developed in the United States in 1943. These antibiotics did not become widely used anywhere until after World War II, tragically too late for so many victims of Japan's bacteriological warfare who might have survived if they had been available only a few years earlier.

In the days of the early advances in identifying disease agents, it was not only the Western scientists who made key breakthroughs in the burgeoning field of microbiology. The remote island nation of Japan, which until the 1850s had remained in self-imposed feudal isolation from most aspects of the outside world, quickly distinguished itself as a world-class center of medical research in the new field. The prominent Japanese bacteriologist Hideo Noguchi isolated pure cultures of the spirochete (spiral) bacteria *Treponoma pallidum* in 1911, and established that it caused the sexually transmitted disease of syphilis after finding it in the brain tissue of victims in 1913. Shibasaburu Kitasato studied under Koch in Germany and in 1894 codiscovered with the Russian Alexander Yersin the bacterium responsible for bubonic plague (a germ originally called *Pasteurella pestis* and now renamed *Yersinia pestis* due to a biological reclassification of the species by the scientific community). In 1898 Kiyoshi Shiga discovered the type of pathogenic bacteria that cause a form of diarrhea dysentery, and both the genus of bacteria (*Shigella*), and the disease itself, shigellosis, were named in his honor by the international community of microbiologists.

European academic and medical institutions granted numerous awards and fellowships to the Japanese microbiologists. The West took note of these impressive accomplishments, as it also took note of a number of Japanese military advances happening at the time. Japan's victory over the Russian Empire in the 1904–05 Russo-Japanese War stunned many, when the fully modernized Japanese navy isolated and demolished the Russian fleet in the Tsushima Straits between Korea and Japan, skillfully picking off the czar's best warships with artillery fire. The rout marked the first time that a nonwhite people had defeated a major European power in a war over hegemony of a contested region, in this case northeast Asia. The peace treaty, brokered by President Theodore Roosevelt at Portsmouth, New Hampshire, in 1905, also engendered the Taft-Katsura Agreement of 1905 that formalized Japanese recognition of the United States' claim to colonize the Philippines. There, the American army and marines were still engaged in a long, bloody war of conquest against the rebellious Filipinos fighting for their independence. (The United States had intervened in the Philippine Islands since the beginning of the Spanish-American War in 1898.) In return, the United States agreed to Japan's claim to suzerainty over Korea, upon which Japanese military and corporate circles had designs, and to the Japanese occupation of China's Kwantung Peninsula and strategic coastal city of Port Arthur. Russia lost the southern half of Sakhalin Island and its control of the lucrative South Manchurian Railway Company to Japan. The major powers' diplomatic game of establishing and trading off areas of conquest continued the movement of nineteenth-century imperialism onward into the twentieth century: Nations were carved up and entire peoples subjugated across the Pacific sphere.

The U.S.-Japan friendship allowed for international acts that vitiated American moral standing and integrity, notably the U.S. military occupation of the Philippines and its subsequent war against the rebellious population, condemned by many observers at the time. Among them was Mark Twain, who wrote bitterly angry essays against both it and the notion of American Manifest Destiny.

Twain's parody, "The Battle Hymn of the Republic Brought Down to Date," written in 1900, was directly inspired by the injustice of the U.S. invasion and conquest of the Philippines:

Mine eyes have seen the orgy of the launching of the Sword
He is searching out the hoardings where the stranger's wealth is stored
He hath loosed the fateful lightnings, and with woe and death has scored
His lust is marching on.

Historians believe that more than 1 million civilians were killed as war continued on into the 1920s; notably targeted were the people of northern Luzon Island, where sometimes entire villages were burned down by American troops, their inhabitants rounded up and shot. U.S. forces also committed frequent massacres of the insurgent Moro people on the islands of Mindanao, Palawan, and the Sulus. The Portsmouth Treaty of 1905 allowed Imperial Japan, in turn, to commence its national and cultural annexation of Korea in 1910, followed by its harsh suppression of the Korean peninsula, while the United States and Europe turned a blind eye.

Between 1910 and 1918 the Japanese confiscated enormous amounts of land for the use of Japanese individuals and business interests, forcing many Koreans into homelessness and desperate immigration to Japan proper, where they faced a life of low-wage employment, ghettoization, and racial discrimination. Although Japan's forces allowed some limited local self-rule in Korea, the Japanese colonists occupied all the major administrative positions in government. The Korean language was banned and Korean schoolchildren were made to learn Japanese as their first language. Korea's largest city, Seoul, was given the Japanese name Keijo. A mass Korean uprising for national independence took place on March 1, 1919, only to be crushed with extreme brutality. The Koreans were never allowed any real representative voice in the Japanese parliament (the Diet), although they were conscripted into the Japanese army in the 1930s as the war with China expanded, but they were not permitted to attain rank commensurate with even that of a Japanese private. (Conscripts from Taiwan were treated similarly.)

Japan in this period had been mimicking the West in its warlike foreign policy and succeeding on these terms, as the nation had also advanced domestically in setting up industrial factories, roads, bridges, railroads, plumbing, universities, hospitals, and electrical infrastructure. Unfortunately, Japan eventually came to exhibit the worst characteristics of a Western imperialist power, including military adventurism and political repression, both at home and in its colonies abroad.

But at the dawn of the twentieth century, it seemed that Japan's rate of progress shaping a modern, industrial society had been truly astounding; it had been only a few decades since Japan had suddenly emerged from isolation and medieval backwardness, and the governors of Japan had dodged the bullet they feared most: becoming a colonized nation, as Korea and the Philippines were to become. The possibility of this fate had become clear to these feudal rulers back in 1853, when a surprise gunboat flotilla of ironclad U.S. navy frigates haughtily steamed into Edo Bay, port of the capital city of Edo (today's Tokyo), and out onto the dock planks stepped Commodore Matthew Perry.

The nation's leaders were shocked and terrified. They had never seen such weaponry and naval technology. Although Japan had guns, they were of the small arms variety and nothing that could compete with the cannons aboard the armor-plated, mechanized, oceangoing ships of the Americans.

The United States had recently gained a hold in the Pacific, owing to its acquisition of California in the Mexican-American War. Perry delivered an ultimatum to the hermetic island nation, veiled in the form of a diplomatic request from President Millard

Fillmore: Open your ports and your markets to American trade interests, as soon as possible, or face the consequences of a war you cannot win. The Japanese reluctantly signed the Treaty of Kanagawa with the Americans the following year, when Perry made a return visit with a larger squadron of warships in tow. The treaty was highly unequal and gave privileged positions to the United States in trade and tariffs. Not surprisingly, this initial opening to the West was considered by Japan's rulers to be a humiliation and a potential disaster.

Japan at this time was led by a military hierarch called the shogun, who presided over the leaders of government, exclusively composed of men from the hereditary aristocratic class of land-lords known as daimyo. They in turn possessed territorial police protection and soldiering forces comprised of the samurai class. This arrangement, known as the Tokugawa Shogunate, had lasted from 1603 onward, and it brought order and stability after an era of chaos and internecine warfare across the Japanese islands. Beneath these classes in the social structure lay the overwhelming majority of the Japanese people: the farmers, bureaucratic officials, merchants, craftsmen, entertainers, and priests of the Buddhist and Shinto sects. The society was rigid in its class distinctions, and social mobility for an individual, either up or down, was unusual.

Although there was some contact with the European powers during the Tokugawa era—mostly Dutch and Portugese mission-aries and traders—the feudal aristocracy saw an invasion of for-eign ideas as upsetting to social stability and thus a threat to their continued power, and they zealously guarded against it.

Perry's visitation made a dramatic impact on the whole of Japan, starting at the top, where the shogun and daimyo set about reorganizing themselves so as to avoid foreign invasion or other humiliating trade agreements. Britain, France, Russia, and other European powers soon followed America in the drive to open up Japan. The Meiji Restoration of 1867–68 marked the beginning of the process by which Japan's leaders sought to guard their nation's sovereignty and culture by adopting Western technology and institutions such as a modern military, parliamentary government, and university system while keeping the basics of the old feudal system in place.

This meant preservation of social inequality and of the power of the ruling families, who now had to contend with rising movements among the lower classes for more freedom of speech, voting rights, land reform, labor unionization rights, and many other reforms as the social democratic influences of the modern world took root among a hitherto repressed and isolated people. But the Meiji transformation saw the replacement of the shogun supreme authority with the emperor (*tenno*), who had been a minor and marginalized figure throughout the Tokugawa period. Now he was back and put in a position of absolute authority by the governing daimyo; ancient Shinto religious practices of emperor worship, which entailed revering the monarch as a living god, were revived and encouraged.

The figure of the emperor provided the Japanese with a sacred personage to rally around, and with a constitution based largely on that of Germany, Japan's Meiji government sought to follow the example of a successfully industrialized and militaristic European state. Governmental branches included the emperor's court, a popularly elected, multiparty diet, a daimyo-controlled House of Peers, and the judiciary. Tremendous behind-the-scenes influence was wielded by the military and the zaibatsu, large, corporate industrial cartels that were usually managed at the top by members of aristocratic families.

The leadership position of the Meiji emperor and his royal descendants alternated between symbolic stature as a figurehead, and the exercise of actual decision-making power in matters of law and military actions. This ambiguity would become an important issue in World War II and the postwar period, when demands arose for answers as to the extent of Emperor Hirohito's responsibility and guilt in such issues as the planning and instigation of aggressive war, his approval of the system of the military's sex slavery of Chinese, Korean, and Filipino women and girls known as *ianfu* or "comfort women," abducted and forced to serve as prostitutes; the Unit 731–led human experiments and germ warfare; chemical warfare; the Nanking Massacre; and various other crimes. (Immediately after World War II the long-repressed Koreans, who had been forced to attend Shinto services and perform Shinto rituals, set ablaze 136 Shinto shrines and other buildings in which iconic photographs of Emperor Hirohito were displayed.)

One Japanese expression that I have often heard repeated is "The nail that sticks out gets hammered down," typically quoted by Americans intent upon illustrating the stifling conformity and compliance of Japanese culture. In accounting for why and how such an appalling phenomenon as Unit 731 could happen, it is easy to cite such traditional regimentation and strict obedience to authority as key contributing social factors, reminiscent of the stereotypical German predilection for order, discipline, and subservience to authority. But the fact remains that for all the bad in Japan, there was also a significant amount of rebellion and popular struggle for the good, the causes of democracy, equality, and human rights. Indeed, it is equally important to recognize that the massive human experiment and biological warfare system Japan developed could not have existed were it not for the preexisting foundation of advanced hospitals and medical universities dedicated to the goals of curing disease and improving the health of all people.

This impressive system, one that produced so many brilliant physicians and top bacteriologists, was based on the ideals of compassionate healing and the betterment of humanity, as necessarily is all medicine that is not involved in the production of weapons. To all the tragic and ironic aspects of the Unit 731 saga we must add the fact that a kind and beneficent medical tradition was turned upside down. Shiro Ishii sardonically referred to himself as "a humanitarian in reverse." The research methods and discoveries of plague and syphilis pioneers Shibasaburu Kitasato and Hideo Noguchi, conceived in their battle against these diseases, paradoxically created an environment that enabled the twisted likes of Ishii to do battle using plague and syphilis *against* the population of China, killing them in germ attacks and secret experiments. The Unit 731 legions coldly preserved medicine's scientific devices while annihilating all its high ideals.

By the 1930s, Japanese culture had gone into a moral tailspin. A country whose conduct with regard to humane and ethical treatment of prisoners of war had once been among the world's best was now speedily building its first bio-war weapons programs and using both prisoner POWs and civilian prisoners as human guinea pigs along the way. Japan was engaged in the severe oppression of the populations in its overseas territories and had abandoned its traditions of battlefield honor and mercy that had existed in the old samurai code (contained in a set of formal precepts known as Bushido).

In the Sino-Japanese War of 1894–95, Japan initiated aggression against China, opening wartime hostilities by attacking Chinese troops in Korea, and Japanese leaders used the war to seize Taiwan, the Pescadores, and the Liaodong Peninsula from China. The Japanese occupiers harshly treated the local populations of these territories as colonial subjects, in much the same manner as it later subjugated the Koreans. Yet the Imperial Declaration of War stated explicitly that Japanese troops should wage the war without violating the tenets of international law. And Japan lived up to its word: None of its 1,790 Chinese prisoners of war was harmed, and all were subsequently released on the battlefield without being held in detention camps, after they signed an agreement not to fight again against Japan. The army command offices even had scholars trained in international law posted to advise the military on how to apply the law to the situations they would encounter, and the Imperial Headquarters kept a retinue of legal scholars and diplomats to oversee the ethical conduct of the armed forces. More than two dozen POW camps were established across Japan for 79,367 Russian prisoners during the Russo-Japanese War, and all demonstrated excellent treatment of the prisoners. The Japanese captors even paid their Russian prisoners a salary that was double the amount paid to Japanese soldiers of the equivalent rank.

The contradictions ran through aspects of everyday life. While Japan was emphasizing ethical military standards in the field during the 1894–95 war with China, its public education system began indoctrinating Japanese youth in militarism and racial hatred toward the Chinese, whose culture and traditions had previously been respected and even admired to some degree. In an elementary school ethics class, a teacher is reported to have "described in exciting detail how our brave and loyal soldiers and officers drive the pigtailed Chinks to Pyongyang [Korea]." Teachers at the school also posted a report on the bulletin board: "Japanese troops defeat Chinese at Pyongyang and win a great victory. Chinese corpses piled high as a mountain. Oh what a grand triumph. Chinka chinka chinka, chinka so stupid and they stinka." The treatment received by residents of the formerly Chinese island of Taiwan was harsh. Almost no self-rule or dissent to Japanese policies was tolerated, even at the level of local municipalities, and Japanese was enforced in schools and publications as the official language.

There was continual tension right through to Japan's war defeat in 1945 between the military and corporate-feudal oligarchs seeking to clamp down on basic rights on the one hand, and struggling intellectual and democratic groups on the other. In the 1870s and 1880s a "people's rights" movement vigorously fought for the establishment of freedom of speech and assembly, and an elected parliament; many in the movement braved imprisonment and severe harassment by the Meiji oligarch authorities. But in the end some limited freedom of speech was granted in the final constitution, and the Diet was formed, which included the pro-rights Jyuto (Liberal) Party. Even more promising was the period from 1915 to the early 1920s, sometimes referred to as the Taisho democracy time (Taisho was the reign title of the then-emperor Yoshihito), when the representative Diet and wide-ranging political expression blossomed. Alas, it also served to trigger a wave of repression through the remainder of the 1920s. The Peace Preservation Law was passed in 1925 as an internal security measure to outlaw socialist assemblies and censor socialist concepts in publications and speeches. Antiwar books from the turn of the century were reprinted in the 1920s, but only with certain passages deleted by the government. At least an undercurrent of antiwar and antimilitary feelings did exist among the populace; some of Imperial Japan's antiwar writings have become classics of world literature, such as "Kimishin tamau koto nakare" ("My Brother, Don't Waste Your Life in the War"), by the renowned female poet, women's rights advocate, and pacifist Yosano Akiko.

Popular democratic, humanist, pacifist, socialist, anarchist, and communist movements all existed in Japan and had their influences in the artistic life of the country as well. But again, as with so many other rebellious and idealistically inspired social facets of Japanese society, they all faced suppression in the 1920s, and were forced deeper underground with the advent of Japan's right-wing slide toward war and fascism in the 1930s.

The core values of health and medical practice were also turned upside down in the 1930s, and the beginning of Imperial Japan's human experiment and biological warfare attacks, led by the brightest university scientists and physicians, is much a part of this phenomenon—a nation on the rise in terms of foreign conquest and war technology and in the gutter in terms of moral principles.

Through it all the United States kept up its friendship with Japan. With the partial exception of an oil embargo imposed by the United States at the urging of President Franklin D. Roosevelt in 1941, American corporations kept up a vibrant commercial trading routine of all manner of goods with the Japanese Empire right through their most infamous and widely known atrocities of the 1930s and early 1940s, up until the attack of Pearl Harbor on December 7, 1941. There were some calls for boycotts of Japanese goods and protests of Japanese-owned stores in the United States after the Nanking Massacre in 1938, but these were mostly from radical-left organizations and had little effect on U.S. policy. The famed "Flying Tigers" squadron of American fighter plane pilots, assisting China in its battle against Japan after the 1937 invasion of central China, basically functioned as a somewhat romantic, quasi-mercenary volunteer force and received no official backing from either the U.S. State Department or Congress (until Pearl Harbor and simultaneous Japanese assaults against U.S. and British territories in the Asia and Pacific region).

Even the U.S. ambassador to Imperial Japan, Joseph Grew, consistently defended Japanese actions and put himself at odds with those in the State Department more inclined to sympathize with the plight of China. "There is no better person than the best kind of Japanese," Grew insisted. The pro-Japan faction had powerful sympathizers also among the more conservative elements of America's leading families and corporations, including those backing the isolationist and anticommunist wings of the Republican Party, who saw Japan's merciless advance across Asia as a bulwark against the Soviet Union and the spread of communism in China.

*   *   *

In Europe, on the Western Front of World War I, at Ypres, Belgium, the age of modern chemical weapons began on April 22, 1915. Rows of French and Algerian soldiers, huddled at dusk in the muddy trenches of the no-man's-land, heard a long silence broken by the first clatter and thunder of machine gunfire and artillery bursts. The weary young men jumped upright to assume defensive firing positions. A division of British and Canadians anxiously clutching their bayonet rifles held the flank to the right of the French and Algerian troops. The Second Battle of Ypres had begun. A fresh German offensive had opened up in an effort to break the frontline stalemate.

Shooting continued back and forth for several hours, and then the German troops abruptly left their positions and disappeared. The French-Algerian platoons charged into the breach, into something new, a greenish-yellow cloud rolling in from the German lines, noiseless, billowy almost, a strange haze suffusing the very air. Their hands went to their mouths reflexively as the young men attempted to breathe. Then came the coughing, handkerchiefs, jacket collars lifted to face, nose, mouth, but to no avail. None had a gas mask. It was not a part of the standard equipment, and no commanders had expected they would need any. The spreading mist had a sharp, choking odor. An acrid metallic taste filled their mouths. Many men found their eyes and skin burning, and many felt their lungs seeming to catch fire.

They fled, some dropping their guns, running for the medics and for good air. With this event, the war to end all wars had given the world a glimpse of chlorine gas in battle. It was a stunning debut for the use of mass-produced chemical weapons, a new form of violence invented by a German chemist named Fritz Haber. Rather than calling for an immediate ban on poison gas, within a short time the Allied nations that had been the victims of

Germany's chlorine volleys began using it too, and continued to do so until peace came in 1918. A year later, Haber actually won a Nobel Prize in chemistry for a process he had invented to synthesize ammonia, despite his infamy as the progenitor of modern chemical weapons and messages of outrage to the Nobel Committee sent from many ethically minded scientists protesting the award. In his acceptance speech he enthusiastically called his chlorine weapons "a higher form of killing."

In the Ypres attacks, the German army launched 5,723 cylinders of asphyxiating chlorine gas at the Allied line. Many men became violently ill, and the Allied regiments disintegrated into chaos and panic. Medical facilities were overwhelmed. The frontlines drew back, creating an opening for a crucial German advance. The Germans, though, were unprepared to follow up on the deadly effectiveness of their strange new weapon, and failed to move infantry forward in time to make a stalemate-ending breakthrough. Five thousand French, Algerian, British, and Canadian troops died in the Battle of Ypres, many from inhaling the chlorine. Ten thousand more were wounded, many with gas-induced chronic lung injuries that would cause pain with each breath.

Before the war's end, chemical gas shells and canisters were being used routinely by nations on both sides of the conflict, including Germany, France, Great Britain, Austria-Hungary, and the United States of America. More than 91,000 men were killed by gas, and approximately 1.3 million suffered persistent health problems due to exposure. Gas masks became a familiar supply piece in the trench soldier's kit, but the emergence and continuing use of advanced poisons as a means of waging war, so technologically advanced and simultaneously so barbaric, had the effect of causing shock, fear, and revulsion in people of all cultures and societies. Despite this popular reaction, the governments of the Western nations continued to employ gas and expand the scope and lethality of their chemical attacks.

Even before Ypres, there had been an international compact banning both chemical and germ weapons, the Hague Convention of 1899. This treaty sought to establish many rules for the conduct of war, such as provisions for the humane treatment of POWs and the protection of civilian institutions from targeted destruction. The Hague Convention states simply that "the use of poison and poisoned arms" is "especially prohibited," a ban that presumably applies to all forms of "poison" including microbes and chemical substances. With the general acceptance of the germ theory of disease and subsequent identification of many disease-inducing microbes had also come the realization that the laboratory methods for studying the germs to cure disease could also be put to work in reverse.

In addition, a separate declaration was issued as part of the convention, specifically and categorically banning "projectiles which have the purpose of diffusing asphyxiating and deleterious gases" from being used as weapons, despite the fact that no such chemical gas weapons had yet been scientifically developed or used by any nation. The framers of the Hague Convention recognized the advancing state of chemistry as an industrial science and envisaged the potentials for its misuse.

Yet within sixteen years, several nations that ratified this treaty had broken their pledge by using chemical weapons, most notably Hague signatory Germany.

The response in the Allied press to Germany's use of poison gas might generally be described as condemning, yet at the same time curiously muted; no one called it an extreme war crime. For example, the first accounts of the Ypres battle published in the *Times of London* on April 26, 1915, cite the chemical weapon attacks as merely one more violation of civilized conventions in a litany of German misdeeds:

"[I]t is certain that asphyxiation was the sole aim [of the gas assaults], and that the spirit of the [Hague] Declaration has been broken, and that the Germans have added one more crime to the long list of infamies."

"While the Germans are thus violating one more of the conventions of civilized warfare upon land," the *Times* stated in a separate article, "and continuing with ostentation to violate them by the drowning of noncombatants and the sinking of merchant ships without notice at sea, they have carried out their threat of exercising 'reprisals' upon their English prisoners, for our refusal to give the crews of the submarines engaged in this murderous and inhumane warfare exactly the same privileges and courtesies, and comforts as we freely accord to our German prisoners."

Thus the lethal use of a chemical warfare choking agent was presented in the British paper of record as a battlefield incident no more remarkable than submarine anti-civilian attacks or POW treatment issues. Instead of raising an international outcry against Germany's chemical weapons upon their first startling, taboo-breaking use, within five months the British and French began launching their own asphyxiating gas canisters at the Germans.

After the war, the newly formed League of Nations was galvanized by the many cruel deaths and cases of chronic illness caused by chemical warfare to make an international treaty banning the manufacture and use of such arms, the 1925 Geneva Convention, which also outlawed bacteriological weapons. In the 1930s, Japan, which had not used chemical weapons in its battles of World War I, flaunted the Geneva prohibition. A scientific unit specializing in chemical weaponry was attached to the Kwantung Army in the central Manchurian city of Tsitsihar, and was known as Unit 516. It manufactured thousands of poison gas shells containing mustard gas, phosgene, lewisite, diphenyl cynoarsine, and other agents, and worked in tandem with the Ishii Unit to test these gases on its prisoners, including children, in a special glass-walled gas chamber located at Pingfan. Beginning in 1937, Imperial Japan used poison gas on numerous occasions against Chinese civilians as well as troops. In the battle at Nanchang lasting from March through May 1939, the invading Japanese army used more than 3,000 gas shells. In another battle, in October 1941, Japanese planes dropped mustard gas bombs on the suburbs of the Chinese city of Ichang, resulting in the deaths of 600 Chinese soldiers and the wounding of more than 1,000 others.

Japan's chemical warfare was brought as an international issue to the floor of the League of Nations in 1939, but the league, distracted from the matter by the unfolding catastrophe of German aggression in Europe, engaged in little discussion on the topic and recommended no action against Japan, which had already resigned from the league in 1933 over its condemnation of the invasion of Manchuria.

The league had, however, been concerned enough about biological warfare after World War I that it had added a prohibition to this new threat in the international treaty banning the manufacture of chemical weapons. Biological warfare (BW) is defined as the use of living organisms (as apart from nonliving chemicals) as agents of destruction, and is distinct from chemical warfare (CW). The distinction is fundamentally important, although the two are often lumped together as CBW, or more recently in the 1990s (the term was first employed by the United Nations in 1947) as "weapons of mass destruction" (WMD), and classed together with nuclear weapons as NBC: nuclear, biological, chemical weapons of mass destruction.

The first allegation of the scientific use of biological warfare had been an accusation lodged against Germany in World War I. The details are somewhat vague; British scientists contended that from 1916 to 1918 a group of German secret agents had attempted to export sheep and horses that had been deliberately infected with the bacteria causing anthrax and glanders. The animals were to be sent from German contacts in Romania into Russia and France, and to Allied troop units on the Western Front, but evidence suggests they never arrived at these destinations. It was claimed that some 200 livestock animals had died of these intentionally spread diseases while they were still penned in Romania. An international panel of experts convened at the League of Nations in 1924, working to help draft the 1925 Geneva accord banning chemical and bacteriological warfare, noted that cultures of the glanders bacterium had been discovered in the German embassy in Bucharest, Romania, together with instructions for the infection of the glanders disease in horses of the Romanian cavalry. Apart from this attempt, which produced no known human casualties, no other credible allegations of biological warfare in World War I had been leveled. But the Romania livestock BW charges against Germany had further aroused the already existing concerns in intellectual and scientific circles over the possibilities of future germ warfare.

While Japan and Germany's biological weapons camps and human medical experiment programs evolved in eerily similar fashion, Japan's descent into fascist imperialism took a different route than did the Third Reich. In the mid-1920s Japan had become a rapidly modernizing state, ahead of every other nation in Asia in terms of its military power, independence from the West, and industrial might. The nation was still nominally a multiparty republic, combining aspects of electoral democracy with a rigid, feudal social structure, and its economy was dominated by the zaibatsu (which translates literally as "wealth cliques"), a dozen aristocratic families who ran corporations that monopolized such key sectors as the coal, aluminum, and timber industries and engine manufacturing. The most powerful zaibatsu families were the Mitsui, Sumitomo, Yasuda, and Iwasaki clans. The Iwasaki family company, which made arms for the military, was called Mitsubishi, the name by which it is still known today and which has become familiar to consumers the world over as a leading automaker. The island nation had also integrated many common aspects of the modern West into its daily life. Americans would feel quite comfortable in the Tokyo of the 1920s and 1930s; baseball had become a popular pastime, Coca-Cola signs were ubiquitous, and American-made cars rolled along the streets. Western books and films flooded the Home Islands and were eagerly absorbed by the growing Japanese middle class.

Unlike Italy and Germany, its allies in the anticommunist Anti-Comintern Pact of 1936, and the military Tripartite Alliance of 1940, Imperial Japan never experienced a governmental takeover by a militaristic, far-right political sect, such as Mussolini's blackshirt *Fascisti* or Hitler's Nazis. Instead Japan's parliamentary system and its laws guaranteeing press freedoms and labor rights suffered slow and steady erosion over the decades, as corporate and military interests became all-powerful, rallying the public behind the sacred banner of Emperor Hirohito.

The society's traditions included a samurai ethic of violence and aggressive war. The emperor was granted virtually unlimited power by the constitution, and made the chief of both the army and the navy. Imperial Japan was also a society of great inequality. Beside the estates of the fabulously wealthy corporate leaders and landowning nobles lived the poor who comprised the vast majority of the Japanese people—the uneducated workers and peasants who often existed on the edge of hunger, usually eating a rice substitute gruel made of cereal grains because even rice was considered too expensive to enjoy on a daily basis. Tokyo was ringed with mile upon mile of grim shantytowns. A theocratic indoctrination of emperor worship held sway as citizens were taught to revere the young Emperor Hirohito as a living god, a direct descendant of the sun goddess Amaterasu, the supreme Shinto deity. His pious subjects, the common people of Japan, would cast their eyes downward when Hirohito and his entourage passed by in a public place, as it was considered improper to glance directly upon the divine emperor.

The ideology of emperor worship (*kodo*) grew steadily in intensity through the 1920s, as the educational authorities encouraged this dogma as a way of uniting Japan's civilian masses behind their leaders' industrial goals for war, and of reinforcing the morale of enlisted soldiers, who were mostly draftees. These men were often poor tenant farmers who did not share the gung-ho ethos of the professional-warrior officer class within the military.

In short, by the 1930s Japan was a land of painful and explosive contradictions, ripe for exploitation by the nationalistic, power-hungry microbiologist Shiro Ishii and men like him. To the outside world, Japan had gained notoriety as an expansionist imperial power, spurred by its burgeoning economy and the efforts of Japanese ruling circles to gobble up overseas empires—matching the moves of Western colonial powers in Asia and the Pacific. In its decision to research biological weapons, Japan mimicked the West again.

Crucial to the history of biological weapons is the way that Japanese-U.S. ties evolved, from a relationship of friendly trading and diplomatic partners willing to look the other way when one or the other made an imperialistic grab, to sharp rivals, and ultimately to bitter wartime enemies—followed by Japan's transformation into a subaltern ally of the United States during the Cold War. "Our unsinkable aircraft carrier in the Pacific" became one frequent way of putting it.

The post-1945 U.S.-Japan friendship made the United States complicit in Japan's biological war crimes when American military and political officials protected Japanese germ warfare criminals from war crimes prosecution and covered up information on their attacks (the details and history of which I discuss in Chapter

Nine). In return, the Japanese gave the Americans their secret data and counsel on lethal human experiment and germ warfare. As a consequence, it was over half a century before the hundreds of thousands of germ warfare victims could pursue recognition and reparations for what had befallen them at the hands of Unit 731.

SIX

THE GATHERING STORM

IN JULY 1937 THE JAPANESE LAUNCHED A FULL-SCALE INVASION of China. The pretext for the Second Sino-Japanese War was the military's claim that the Chinese had attacked first, by firing shots at a Japanese regiment conducting night maneuvers in a Japan-leased section of Peking, near the Marco Polo Bridge. The next day, when the Chinese commander of a nearby fort refused to allow Japanese troops inside to search for a missing soldier, the Japanese garrison fired artillery rounds at the fort, beginning hostilities that resulted in the rapid Japanese conquest of Peking (now Beijing) by August.

Prior to this incident, Imperial Japan had been provoking skirmishes and installing Chinese puppet administrators in several of China's northern provinces near Manchuria. In Tokyo, cabinet officials became nervous. The Japanese militarists seemed to be repeating the 1931 invasion of Manchuria, this time on an even grander scale, with unknown consequences. Japan had already received the opprobrium of all forty-two other members of the League of Nations for its Manchurian occupation, and in response had resigned from that organization. This new invasion would only deepen Japan's diplomatic isolation.

Prime Minister Fumimaro Konoe and the Foreign Ministry had not been apprised of the military's attack plans and did not know its strategy for conducting the war, or how far into China they intended to go. Imperial Japan's militarists, its zaibatsu corporations, and the emperor had become a force unto themselves, accountable to no one—not the prime minister, or his cabinet or the Diet—and with an unstoppable war machine. The military continued to increase its grip on society from 1937 onward, drawing millions of Japanese soldiers and civilians deeper into its wars of aggression. All the while, millions of yen were poured upon Ishii and the network of human experiment and biological warfare stations. Perpetual war was an ideal situation for the BW scientists, for there would always be keen military interest in the promise of their work, Japan's version of the Manhattan Project.

Thus from the time of Pingfan's inception in 1936, Ishii had made sure to set up a network of satellite sub-unit bases across the Manchurian plains and the Liaodong Peninsula. These posts, employing about 300 people each, trained personnel for germ warfare field trials and attack operations in addition to cultivating large amounts of bacteria, insects, and animal-disease hosts in their own laboratories. At the Songo Unit, also known as Branch 673, where Masaji Kitano began investigating the cause of Songo fever, white rats, mice, and guinea pigs were bred along with large quantities of fleas produced for use as bubonic plague carriers. Branch 673 members also caught wild rodents living in the vicinity and brought them to the lab, breeding them indoors for future release as flea-infested plague BW vectors. Branch units similar to this one were located at Hailar (Unit 543) close to the Soviet border, and at the Manchurian towns of Linkow and Mudanjiang. Such outposts were useful for conducting experiments on nearby villages and isolated population groups in remote areas of Manchuria.

Another unit, situated in the strategic coastal city of Dairen, near Port Arthur in Liaodong Province, was called the South Manchurian Railway Sanitary Institute; large quantities of vaccines were produced there. Other urban Unit 731 detachments were to be found in Harbin (the original 1932 facility in a converted sake distillery) and in the large city of Mukden, near a POW camp where Unit 731 scientists performed experiments on some Allied prisoners, including Americans who had been captured in the Philippines. The commanders of these bases had in mind as their primary strategic goals the development of microbes and chemical poisons to be used either in the event of war with the Soviet Union or in their ongoing attacks with both germ and chemical warfare against the Chinese.

After Pingfan, the most active BW installation in Manchuria was at Changchun. Known variously as Unit 100, the Wakamatsu Unit, and the Kwantung Army Administration of the Anti-Epizootic Protection of Horses Unit, Changchun was where much research on the use of biological weapons against animals and plants took place. Its commander, a veterinarian named Major Yujiro Wakamatsu, headed the organization from 1936 until the Japanese surrender in 1945, by which time he, like Ishii, had attained the rank of major general. Wakamatsu worked closely and continually with the generals in charge of the Kwantung Army Intelligence Division and the Kwantung Army Veterinary Service. While Wakamatsu was a quiet, polite man, in marked contrast to his counterpart at Pingfan, he was no less dedicated to the pursuit of biological and chemical warfare. Unit 100 covered an area of twenty square kilometers and included farmland on which was conducted research into chemicals, bacteria, fungi, and germs that could be used to destroy crops. Scientists there experimented with plant pathogens that could spread like wildfire through tobacco fields, sabotaging a civilian economy. Other experiments involved pathogens that could wipe out wheat or rice crops. Unit 100 conducted many projects that involved infecting livestock with contagious diseases and then leaving the animals behind Soviet enemy lines or in the Mongolian People's Republic, Manchuria's other communist neighbor.

China had been plagued with famines due to crop failures for many centuries; there was a major famine in Henan Province in 1942–43 caused by the combined effect of crop failure due to drought and wartime disruptions, and an estimated 2 million to 3 million people died. Entire regions of the country, the Japanese knew, could be brought to its knees by artificially induced famines.

Buildings on the Unit 100 grounds contained veterinary housing for animals; laboratories; dissection rooms for both animals and human prisoners; and factories to make clay, ceramic, and glass-hulled germ delivery bombs, flasks, and bottles. The large, two-story headquarters building dominated the camp. Administrative offices were located on the second floor of the building, with laboratories on the first floor and in the basement. As with the Ro quadrangle at Pingfan, the Changchun Unit's administration, lab space, and prison cells were clustered together. And as at Pingfan, this central structure had a catacomb of tunnels leading to other animal housing and laboratory facilities.

As many as 800 scientists, technicians, and guards worked at Changchun. A great deal of research focused on horse diseases and blood, and a total of 150 horses were lodged in three stables. Among the contagious horse diseases studied were glanders, equine infectious anemia, a viral illness that destroys the immune system and red blood cell production, and piroplasmosis, a protozoan infection of red blood cells carried by ticks. Unit 100 scientists also kept a variety of rodents in buildings across the camp, among them mice, rats, squirrels, and rabbits. Cattle, sheep, and oxen were kept at the camp also, living in large pens.

Unit 100 concentrated on pathogenic animal microbes that could be used to infect and sicken people, such as the germs of anthrax and glanders. Its scientists also worked on mosaic virus and red rust fungus, both crop-killing organisms. Microbiologists and veterinarians searched for the best ways to kill entire herds of livestock, and researched rinderpest, or cattle plague, and ox plague.

Germs and chemical herbicides were tested on plant species.

Throughout its existence, Unit 100 remained fairly independent of Unit 731, and it expanded to form its own network of branch units in Manchuria. Of course, there was still much overlap of scientific personnel, sharing of research data, and coordination of germ warfare operations between Unit 731 and Unit 100. Wakamatsu's men also worked closely with the Kwantung Army's "hippo-epizootic detachments"—from the Greek *hippos*, or "horse"—which were tasked with spreading animal disease. These BW units were created within the Kwantung Army in 1941, at the behest of the General Staff, and stationed in the towns of Tunan, Tunging, Koshan, and Chining. The Army sent cadres of soldiers to the detachments for training by Unit 100 personnel on how to conduct disease-spreading missions.

Unit 100 scientists treated their prisoners in much the same way that their Unit 731 peers abused the prisoners of Pingfan. Wakamatsu's doctors tested a variety of germs and poisons on human subjects, and performed some vivisections to chart the effects of a disease. Two thick sets of Unit 100 victim autopsy reports, one covering thirty cases of anthrax, the other twenty-one cases of glanders, surfaced after the war. "The Report of 'A'" and "The Report of 'G'" both contain hundreds of photographs and panels with color pastel illustrations, each panel framing images of precisely labeled tissue sections and individual cells. Full-body illustrations of the victims are given case numbers to go along with the text references; there are no names. All are drawn with the same face and body, with the right arm outstretched at shoulder level. Within the torso of each body a set of organs is drawn, color-coded to show the infection route and tissue damage, with accompanying notes. Each figure's head is bald, with a small horizontal slit for the mouth.

The panels showing organ tissue close-ups and individual cells contain either pastel drawings or photomicrographs. "The

Report of 'A'" covers its thirty human guinea-pig cases of anthrax in 406 pages; "The Report of 'G'" takes 372 pages to discuss the twenty-one glanders-infected prisoners of the Wakamatsu Unit. The effects of the pathogen are recorded in fine detail: The microscopic alveoli and bronchial changes in the lung are depicted by color-coded drawings, with each drawing corresponding to a case number. Cross referenced with the case numbers are concise technical descriptions of the changes that happened to the lung tissue as the disease progressed.

The "A" report contains notes on nine people made to eat tainted food and infected with the gastrointestinal form of anthrax, an extremely rare disease. (Anthrax has two other manifestations: cutaneous, or skin anthrax, which is generally not fatal, and the much rarer inhalation form, called pneumonic anthrax, which has a 90 percent mortality rate if not treated quickly with antibiotics—drugs not widely available until after World War II.) The report states that these nine experiment victims "were infected . . . with some food stuffs, which contain some quantity of anthrax bacillus and all patients died definitely after several days by acute abdominal symptoms and severe hemorrhagic ascites." In other words, they internally bled to death. One prisoner, labeled Case Number 32, had his death summed up in one pathologist's brief note: "Remarkable congestion and plenty of bacterial accumulation."

In another anthrax experiment on Case Number 54, the pathologists noted the changes organ by organ: "Heart: intense degeneration and interstitial edema. Liver: Hepatitis serosa III, accompanied with some hemorrhagic changes. Kidney: Glomerulo-nephrosis . . ." These observations describe what must have been an excruciatingly painful state for the victim, his inner organs swelling, bleeding, and disintegrating. The characteristic skin lesions of anthrax on this person were recorded as "Localized cutaneous ulcers and perifocal phlegmons (r-thigh)."

The doctors' painstaking attention to detail is also evident in the reports' drawings of individual cells and their annotations. On this micro-level, the report on another individual's anthrax infection shows a careful analysis of how the bacteria affected the person's liver cells: "Slight congestion and slight exudative changes in Disses' spaces . . . slight fatty degeneration of parenchymatous cells." At another stage of infection: "Hepatitis serose II-III with bacterial emigration in capillary-nets in sinuses."

The Report of "G" reveals that Case Number 180 lived for twelve days before succumbing to glanders. It notes that this person's liver tissue suffered damage: "Miliary glanders—Knots in exudative form . . . some parenchymatous degeneration in the Liver." The report for Case Number 16 describes spreading inflammation in the back of the mouth and throat—"Metastatic Tonsilitis acuta"; that person survived thirteen days, the longest-lived of all the report's subjects. The crematoria at Unit 100 evidently proved insufficient for eliminating the bodies of all the people who had died in experiments, because in 1949 Chinese peasants out in the fields planting crops near the former Unit 100 grounds made a grim discovery. They reported finding human corpses scattered over an area of 500 meters. "Even after digging two to five meters deep," one said, "we found that there were still human bodies."

Kazuo Mitomo, who assisted in the mass production of glanders bacteria at Unit 100, confessed after the war to administering a lethal injection of potassium cyanide to a Russian prisoner who had survived the unit's experimentation. Mitomo said that he and his superior officer Matsui tricked the Russian into willingly allowing the injection by first infecting the prisoner with a germ that caused diarrhea. He deceived the man into believing that the injection was a treatment for the diarrhea. He then took the Russian's body to what he described as a "cattle cemetery, at the back of the detachment premises," dissected the body there, and buried it. In another experiment, Mitomo mixed a gram of heroin

into the porridge of a Chinese prisoner, who "after eating the porridge . . . wandered about distraught for several hours and then
died." This prisoner too was buried in the cattle cemetery. Mitomo said he also knew of one Chinese and two Russian prisoners
who were shot dead at the cattle cemetery.

On April 18, 1939, Ishii and a group of high-ranking Unit 731
physicians established another major biological warfare operation, Unit 1644, in the conquered city of Nanking.

The events leading up to the December 1937 Rape of
Nanking were these: In November 1937, Shanghai fell to the
Japanese, after a hard, three-month battle—longer than Japan's
militarists had expected. But further, prolonged resistance to the
Japanese invasion was made impossible by the ineptness, repression, and corruption of the Chinese Kuomintang government's
dictatorial leader Chiang Kai-Shek and his ruling circles. Kuomintang vice, coupled with the disunity and chaos caused by
China's partitioning into regional warlord-ruled fiefdoms across
vast areas of the country and the deep class divisions within Chinese society itself, allowed for rapid Japanese colonial consolida-
tion. Then in December 1937 Japanese troops commanded by
General Iwane Matsui breached the defensive fortifications of
Nanking, the capital city of Nationalist China.

Upon entering Nanking through February 1938, they perpe-
trated the orgy of civilian and prisoner-of-war killings, rapes,
looting, torture, and burning known as the Rape of Nanking.
Tens of thousands of women and girls were assaulted, including
elderly women and girls under the age of ten. Estimates of the
number of Chinese civilians and prisoners of war killed usually
range from about 100,000 to more than 300,000 over the course
of the troops' six-week rampage.

The violence and destruction committed in this ancient city on the banks of the Yangtse River garnered worldwide attention and condemnation. But the Nanking carnage was not an anomaly, it was a more intense manifestation of the thousands of underreported army massacres and rapes that had preceded it in occupied Manchuria, Korea, and other places under Japanese control. Less than a month before the Rape of Nanking, for example, the ancient, canal-laced city of Suzhou, with a population of 350,000, had been burned and sacked by General Matsui's troops. Following Nanking, the rounding up and slaughter of civilian populations in retaliation for acts of rebellion against Japanese rule became standard procedure for Japanese troops.

Nanking was strategically situated at the crux of central and southern China, and the prospects for spreading new epidemics and field-testing germs in this southerly environment tantalized the members of Unit 731. Characteristically, Ishii saw an opening in Nanking for his ambitions and swooped in soon after the massacre to set up his new BW detachment inside an expropriated Chinese hospital complex. The hospital, a landmark in the city because of the giant red cross painted atop the six-story main edifice, was located in the heart of Nanking, on East Zhongsan Street. From the hospital one had a magnificent view of Zhilin Mountain, famed for its acres of cherry trees, and the complex was only a short walk from the tomb of Sun Yat Sen, the founder of the modern Chinese republic.

Why the BW units were numbered as they were is something of a mystery, but the number 1644 is significant in China as the year in which the Manchu warriors charged southward from their native Manchuria to defeat the Han Chinese forces and founded the Manchu-ruled Ching Dynasty. The Manchu heir to this dynasty, overthrown in 1911 with the founding of the Republic, was Henry Pu Yi, "the Last Emperor." Pu Yi was reenthroned by Tokyo in 1934 as the figurehead emperor of Japan-occupied

Manchuria. Some have surmised that Ishii's choice of the number 1644 was intended as a humiliation to a beaten-down China. The unit was also referred to as "Ei 1644," from the Japanese character "ei" meaning "prosperity."

With his usual Orwellian flair, Ishii designated Unit 1644 to be a branch detachment of the Central China Anti-Epidemic Water Supply Unit, and he appointed his friend from childhood, Tomosada Masuda, as one of the principal directors of the facility. Masuda held a medical degree and a Ph.D. in microbiology from Kyoto Imperial University, and had coauthored a scientific paper with Ishii early on in his career. Masuda looked up to Ishii as a mentor and brilliant innovator, and had helped him and the Kwantung Army scout out possible locations for their initial Manchurian BW stations in 1932.

Still, the two were something of an odd couple: Masuda was reserved and studious, in contrast to Ishii's voluble aggressiveness. But Masuda was no less intensely dedicated to waging biological warfare. Like Ishii, he taught at the Army Medical College in Tokyo, and in 1936 became a staff member of the Army Medical Bureau. In 1937 he became the director of a Unit 731 branch BW facility, the Dairen Anti-Epidemic Center. Masuda was frequently absent from his post, however, spending much time with Ishii in Harbin, consulting on experiments and germ warfare projects.

When Masuda moved to Nanking in 1939, he and his wife took up residence in an elegant townhouse within walking distance of the new BW base. A total of about 1,500 personnel were attached to Unit 1644. A central office and headquarters were located inside the hospital, while a four-story annex to the hospital housed laboratories and equipment relating to biological research, as well as a prison for experiment victims. A barracks for civilian and military personnel being trained in germ warfare techniques was built on the complex, and approximately 300 microbiologists a year were schooled in biological warfare at Unit

1644, then sent out into the BW system. One former army private assigned to training in Nanking remembered being organized into squads of ten people and that they were required to wear white surgical masks and surgical garb while performing laboratory work. Rubber boots and long rubber gloves were worn at all times during training duties. The former private recalled being taught how to breed lice and bacteria, and the various ways to scrutinize water for the presence of certain microbes.

As at Pingfan, the Nanking base offered its workers and visitors a swimming pool, library, auditorium, and recreation center for leisure activities. The security model of Pingfan was also duplicated. The entire perimeter of the hospital and adjacent grounds were surrounded by an eighteen-foot-high wall, above which barbed and electrified wire were stretched. Entry was possible only through well-guarded gates in the wall. Policemen and guard dogs constantly prowled the city blocks surrounding the base. Across the road from the hospital base was a military airport through which the Japanese army flew scientists, physicians, and military personnel who came to visit Unit 1644. The corpses of experiment victims and lab animals were burned in an on-site incinerator.

The Nanking unit's bacteria factory was designed to mass-produce germs for the purpose of battle and sabotage. The facility could create, at peak output, about ten kilograms of bacteria per production cycle, enough, theoretically, to infect thousands of people. In one room at the factory were about 200 bacteria incubators, which were referred to by BW personnel as "Ishii cultivators." The room also held two large, cylindrical autoclaves for sterilizing laboratory equipment.

Gasoline cans functioned as the breeding homes for mass quantities of fleas; about 100 such cans were employed at Nanking. Unit 1644's Bacteriological Division set up a special section for the breeding of fleas and production of bubonic plague bacteria. Its plague bacteria and plague-carrying fleas were dispersed by airplane at Ningbo in 1940, the city of Changde, Hunan Province in 1941. Unit 1644 also did many experiments involving poisonous chemicals, in collaboration with a secret weapons facility back in Japan, located in Kanagawa prefecture. This unit, the Ninth Army Technical Research Institute, was often referred to simply as the Kyu Ken. In 1941 a group of Kyu Ken officers and physicians traveled by ship to Nanking, and together with Unit 1644 scientists tested a variety of exotic poisons on the captives of their secret prison at the base on East Zhongsan Street.

The prisoners of Unit 1644 were kept in metal cages on the fourth floor of the hospital annex, like animals. The floor had a maximum capacity of about 100 prisoners, but it usually held only thirty or forty inmates at a time. Armed guards watched them always. The prisoners were mostly Chinese, with some other ethnic groups including Russians, perhaps taken from the White Russian expatriate communities in Shanghai and other Chinese cities. Proportionally more women and children prisoners were used at the Nanking unit than at other units in the BW system.

When the Kyu Ken doctors arrived, each inmate was led from the fourth-floor prison to the third-floor laboratory, put on a bed, and told through an interpreter not to be afraid, because the doctors were there to give him or her a healing medicine. Once lulled, the victim was injected with a toxin. One assistant said that he gave the lethal injections to prisoners "very quickly" because the team didn't want the victims to "catch on and thrash around."

The substances tested on prisoners included various species of bacteria, and extracts squeezed from venomous snakes, including cobra poison. The toxin found in the flesh of the *fugu* pufferfish was another biochemical agent used on inmates. An arsenic compound called arsenite was fed to prisoners in dumplings, but the poison failed to sicken them, as digestion thwarted the absorption of the toxic chemical. Cyanide hydric, nitrile prussiate (both cyanide acids), and acetone (a common industrial solvent) were a few of the many deadly chemicals used on Nanking's human guinea pigs.

A former Unit 1644 researcher, speaking on condition of anonymity, said, "The *maruta* were kept in cages . . . one had to pass through the main offices in order to get to where the cages were. The area where the prisoners were was sealed off with a door. One meter in front of the door and on its other side were disinfectant mats to prevent bacteriological contaminants from being carried outside on people's shoes.

"Most of the *maruta* in the cages were just lying down. In the same room were oil cans with mice that had been injected with plague germs, and with fleas feeding on the mice. These were not the usual types of fleas, but a transparent variety. Around the perimeter of the room was a thirty-centimeter-wide trough of running water." The trough acted as a moat that prevented the fleas from jumping out of the room and escaping.

The researcher said that at Nanking new members of the unit were assigned to the specimen room, as a kind of desensitizing initiation rite that would numb the novices to the realities of the world they had entered. "Every year, when the new soldiers came in," he said, "the first job they got was cleaning up at night around the human specimen room. The other soldiers would put a dish of fireflies in the specimen room by the window facing the corridor." In Japanese culture, fireflies are associated with happiness and luck. Whether they were placed in the room to countervail the awful environment, or as a ghastly joke on the new recruits, is unclear. "The fireflies swarming around the specimens of body parts created an eerie feeling, and some of the young recruits suffered emotional problems from the experience."

Another Unit 1644 member, Hiroshi Matsumoto, said in a 1997 interview that the prisoners "were all naked and kept in cages that looked like cages for birds or animals, very small, in the size of 1.2 meters to 1.30 meters in height, side, and width.

They had to always have their legs crossed. . . . After we injected live germs into prisoners, we would wait until the germs spread in the blood, then we would take out all their blood."

In describing the usual method of draining the prisoners' blood so that it could be harvested for germ warfare purposes, Matsumoto recalled that after about six months of captivity, the *maruta* would be taken to the "treatment room," put to sleep with chloroform, and cut open at their inguinal artery, in the center of the thigh.

"After a considerable amount of blood was gone, the whole body would start shaking in convulsions," he said. The blood would then be used "probably to culture germs for contaminating food, or for feeding [on a blood meal] fleas that would be scattered over an enemy area. . . ."

Lice were bred in large numbers by technicians on the second floor of the annex building. Typhus rickettsias were cultivated on the first floor to be transmitted to their louse host carriers, and bubonic plague bacteria also were bred on this level for eventual transfer to host vector rodents and fleas, housed on the second floor along with the lice.

Unit 1644's central location in Nanking allowed it to serve as a forward base and hub to project diseases into middle and southern China after receiving the personnel, germs, and infected insects that had been transported from the Unit 731 Pingfan complex in Manchuria, and flown south directly to Nanking, or to the Unit 731 airport in Hangzhou, near Shanghai, where BW teams from Pingfan and Nanking would connect in coordinated BW missions. The strain of plague or cholera bacteria cultured for extra virulence in the blood of an infected prisoner at Pingfan would eventually be scattered over the Chinese citizens of Ningbo, a thousand miles from Pingfan, or Changde, a city 500 miles from Ningbo, or at other places in central China far away from the original Manchurian BW nexus where that prisoner had been vivisected on a sterile operating table. Doctor-made epidemics raged in cities and villages across China.

The experiences of Tsuruo Nishishima, a former member of the weather section of the Unit 731 air corps, underscore the expanded reach into China that the Japanese bio-war program attained. As a meteorological specialist, he reported on weather conditions for BW airplane flights and the wind, sunlight, and temperature factors relevant to the aerial spraying of germ-laden plumes and the dropping of germ bombs. In a 1998 Osaka interview, the eighty-five-year-old Nishishima remembered a germ warfare expedition from Pingfan to Nanking, and from Nanking into the east-central cities of Quzhou and Nanchang: "It was in the summer of 1941 as a part of the Zhejiang campaign. That particular one was called the Nanchang campaign. A total of thirty to forty staff including ten of the weather team, ten radio operators, mechanics, surgeons, and pilots were flown to Nanking by a heavy bomber plane. There was no chair inside apart from those for the crew, therefore we all had to sit on the floor.

"We left Nanking for Quzhou by truck. The whole town was empty. We made a base inside of Quzhou Castle. The airplane was also moved to the small airport outside the town. We could not see the attacking team during our stay in Quzhou because the airport was away from the town. . . .

"Before spreading germs, it was usual practice for the BW corps to send Chinese spies to spread the rumor of epidemics. As soon as spies came back, the airplane sprayed germs in between Quzhou and Nanchang in order to prevent the enemy from coming back to the area. We also left the area soon.

"I don't believe they used bubonic plague in this case because there would have been much stricter precautions taken. I would think they used cholera, typhoid, and dysentery."

*   *   *

During the summer of 1939 Unit 731 engaged in its first battle-field biological warfare attack, against Soviet and Mongolian troops in the Nomonhan Incident engagements (known to Russians as the Khalkhin-Gol Incident). At Nomonhan the Japanese engaged in an unprovoked incursion across the Soviet border with tanks and mechanized infantry and artillery units. The main purpose behind their attack was to probe Soviet defense strength, as they considered the possibility of launching an all-out war against the Soviets from the Kwantung Army base region in Manchuria.

The attack involved throwing typhoid germs into a river upstream from where Soviet and Mongolian troops were camped, but the Japanese apparently had no way to assess the results of their disseminations. Unlike with their prisoners, they couldn't interview the Soviet soldiers for their reactions.

We do know, however, that more than forty BW team members who worked on the Nomonhan attack accidentally contracted typhoid fever and died in the hospital as a result of becoming infected by their own bacteria. Among those killed in this way was a BW squadron leader who had been spraying typhoid germs with his men toward the end of August.

The former Pingfan technician Yoshio Shinozuka recollected first arriving in Harbin, as a member of the Junior Youth Corps, during the Nomonhan Incident. "The Japanese army had just started to attack the Soviet army. At the end of July, mass production of germs to be used as biological weapons was begun and we Junior Youth Corps were ordered to assist that production.

"I was dispatched to Hailar from Harbin by night-train. We kept a box full of deadly germs on the deck of the train and took turns guarding it. Two of my fellow Junior Youth Corps members actually participated in germ warfare. I heard from them that they had flung the germs in that box into the River Horustein, at the point upstream were it meets the River Haruha."

A 1989 Japanese newspaper article published confessions by three former Youth Corps members who had engaged in the Nomonhan BW actions. These veterans confirmed that their group was ordered to dump typhoid germs into a river. The germs were stored in eighteen-liter oil drums carried on two trucks, and these trucks drove at night, without their lights on, near the Horustein. The team then "crossed over swampy ground to a point near the riverbank, watching Soviet-Mongolian flares shoot up from the opposite side." The team members then poured each can's "jellylike contents" into the river.

While the typhoid fever bacterium, *Eberthella typhosa*, can survive in pools of still water, food, and beverages, it cannot survive the currents of a river; any microbiologist could have guessed that the bacteria would soon die in the conditions of the Horustein. Ishii must have known beforehand that this was likely to happen, and that few if any Soviet or Mongolian soldiers would become ill. And clearly he underestimated the need for special standards in handling the germs, given the infection and deaths of dozens of his own troops.

So why did he do it? It is likely that Ishii had an ulterior motive in participating in the Nomonhan combat. Because it was the Kwantung Army's first major military engagement with the Soviet Union, he may have wanted to get in on the ground floor, as it were, thereby increasing his prestige and status—and Unit 731's funding. His inability to monitor the results of the typhoid river contamination on the enemy could work in his favor too; no one could charge him with failure.

Indeed, Unit 731 received a special award from the commanding general of the Kwantung Army on October 1, 1939, shortly after the army's disastrous defeat at Nomonhan. Still, it was important in 1939 for the Japanese militarists to put a false face on their defeat and spin a tale of some kind of heroic victory, especially when Imperial Japan had already become deeply sunk in the quagmire of a war against both Chinese Nationalists and the communist forces. The official commendation that went along with the award reads in part, "the unit . . . contributed to the securing of an advantageous tactical operation position of a large bridge force."

The wording of the entire commendation is vague with no mention of biological warfare. Likewise, when the text of the army's special award to Unit 731 appeared, along with Ishii's photograph, in the Tokyo newspaper *Asahi Shimbun*, readers likely wondered what this man had done to deserve such a prominent decoration and why neither the award citation nor the *Asahi* article provided any details about the mysterious "tactical operation" of the medical unit.

Ishii himself received a high military honor for his service at Nomonhan, the Third Order of the Golden Kite and the Middle Cord of the Rising Sun, on April 29, 1940, as did another Nomonhan combatant, a Kwantung Army colonel named Yamamoto who had helped coordinate the typhoid BW dispersals.

Ishii's Nomonhan biological warfare had been a debacle, yet he and his Epidemic Prevention and Water Supply Unit, as it was now officially known, received, under a 1940 decree by Emperor Hirohito, a large increase in the number of researchers, laboratories, and territory under their command. Hirohito's decree also authorized the formation of multiple Ishii unit branch detachments in Manchuria, and raised the number of personnel employed at Pingfan to 3,000. A vast acceleration in the funding and scope of Japan's biological warfare activity got under way in 1940, as heavy fighting continued in China and Japan's hostility toward the USSR, post-Nomonhan, remained high, despite the official neutrality between the two countries.

A year after Nomonhan, Unit 731 attacked again. This time they chose as their enemy a soft target: the civilian population of

the port city of Ningbo in Zhejiang Province, a strategic location
not under Japanese control but on the front lines of a military
stalemate between the armies of Japan and Nationalist China.

The men loaded a heavily guarded train with fifty kilograms
of cholera bacteria and seventy kilograms of typhoid bacteria and
millions of plague-infected fleas, and in May 1940 the train traveled from Pingfan on South Manchurian Railway lines, south to
the city of Hangzhou, located over 1,000 kilometers from Pingfan and 250 kilometers southwest of Shanghai. Ishii maintained a
hangar at Hangzhou airport, which had belonged to the Chinese
air force prior to the Japanese invasion. There a Unit 731 team
transferred the fleas to airplanes specially rigged for spraying over
Ningbo. These were dropped by hand into wells and poured on
food stocks. Naoji Uezono, a former Unit 731 member, described
the germ transport process at Pingfan. "Unit 731 received 'Bin
#659' order from the Kwantung Army. The members of the expe-
ditionary detachment rode in ten railway coaches at 5:00 P.M.
July 26. Forty germ warfare army men were in one coach. The
other nine coaches were equipped with germ armaments, aircraft,
and seventy kilograms concentrated liquid of typhoid."

Upon the train's arrival in central China, the soldiers gave the
typhoid bacteria to BW squads operating in Zhejiang Province.
That summer, they emptied flasks and bottles of typhoid into the
village wells of the Chinese population, resulting in localized outbreaks of the lethal disease. It is not known how many people died,
but the quantity of seventy kilograms that Uezono cites was sufficient to wipe out scores of villages. The plague-infected fleas were
sprayed over Ningbo in October, resulting in an urban plague epidemic.

The germ warfare researchers' intentions were primarily to kill
large numbers of people with contagious disease, and inflict misery,
terror, and hardship on those who didn't succumb. There was also
an experimental dimension to their BW, and a variety of bacterial

Biowar program founder and leader, Shiro Ishii.

Shiro Ishii in lieutenant general's uniform.

The Ishii family. Shiro Ishii in military uniform with his brothers: Standing first on the left is Takeo Ishii, in charge of Pingfan human prison section; and second from left is Mitsuo Ishii, director of the Pingfan animal breeding section.

Front view of the Unit Ei 1644 complex on East Zhongsan Street in Nanking.

Ruins at Pingfan of the boiler building that generated heat for the complex.

The site of the anatomy room of the human experiment and germ warfare station in Beijing, Unit 1855.

Japanese germ warfare squad studying the site of an epidemic.

Biological troops in gas masks at a field test site.

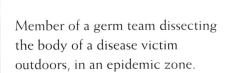

Member of a germ team dissecting the body of a disease victim outdoors, in an epidemic zone.

Unit 731 scientist examines slide samples.

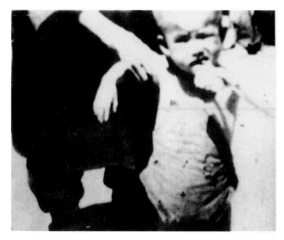

A Chinese boy afflicted with disease from a germ test.

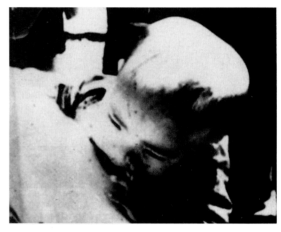

Another infected Chinese boy, victim of an experiment.

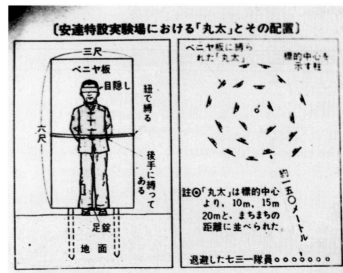

Sketch map of Unit 731 experiment prisoners tied to posts in a circular arrangement around a biological bomb, at the outdoor Anda field test site.

A 1980 photograph of Dr. Ryochi Naito, close associate of Ishii and perpetrator of Unit 731 human experiments who directed the Green Cross drug company in the postwar era.

Postwar photo of Kozo Okamoto, former Unit 731 pathologist and anatomy section leader who became medical director of Osaka Kinki University.

Site of Pingfan's aviation section, a branch of Unit 731 that organized flights for spreading epidemic disease germs by aircraft.

Pingfan underground corridor leading through the administration building into the "special prison" of cells for human experiment victims.

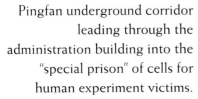

Japanese biowar team members tending to a fellow soldier accidentally sickened in one of their own operations.

Pingfan ruins beside the secret railway line that carried "special transport" captives to the Unit 731 prison.

Ruins of Hisato Yoshimura's frostbite experiment building at Pingan.

Airplane used in germ-spreading missions.
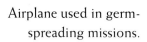

Postwar photo of Dr. Hisato Yoshimura, chief of frostbite experiments at Pingfan who became president of Kyoto Prefecture Medical College and a leading Antarctic researcher.

Postwar photo of Dr. Tachiomaru Ishikawa, former Unit 731 pathologist who became president of Kanazawa Medical School.

Biological warfare team conducting on-site sterilization after a germ test.

Ruins of Pingfan crematorium used for prisoners killed in experiments.

Chinese eyewitness Fang Zhenyu, who saw victims being unloaded from train cars at Pingfan and escorted by guards to the Unit 731 prison.

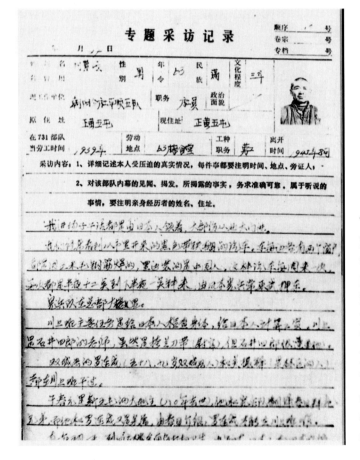

Testimony of Fu Jingqi, a former Chinese laborer at Pingfan. He describes how Staff Sergeant Ichigo Sohara of the Unit 731 Military Police Office, sent "special prisoners" under escort to be used in lethal experiments.

spreading methods were tested on the Ningbo area population. They sprayed from low-flying airplanes bits of wheat that were coated with bubonic plague bacilli, and also tried dropping contaminated cotton and simply spraying live plague-carrying fleas. In the same region, they also poisoned water supplies by dropping the bacteria of lethal water-borne diseases, cholera and typhoid, into the small backyard wells of unsuspecting families, and also large community water sources like reservoirs. Ishii's men took notes, studying the effects of these pioneering efforts in BW by following the local media accounts of the outbreaks that followed.

They noted the antiepidemic countermeasures taken by the people and local government, and whether the Chinese managed to identify Japanese germ warfare as the cause of the epidemic. (They did.) Major Tomio Karasawa, the former head of a germ production unit in Pingfan's Division 4, said, "a special group was left behind [in Zhejiang Province] to gather information as to the results of the operation. It was headed by Major Nozaki, who managed to get hold of newspapers which told of the outbreak in the [Ningbo] area."

The Unit 731 doctors made a film of their accomplishments at Ningbo and its environs and held special screenings for select military officers and civilian scientists at universities back in Japan. In fact, the BW units produced a number of documentaries of their germ warfare and human experiments. Ishii hoped the films would inspire medical researchers to join or at least support his BW unit network, and that they would help secure more financing for his achievements in defense and medical science.

"I saw a documentary film showing the Detachment 731 expedition in Central China in 1940," said Lieutenant Colonel Toshihide Nishi. "It first showed a receptacle containing plague-infected fleas being attached to the fuselage of an aircraft. Then the spraying apparatus was shown being fastened to the aircraft's wings. An explanatory text was thrown on the screen, stating that the apparatus was charged with plague fleas. After this, four or five persons boarded the plane, but who they were I could not make out. The plane took off, and it was explained that it was on its way to the enemy's territory. The plane was next seen flying over the enemy's positions. Then followed shots of the aircraft, of Chinese troops in movement and of Chinese villages. A cloud of smoke was seen detaching itself from the airplane's wings, and it transpired from the explanation that this smoke consisted of plague fleas, which were being sprayed on the enemy. The plane then turned back to the airfield, and a caption appeared on the screen: 'Operation Concluded.' We then saw the plane landing. A squad of disinfection orderlies drove up to it, and the plane was shown being disinfected. People were seen alighting from the plane: the first to alight was Lieutenant General Ishii, and he was followed by Major Ikari. Who the rest were, I do not know. This was followed by a caption: 'Results,' and a Chinese newspaper was shown, with a translation in Japanese. The explanatory text stated that a severe epidemic of plague had broken out in the Nimpo [Ningbo] area. The concluding shot was of Chinese orderlies in white overalls disinfecting the plague area. It was from this film that I learned quite definitely that the bacteriological weapon was employed in the Nimpo [Ningbo] area."

Nishi said that he first heard of the biological assaults against Ningbo while he was stationed at the Unit 731 branch in Peking when the unit received a document from Unit 1644 in Nanking stating that bacteria had been used in Ningbo. Later Nishi recalled, "my friend Major Seto told me that he had just returned from the operation in Central China."

Archie R. Crouch, a missionary from California, was living in Ningbo when Unit 731 struck. At that time, he lived in an ancient house on a church compound with his wife, Ellen, then nine months pregnant, and their two-year-old son, Edward. In an unpublished memoir he describes the attack.

October 27, 1940 The air-raid siren shrieked a warning that Japanese bombers were approaching. This alarm was different from the 250 previous alarms during the nine months since we had moved into our home in Ningbo, China. It was just before twilight, and all other raids had been during the middle of the day, generally from about 10:00 AM to 3:00 PM. That single-seater plane, flying slowly for a few minutes over the center of the city, caused a greater and more prolonged disruption of life than all the other raids we had witnessed. We would soon learn that fleas carrying bubonic plague can cause more civilian and economic destruction than squadrons of planes carrying bombs.

[W]e were together in our home in Ningbo late in the afternoon of October 27, 1940, a few days before [the baby] Carolyn was born . . . We kept a cache of essential foods and clothing packed in small bags, ready to snatch and run if necessary. I opened windows all over the house to protect against shattered glass from bomb explosions, then went outside to spot the planes and try to determine where they would bomb.

It was strange. I heard nothing until the plane was over the center of the city. It was flying very low, and that, too, was unusual, since the bombers usually came in groups of three, six or nine. . . . A plume of what appeared to be dense smoke billowed out behind the fuselage. I thought it must be on fire, but then the cloud dispersed downward quickly, like rain from a thunderhead on a summer day, and the plane flew away.

Puzzled I went back into the house to report to Ellen, who was reading a story to Edward. A few minutes later the all-clear siren relieved the tension, and the life of that autumn afternoon and evening went on with its usual routine. We did not realize the significance of that single plane's appearance until a few days later when the first bubonic plague symptoms appeared among people who lived in the center of the city.

October 28, 1940: The gossip around the city was that the plane had dropped a lot of wheat, so much in some streets that the people were sweeping it up for chicken feed. By the time I got to school the students and faculty were trying to figure out what it meant. Some wondered if it might be a kind of biological warfare, and we all felt a tension we had not felt during the conventional bombings.

November 1, 1940: We heard that 20 people from the central part of the city had contracted a severe disease. Although the laboratory tests were not complete, the symptoms were clearly those of bubonic plague, so the doctors made plans for plague control. They asked the city authorities to cordon off an area in the heart of the city from which the patients were coming. No persons except doctors were allowed to go into or leave that part of the city . . . We put batches of rat poison all over the schools and our homes. Edward was not allowed to leave the yard.

November 2, 1940: My diary noted that 16 more people died and that the disease had definitely been established as bubonic plague. The Chinese newspapers carried full descriptions of the causes, symptoms, and cures. Prior to the outbreak of plague there had been rumors that the Japanese army was advancing toward Ningbo from the south but similar rumors in previous months had proven to be false. Now there was more fear of the plague than of the Japanese army!

November 3, 1940: Schools with no boarding facilities were closed. . . . Traffic in and out was limited to the essentials. City authorities were collaborating with the hospital staff in preventative programs. . . . Armies of brick masons were organized to build a fourteen-foot-high wall around the six square blocks in the center of the city where the plague was concentrated. The plan was to burn that section of the city as soon as the wall was completed and the people evacuated. Rats can climb walls, but the authorities figured they would not all get away.

People with plague were taken to a large building which was set up as a plague hospital outside the city. Family members . . . were isolated in another building until it was determined that they were free of the disease.

No one who lived in the area enclosed within the wall was allowed to leave except through the decontamination sheds which were adjacent to the gates . . . The area was manned by specially trained decontamination squads clothed in green uniform, flea proof boots, and helmets which might have been the mock-ups for space helmets used many years later.

December 1, 1940: The heart of the city was quickly reduced to a pile of glowing embers, and the assumption was that no rat and no flea could possibly have escaped. The next step of the hospital and city authorities was to get enough anti-plague serum for compulsory injections for the entire population. The Japanese authorities cited Chinese records, which stated that 99 of the plague victims died.

December 2, 1940: A new fear spread through the city with the news that one of the orderlies at the hospital died of *pneumonic* plague [a more virulent and contagious strain of the bubonic plague bacteria]. The Chinese newspapers confirmed the rumor that the plague had been spread by a Japanese plane. . . . Fifty-two years later we discovered that this was the first major tactical experiment, which provided the impetus for a full-scale advancement of biological warfare in China. The invading [Japanese] army had a plague decontamination unit which forced the entire population, including our family, to be injected with its anti-plague serum, even though we had already been injected with serum provided by the Chinese.

That Ishii's Epidemic Prevention and Water Supply Unit did actually practice public health care from time to time highlights the thin line that exists between germ warfare and epidemic containment and prevention. Virtually all the units in the network did in fact do some real epidemic prevention work, such as hygiene improvement studies or the creation of vaccines, even as they engaged in germ warfare research.

Indeed, it has often been noted by those seeking to enforce treaties that prohibit use of biological weapons that vaccine development unfortunately blurs the distinction between germ weaponry and disease defense because both involve the same methods of culturing of harmful bacteria and viruses and the injection of live or inert strains of these microbes into people. Vaccines could also serve an offensive purpose in that they could allow troops and other military agents to safely operate in territory that had been contaminated by germ warfare with a pathogen for which they had been immunized.

Finally, by doing good public health work, the Japanese BW doctors could maintain the façade that they were in Manchuria to vaccinate the people and improve the sanitation standards—and indeed to purify the water of some civilian areas. Causing sickness and death through microbiology was simply the inverse of public health care.

Hu Xian Zhong, who lived in Ningbo in 1940 and still lives there today, is one of 180 plaintiffs who sued the Japanese government in 1997 for damages from biological warfare. "I am the sole surviving member of a family exterminated by germ warfare carried out by Unit 731, The Imperial Japanese Army, in Ningbo in China," he testified in Japan in 1997. "My name is Hu Xian Zhong and I am at present 66 years of age. . . . In the end of October 1940, Unit 731 aircraft flew low over Ningbo and hovering over downtown Kai ming jie, dropped plague-infected fleas along with wheat and corn.

"At the time I was 8 years old and our family lived on No. 70 Kai ming jie. I saw myself, along with the people of our neighborhood, the mixture of fleas, wheat and corn forming a hazy spray in the sky as it fell on us. In Kai ming jie, my father ran a Mah-jongg tile shop called Hu Yuan Xing. He both made and sold them. The first victim of the plague was my sister, Hu Ju Xian. At the start of November she started complaining of headaches and developed a fever. Her face was completely red and the lymph nodes in her thighs were swollen. She lost consciousness. With no appetite and ability to even gulp a drop of water, her condition continued to deteriorate.

"Despite our mother's best tries with different medications, her illness did not reverse its course and soon, with our family gathered around her bed, my sister, who had always been so affectionate to me, left this world. I remember my thoughts of that time. 'Why have you left us for that world so soon, dear Sister? I still wanted you to play with me and study with me. I am so small and can't live without you,' I remember crying out loud.

"Barely 10 days after my sister's death, my brother, then my father and mother, passed away infected with the plague. My brother was such a cute and naughty boy. I just couldn't believe that he was no more. Soon, my father was undergoing the same pain and agony as my brother and sister. Men in white caps, white body suits and long boots came over to our house and took my father to the Jia bu Quarantine Hospital, a sanitarium for plague patients. I saw my mother crying and was informed that he had died. 'How shall we continue to live?' cried my mother.

"My mother's own condition was itself deteriorating. Lumps had formed under her armpits and she was saying that she herself would soon be taken away to the sanitarium and die. And that is what happened.

"And in such a manner, in no time, I became an orphan. I did not know what to do and how to live. I was full of fear about my future and the more I thought about it, the gloomier I got. I cried and cried. It is an experience I still cannot put into words. As a result, I can never forgive the Imperial Japanese Army's Unit 731 and its germ warfare on us that completely changed my life and filled it with misery and agony. Furthermore, a month after the outbreak of the plague, in late November, more than a hundred buildings in the infected areas were burned to the ground to prevent the disease's further spread. Five hundred people or so were thrown out of their houses to live on the streets, having lost their families, their possessions. I was one of them."

The mortality rate statistic most often cited in medical books for plague is 90 percent, but the Ningbo patients suffered a 99 percent mortality rate. As with other plague outbreaks caused by germ warfare, the organisms dropped on Ningbo were especially deadly as the result of having been bred for this purpose in the labs and cultured in the blood of human test subjects at Pingfan, Nanking, and Changchun. Of the 100 people in Ningbo who came down with plague, only one survived.

In 1995, researchers in the archives of Japan's Defense Agency discovered the journal of Kumao Imoto, an army captain who coordinated operations and communications between Unit 731, army support personnel, and the general staff of the China Expeditionary Army. Imoto functioned as "operational sections chief" for the general staff. The Imoto diary, as it has become known, reveals the secret transmissions and code names stating in precise detail how and when the germ attacks of 1940 were carried out by airplanes and by BW personnel on the ground. The journal reveals how the BW squads disseminated germs and evaluated the disease epidemics they caused.

An entry by Captain Imoto for July 5, 1940, refers to planned germ warfare attacks along the strategic "zhe gan line" in Zhejiang Province, where Japanese and Chinese armies fought over control of the key railroad:

1. Period not-decided (In July)
2. Airport Juyang
3. Object cities in the area along a line zhe gan
4. Direction to Command troop general headquarters conduct directly
     (colonel Ishii in charge)
5. altitude will be more than 4000 generally
6. kinds, raining, flea

The "flea" here refers to plague-infected fleas provided by Unit 731; "altitude," "raining," and "airport" suggest an aerial flea-spraying operation to spread bubonic plague. Residents have corroborated that such airplane flea scatterings were conducted in the area in 1940.

A few months later, on September 10, an entry elucidates part of the planning phase for the Ningbo plague spraying. It refers to communication between two officers, Lieutenant Colonel Sumi Ota and Captain Yosiyasu Masuda, about bacteria transportation and the targeting of Ningbo and vicinity:

September 10th
1. Nara Unit, lieutenant colonel Ota got in touch with captain Masuda
2. (1) Searching objective in Sep. 10th, Ningbo county and Qu county are appropriate for aim
     (2) Sep 10th the first transportation . . . was delayed will reach within a couple of days

An October 7 entry outlines plans for shipping germs to the Ningbo attack deployment zone, and mentions the number of plague fleas used per gram of flea weight. It also reveals the "future code name" for Zhejiang germ warfare, the "HO" operation:

October 7, 1940
  1. Condition of Nara Unit
    (1) Transportation six times so far (including shipping twice). Air transportation can reach within a day, and shipping takes six days. In the future airplane would be desirable.
    (2) The numbers of attack . . . flea about 1700 per gram
    (3) Expect the evaluation of its effect.
       Spy.
    (4) Weather fact is measured in Hangzhou, and transferred to the local area with parachute (only in Ningbo)
    (5) Wenzhou was once to be the target but Taizhou etc. was regarded as unsuitable. In case Wenzhou becomes a target, decision will be hard to make to check weather factor without parachute
    (6) (By Yamamoto) Target and way to attack have to be flexible. (decision) the ways to attack can overlap
    (7) Personnel matter
    (8) Geographical description for military use
    (9) Future code name "HO" operation

The "Yamamoto" referred to in the entry is Yoshiro Yamamoto, a member of the Nara Unit organizing the BW assaults. Line 5 ambiguously refers to the towns of Wenzhou and Taizhou as targets but now perhaps regarded as unsuitable as targets. The Japanese in fact had already hit Wenzhou and Taizhou with plague the month before, so this comment may be expressing some dissatisfaction with the results of those attacks.

On October 27, 1940, the cities of Ningbo and Quzhuo suffered plague-flea dispersals by Unit 731 teams. In November the Quzhuo plague spread to the neighboring city of Yiwu, and the city of Jinhua was aerially sprayed with odd whitish-yellow granules containing plague bacillus. No fleas were dropped along with the granules. But this attempt ended in failure, as no plague cases occurred in Jinhua. In December the village of Tangxi near Quzhou experienced an outbreak of typhoid caused by Japanese soldiers dumping germs into the water supply. The following year, on November 4, 1941, Unit 731 again sent out an aerial plague-spreading mission, this time to the city of Changde in Hunan Province, located behind Chinese lines in the interior of the country. A single plane, flying very low, dropped a mixture of plague-infected fleas, bacteria-coated wheat and rice, cotton wads, and pieces of paper. Positioned near an enormous body of water called Lake Tung Ting Hu, Changde had high strategic value as a major commercial center, trans-shipment point, and railway nexus. The mission was directed by Colonel Kiyoshi Ota, who had performed aerial plague-flea-scattering tests on Pingfan prisoners tied to posts, at Unit 731's outdoor experimental field at Anda.

On the November morning of the attack, the Changde air raid sirens blared, but city residents were surprised to see only a single plane in the air. That plane dropped a mixture of bacteria-coated wheat and rice, cotton wads, pieces of paper, and what China's National Health Administration investigators referred to as "unidentified particles." The Khabarovsk testimony of General Kiyoshi Kawashima reveals that, in addition to the unloading of this mixture, fleas were also sprayed. The Imoto Diary, corroborating the Khabarovsk information, states that a total of 36 kilograms of plague fleas were sprayed over Changde at this time. A few days later, the first human plague fatality occurred: an eleven-year-old girl named Tao-erh Tsai. She died of plague at the Changde Presbyterian missionary hospital, within three days of initially collapsing with a high fever. Six more Changde residents died of plague that week before a medical investigation team of plague specialists arrived in Changde, headed by Dr. Wen-Kwei Chen, a consultant to the Chinese Red Cross Medical Relief Corps, and the director of a university department of laboratory medicine. Based upon blood tests, organ examinations, and animal studies, they quickly concluded that the bubonic plague outbreak under way in the city had been caused by the November 4 germ bombing of the Japanese plane.

The Changde plague epidemic spread through the city and beyond to eventually encompass hundreds of neighboring villages. A comprehensive research survey, conducted in the 1990s over the course of seven years, found that at least 7,643 people died of plague in that epidemic, based upon approximately 30,000 separate interviews with local residents.

The Chinese government held a press conference in April 1942 in Chongqing to announce the Chen Report's findings that the Japanese had engaged in biological warfare. It was the first official accusation by a government that a Japanese BW program existed.

In Zhejiang Province, at least thirteen towns suffered epidemics of plague and typhoid from Unit 731's first large-scale biological warfare operations. The vast majority of the attacks by Unit 731 and its affiliates did not involve aerial germ bombing. Instead, the dissemination was usually carried out by scientists and trained military teams surreptitiously scattering their germ weapons in or near people's houses and neighborhoods.

In 1940 Ishii and scientists from Wakamatsu's Unit 100 spread cholera bacteria on the outskirts of Changchun. Ishii then urged the health authorities in Changchun to organize an immunization drive to protect the citizenry from the real threat of cholera reaching into the city. In parts of Changchun, the people, not realizing that the existing cholera outbreaks had been caused by Japanese germ warfare, lined up for their government-mandated cholera vaccine shots, exposing themselves to the epidemic. The Japanese tainted those vaccines with live, virulent cholera bacteria, and many who received the injection fell ill with the disease, spreading it further still. Once Ishii had created a cholera epidemic by spreading the bacteria, he then created a second opportunity for his units to test the effectiveness of fake vaccine shots as a method of causing epidemics.

One Unit 731 veteran, Tsuro Shinohara, remembered a story his BW training instructor at Pingfan had told about an experiment conducted on children in Jilin, a city in central Manchuria. "Once, he recalled the time when he was part of an operation in the city of Jilin," Shinohara said. "They carried plague bacteria there and conducted tests. The method involved placing the pathogens into buns and then wrapping them in paper. The Unit 731 men went into an area of the city where children were playing and started eating buns similar to those in which they had planted the germs. The children saw the men eating, and came over. Then the men gave the children the infected buns. Two or three days later, the strategy team went to the village to investigate, and noted stories about the outbreaks of disease."

Such operations suggest that people in the BW network realized that to most efficiently create epidemics within a population it was necessary to get close to children and the elderly, who with their underdeveloped or compromised immune systems were most likely to catch the disease and spread the contagion to others.

In July 1994 a former Unit 731 hygiene specialist confessed to his detachment's pathogen-spreading activities on condition of anonymity. It is clear that the germ used by his team induced a type of illness that can be water-borne, since it infected people after being dropped in a water supply, but the exact bacterium that they employed remains unknown. This veteran had worked at the Unit 731 branch at Hailar, in the far north of Manchuria close to the Soviet border. He remembered conducting BW assaults on small civilian communities in Manchuria. These Unit 731 targets were hamlets and villages in the vast Manchurian hinterlands, often composed of ethnic minorities like Mongolians and Manchus. The isolation of these people, in terms of both geography and culture, from the Han Chinese majority and Manchuria's sophisticated Russian communities, made them ideal targets for BW experimentation and the field testing of pathogens. The Japanese researchers could spread disease without fear of arousing too much suspicion. Sometimes they were even welcomed into these villages with open arms—at first.

"There was a Mongolian settlement we came to," the hygienist recalled. "They were all happy to see us, and the little girls picked flowers for presents. We exchanged things with them for dried fish and meat," said the former hygiene specialist. "We conducted field strategy there two or three times, then everyone in the settlement suffered from diarrhea and came down with sickness. The last time we went there, they didn't bring flowers and they didn't want anything of ours. Our interpreter told us that they said we had thrown something into the well and made everyone sick. Our officer in command joked about it and told the Mongolians, 'You're the ones who threw it into the well.'

"I had some creosote [an antiseptic medicine, commonly used as a remedy within the Japanese military] and gave it to the Mongolians," the hygienist said. "They were glad to get it. The officer saw that and told me not to give them any medicine, but he didn't press the issue any further. He just said, 'Better stay away from them,' and later told us never to go back there again. . . . I found out later about our team throwing bacteria into the well."

In other attacks against water sources, Pingfan personnel dropped typhoid bacteria in more than 1,000 wells in Harbin and surrounding territory in 1939 and 1940. Sometimes a handful of people were killed, at other times the casualties numbered in the hundreds and entire communities were wiped out. The Unit 731 scientists surveyed the damage and took note of how to improve the efficiency and raise the death toll of their BW with each additional contamination they carried out. The people of Manchuria, in their own cities and villages, were becoming *maruta*.

SEVEN

EPIDEMIC

IN JUNE OF 1941 NAZI GERMANY SUDDENLY INVADED THE Soviet Union. The chief of the Japanese General Staff issued an order insisting on the speeding up of research work on plague bacteria as a means of bacteriological warfare. "The order," said one major general, "made special mention of the need for the mass breeding of fleas as plague carriers."

Word went out quickly from Lieutenant General Ishii's office that the breeding of plague bacteria, rodents, and carrier fleas should be escalated. He and his colleagues at the other BW branches planned the spreading of massive epidemics inside Russia to assist conventional Japanese warfare.

Three months later General Yoshijiro Umezu, the commander-in-chief of the Kwantung Army, ordered Unit 100 to prepare to conduct bacteriological warfare and bacterial sabotage raids, chiefly targeting the Soviet Union. At the time the Nazis were having good success in their campaign against the USSR, and the Kwantung Army High Command anticipated that Japan would invade the Soviet Union from the east in tandem with the Third Reich's advance from the west and crush the surrounded country. It seemed likely that Japan would then take Mongolia, Siberia, and the Russian Far East as its spoils of war.

In preparation for war against the Soviets, the chief of the operations division of the Kwantung Army, Tamokatsu Matsumura, recommended that biological weapons be deployed against the Russian cities of Voroshilov, Khabarovsk, Blagoveshchensk, and Chita, using Kwantung Army planes to drop bacterial bombs and spray germs.

In short order Pingfan shipped to the Mudanjiang Unit six large boilers for growing typhoid and paratyphoid bacteria, together with seventy-five tons of agar-agar jelly, meat extract, peptone, and salt used to make the medium in which the bacteria colonies were cultured. Mudanjiang also received 200 cans from Pingfan to be used for breeding plague fleas. One or two rats infested with the fleas were placed in each can, along with a thin mat of straw (which facilitated the flea reproduction), and batches of 100–150 white rats and 150–200 white mice were sent every month from Mudanjiang to Pingfan for research in the development of plague weaponry. At Hailar 13,000 field rodents were bred and infected with disease-producing fleas, ready for release into the countryside.

The Japanese planned for every contingency. In the event that war with the USSR broke out and didn't go well for the Kwantung Army, Umezu instructed the leaders of Unit 100 to come up with a plan for infecting cattle belonging to the population of Manchuria's North Khingan Province, along the Soviet border. The idea was to sabotage the livestock behind enemy lines. Unit 100 sent out reconnaissance teams to North Khingan and other areas near the Soviet border, to inspect pastures, count the total number of cattle roaming, and in some cases, conduct experiments on the livestock.

In the summer of 1942 Unit 100 sent an expedition to the Tryokhrecheye area, bordering both the Soviet Union and the Mongolian People's Republic. There, a team clandestinely sprayed the ground with anthrax germs and contaminated the reservoirs and rivers with glanders, testing the "durability" of the organisms. One Unit 100 researcher recalled that this contingent was composed of about thirty men. He described the group's work as "experiments under field conditions." In addition to the Tryokhrecheye experiments, the group also spread germs in North Kinghan Province and contaminated the Derbul River with glanders bacteria. The Derbul flows into the Argun, which runs along the Soviet-Manchurian border, and Soviet army units were stationed along this river at the time. What effect the glanders contamination had on the soldiers or any animals that may have been with them is unclear, but by March 1944 Unit 100 had produced 200 kilograms of anthrax microbes, 100 kilograms of glanders, and 20 to 30 kilograms of the wheat-destroying red-rust fungus—enough pathogens to theoretically wipe out entire cities and provincial crop harvests.

The report that came back to Wakamatsu, painstakingly illustrated with maps and charts, indicated that there were 1.5 million head of cattle in North Khingan. Wakamatsu instructed his men that if war with the Soviet Union broke out, 500 sheep and groups of horses and cows numbering 100 each were to be infected with epizootic diseases, in particular anthrax and cattle plague germs, by aircraft and a special sabotage squad. Should the Japanese have to retreat from northern Manchuria, they'd be leaving behind a present for the Soviets and Manchurians.

Meanwhile, the war against China was dragging on interminably. Ishii's invisible bio-atrocity empire expanded into mobile "Water Purification Units," integrated within Japanese regular divisions occupying central and southern China. The Water Purification Units, operating under the cover of providing hygiene and water-filtration support for the military, abducted farmers and committed vivisections of the prisoners, in addition to carrying out countless acts of BW bacteria spreading within the territory they controlled, and sometimes behind Chinese lines in covert sabotage missions.

Such units were led by army colonels, and each included within its ranks up to 500 soldiers and medical specialists trained in germ warfare. These detachments existed within the Kwantung Army, the Shanxi Army in northern China, the Armies of Central China, and army divisions stationed in remote, subtropical places such as Burma (now Myanmar), the Philippines, and the island of Rabaul, off New Guinea. Unit 1644's Colonel Masuda, carrying an eight-millimeter movie camera, filmed the daily goings-on at permanently stationed Water Purification Units in Bandung on the island of Java; Bangkok, Thailand; Saigon, Vietnam; and in Burma, at the cities of Mandalay and Rangoon. In all, the Japanese military had thirteen of the large WPUs and more than forty WPUs with about 250 men each, scattered among regular army divisions. By the early 1940s operations of the once unthinkable had become commonplace acts committed by army personnel in thousands of places across Asia and the Pacific.

Ken Yuasa, the doctor who explained that Ishii was like an "idol" to his employees, was a surgeon serving with the Japanese army in Shanxi Province in northern China, where Imperial Japan's troops constantly engaged communist fighters in pitched battles. At the age of eighty Yuasa was still practicing medicine at a hospital in Tokyo, but in 1993 and 1994 he gave a series of sorrowful speeches as part of the traveling Unit 731 historical exhibition in Japan, recounting what his life was like as a military physician pressured by those around him to perform vivisections on Chinese captives.

"It was practice for army doctors for winning a war," he said. "If you made a disagreeable face, when you returned home you would be called a traitor or turncoat. If it were just me alone, I could tolerate it; but the insulting looks would be cast on parents and siblings. Even if one despises an act, one must bear it. From there, a person becomes accustomed.

"Once at the Shanxi First Army Headquarters, there were

some forty doctors gathered from base and field hospitals. There was a lecture on military medicine, and afterward we were led to the prison cells. There were two Chinese in a cell. The jailer took out his pistol and fired two shots in each of their bellies. One of them was vivisected right there in the room. There was no anesthesia. While this was going on I heard four more shots fired. That meant two more people. Our object was to keep the person alive until the bullets were removed. Since we neither tried to administer ether nor stop the flow of blood, the men died soon . . .

"A secret order came to the hospitals in northern China: 'The war is not going well. Perform vivisections!' Thousands, or tens of thousands, of doctors used live subjects for dissection practice and research. What are those people doing now?"

At the same time, a much larger scheme, involving both field experimentation and coordinated military campaign strategy involving not just plague but also anthrax, cholera, typhoid, dysentery, glanders, and paratyphoid, was behind the 1942 biological warfare atrocities. This larger wave of BW attacks transpired at the directive of General Umezu, who ordered that a group from Unit 731 be sent down to Central China to carry out bacteriological contamination of the Chinese population. Their germ attacks in the Zhejiang region occurred in concert with a large-scale conventional campaign of infantrymen totaling about 140,000 soldiers, who fought pitched battles with even larger divisions of Chinese Nationalist forces.

The order to up the pace and scale of biological warfare was the result of a group decision arrived at by the chief-of-staff generals commanding the Japanese military, and enforced by General Umezu, who would later attain worldwide recognition when he stood with General Douglas MacArthur aboard the battleship

USS *Missouri* and signed Imperial Japan's surrender agreement on September 2, 1945. The general ordered Ishii to assemble a group of 150 to 300 men to coordinate these BW assaults, and transport these expert squads by train and airplane to the vicinity of Zhejiang and Nanking, farther inland, where they would work with Unit 731 and Unit 1644, which was run by Colonel Masuda. Ishii's teams were also instructed by the Japanese generals to work with the Japanese occupation divisions of Central China, and Japan's Shanxi Army of northern China, as they had earlier worked with military personnel of the northeastern Kwantung Army. Japanese germ warfare campaigns in Zhejiang and Jiangxi provinces in 1942, aimed at contaminating regions supportive of Chinese Nationalist troops, killed tens of thousands of people.

That summer Unit 1644 collaborated on the Zhejiang assaults with an expeditionary group of Unit 731 that had come down from Pingfan. Ishii and Masuda carefully planned and organized their bacterial epidemic attacks among Zhejiang residents to further the aims and territorial advantages of Japan's conventional army forces in the region, then fighting, in a stalemate, the Chinese Nationalist troops. The Japanese troops faced hostility from the civilian population in the cities and villages and on the farms, but as in the 1940 Zhejiang campaign, special attention was given to populated areas along the province's main railroad line, the Zhe Gan Railway, which served as a supply route for the Chinese forces. Thus it became a prime target for the creation of a zone of contamination with infectious disease.

According to Takayuki Mishina, the former chief of the intelligence division of the Thirteenth Army Headquarters, the Zhejiang germ campaign was conducted on the orders of General Shunroku Hata, the commander-in-chief of the Japanese Expeditionary Force in China from March to November 1942. Its objective "was to exterminate China's armed forces, namely the Zhejiang camp and other forces located in the region of Zhejiang along the main railway line that connected the towns of Jinhua, Lungyu, Quzhou and Yushan."

Japanese forces had made incursions into Zhejiang since 1937, when they occupied the province's capital city of Hangzhou, near Shanghai, in the north of Zhejiang. But the fighting had become especially acute in 1942, when Japan launched a major offensive, aimed primarily at seizing control of the region that had protected the flight crews of the American bombers in the famous Doolittle raid. The raid was the U.S. response to Pearl Harbor, a daring strike on Japan's home soil. Led by Army Air Corps colonel James H. Doolittle, the mission's sixteen twin-engine B-25Bs ascended from the deck of the carrier USS Hornet on April 18, 1942. They flew across the western Pacific, bombed industrial and military targets in Tokyo and other Japanese cities, and then made for their planned landing at Chuchow airfield, deep within the area of Zhejiang controlled by Nationalist China. But the planes ran low on fuel, the weather was quite cloudy, and the prearranged radio homing beacon that was to be emplaced at Chuchow failed to materialize, leaving the planes flying at night with nothing to guide them toward a friendly landing strip. Fifteen out of the sixteen planes were forced to crash-land or to have their flyers bail out in the dark, over land where Japanese forces may have been present, in Zhejiang and adjacent Jiangxi Province (the sixteenth plane landed safely in the USSR).

Sixty-four U.S. airmen were rescued and hidden from vengeful Japanese patrols by Chinese peasants, who assisted the Americans at great risk to their own lives. These Doolittle raiders were all successfully shepherded west to the safety of areas fully under the control of the Chinese government, where they were officially welcomed as heroes.

But eight flyers were captured when they came down in a Japanese-occupied area south of Shanghai. A Japanese military tribunal sentenced them to die for "indiscriminate attacks on civilians." Three were executed by a firing squad in Shanghai; the remaining five had their sentences commuted to life imprisonment. One of the men, Lieutenant Robert Meder, died in captivity of malnutrition and beri-beri, the result of atrocious living conditions and the withholding of medical care by his prison doctors. The remaining four suffered years of continual hunger and torture before being released in 1945, when Japan surrendered.

In its 1942 post-Doolittle advance through Zhejiang, the Japanese army was ferociously brutal to Chinese civilians in places that had helped the Americans. Those suspected of abetting the rescue of the airmen were tortured to death, along with their family members. Japanese officers conducted reprisal massacres of entire villages, and thousands of innocent people were rounded up and killed.

While Japan's flea drops over Zhejiang Province were retaliatory in nature, they also had the practical objective of allowing the Japanese to control territory that possibly could provide airfields for future United States bombing runs against the Japanese Home Islands. The key to controlling Zhejiang was successful occupation of the Zhe Gan Railway and supply stations along the "zhe gan line" referred to in the Imoto diary entry of July 5, 1940. This line of control extended from Zhejiang's border in the southwest with Jiangxi Province, up the length of Zhejiang to the northeastern area already occupied by Japan, south of Shanghai.

Beginning in May 1942, the Japanese Eleventh Army, made up of two infantry divisions, advanced eastward from Nanchang, while the Thirteenth Army, consisting of five divisions, moved westward from Hangzhou. The two armies, totaling more than 140,000 soldiers, aimed to crush an even larger number of troops of the Chinese Nationalist Army, then defending Zhejiang and Jiangxi provinces. Ultimately the Japanese failed in this objective and had to retreat by 1943, but not before the special army units from Units 731 and 1644 had assisted the battle efforts of Japan's conventional forces by contaminating twenty-two counties with plague, anthrax, typhoid, cholera, dysentery, glanders, and paratyphoid.

Major General Kiyoshi Kawashima recalled that

> in June 1942, Lieutenant General Ishii, Chief of Detachment 731, called together the leading personnel of the detachment and informed us that an expedition to Central China would shortly be organized for the purpose of studying the best methods of employing bacteriological weapons . . . its chief purpose was to study what was called the ground method of contamination, that is, the dissemination of germs from the ground. An order was then issued by [General Umezu] to send a special group to Central China.
>
> The drawing up of the plan of the expedition was entrusted to Lieutenant Colonel Murakami. . . . The group was to consist of from 100 to 300 men. It was decided to employ plague, cholera and paratyphoid germs . . . the expedition proceeded in several contingents by air and rail to Detachment Ei [1644] in Nanking.
>
> The expedition was to carry on its bacteriological activities in conjunction with the Zhejiang operation of the Japanese Army in Central China. The operation was appointed for the end of July. But owing to the fact that the Zhejiang operation, which was to be a strategical retreat of the Japanese forces, was somewhat delayed, the bacteriological operation was carried out at the end of August. This Detachment 731 expedition to Central China operated from the territory of Detachment Ei [1644], where it set up its support bases.

According to General Kawashima, his section of Pingfan, Division 4 of Unit 731, prepared 130 kilograms of paratyphoid

and anthrax bacteria. These germs were sent by air from Pingfan to Central China. "The bacteriological operation was to be carried out in the area of the cities of Yushan, Jinhua and Futsing," said Kawashima. "I learned after the operation that plague, cholera, and paratyphoid germs were employed against the Chinese by spraying. The plague germs were disseminated through fleas, the other germs in the pure form—by contaminating reservoirs, wells, rivers, etc. . . . The advancing Chinese troops entered the contaminated zone and came under the action of the bacteriological weapon." Kawashima said that the operation had been "a complete success . . . from what General Ishii told me," but claimed that he did not know the details of these results.

Near Futsing, a town located in the border area between Zhejiang and Jiangxi, Japanese planes also dispersed anthrax germs by scattering feathers that had been coated with a preparation of anthrax in the laboratory. In some aerial drops, BW personnel released live birds from planes flying at low altitudes. The birds' bodies had been smeared with anthrax, and Unit 731 scientists hoped they would shed feathers as they flew over populated areas, transferring the germs to people as feathers or bits of feathers landed on their skin and clothing. The number of Chinese people infected with anthrax from these attacks is the subject of ongoing research by historical investigators.

Feathers were a more effective way to deliver anthrax than aerosol-type spraying. The quills of a feather enclose the anthrax cells and shield them from exposure to open air and sunlight, which tend to kill the germ, a soil-dwelling organism. In this respect, feathers mimic the fibery places that harbor anthrax germs in nature: the hides of cattle, the bristled coats of goats and pigs, and the wool of sheep. Anthrax is sometimes referred to as "wool-sorter's disease," and its human victims are almost always people who jobs involve close work with farm animals, or animal hides.

The use of feathers to carry anthrax, and a variety of other bacterial and viral diseases, had also been the subject of much research in the germ warfare programs of other nations during World War II. The United States and United Kingdom both conducted laboratory tests using feathers to infect animals during and after World War II. Feathers and other types of fibrous materials proved an effective way to carry germs on the wind toward human targets, while protecting them to an extent from the outside environment.

Another target on the strategic Zhe Gan Railway line that summer was Shangrao, a village with a train station. An entry in the Imoto diary of August 28, 1942, depicts the spreading of bubonic plague through animal vectors and food, an example of what Kawashima called the "ground method of contamination" under study by Ishii and his cohorts as they employed it to practical ends in contaminating areas of supply lines to Chinese troops, and exterminating Chinese villagers. Captain Imoto wrote: "Spread fleas and rats on Shangrao, Guangfeng, [County,] they carry plague germs already. Put the dry plague bacteria on rices at Yushan. At Jiangshan, either put cholera bacteria into the wells, or on foods, or injected into fruits."

The phrase "dry plague bacteria" probably refers to freeze-dried plague bacillus. The freeze-drying of bacteria, a process known as lyophilization, was the subject of intense research and development by Ishii at Pingfan. Unit 731 scientists converted the plague germ *Yersinia pestis* and other bacteria into a powder form that could be stored indefinitely, transported easily in canisters, and then sprinkled as a powder. The lyophilization process is similar to that used to freeze-dry foods kept in the frozen foods section of a modern grocery store. The powdered bacteria regains its normal life state and power to infect when moistened into an emulsion.

In addition to the scattering of fleas on the ground, the effects of the aerial dispersion of fleas by specially rigged planes, which had proved successful at creating plague epidemics at Ningbo, Quzhou, and Changde in 1940 and 1941, again emerged in 1942. In September of that year, with Japanese and Chinese troops still locked in battle nearby, the villagers of Chongshan observed a single Japanese plane flying low in the sky, trailing a smoky plume behind it.

Chongshan is a farming village located near Yiwu City, in Zhejiang Province. Like Shangrao, it had the misfortune of lying along the Zhe Gan Railway supply line, thereby situated in prime territory for Japanese germ warfare epidemics. One-third of the population of Chongshan died of the plague. In 1997 Wang Xuan, a woman who was born a decade after the bio attack and who is the daughter of a former Chongshan resident, spearheaded the 1997 Tokyo civil lawsuit that produced so much testimony about what happened in China in the 1940s. Wang is a linguist and interpreter by profession, fluent in Japanese, English, and several dialects of Chinese. She was the lead plaintiff in the lawsuit, and her language skills, intelligence, and intrepidness have made her an invaluable resource for gathering information and bringing it to the public eye.

She lost eight members of her family to that bubonic plague attack, including her uncle, who was thirteen years old at the time he fell ill. Another Chongshan plaintiff, Wang Lijun, described her experiences in 1942 in written testimony for the court:

> In 1942, when I was 10 years old, suddenly the plague was severely prevalent because of the germs the cruel Japanese army scattered over the village. Every patient showed the same condition: a high fever, splitting headache, feeling thirsty, and swollen lymph nodes. I saw dead people being buried every day, and heard many neighbors dying. We were afraid of losing our lives and all the villagers were terrified. At the height more than 10 people died in one day. [In] just . . . a couple of months

one third of the villagers, that was more than 400 people, were killed by the plague. All members of about 20 families died out. Seven of my family members, my mother, oldest and second oldest sisters, and second oldest brother were infected with the plague. My brother showed the symptoms of the plague first; he was 17 years old at that time and died within a few days. Next, my mother and oldest sister came down with the plague. After a while my 15-year-old sister was taken with the disease, she was killed in three days after painful suffering. Luckily my mother and the oldest sister survived but they had to spend very hard days.

When the village was filled with patients, Japanese soldiers in white robes and gas masks came. They compelled the villagers to come to a public square in a hill at the back of the village, and then inspected the villagers' bodies and injected some unidentified drug into the villagers' bodies.

The Japanese army also enclosed the patients at Linshansi in the outer area of the village. However, they did not cure the patients. Rather, they treated them in a terrible way. At that place an 18-year-old girl, named Wu Xiaonai, was dissected and had her internal organs taken out while she was still alive, which was exactly a devil's act. Zhang Julian who saw that bloodcurdling scene was frightened and barely escaped with her life. She used to live next door to my house, so I heard this fearful story over and over. Further, there were many cases of the villagers finding dead bodies without arms or legs when they tried to bury the corpses.

After a while the Japanese army struck our village again and burned many houses out. On that day the Japanese soldiers forced all inhabitants to go together to a public square on a hill at the back of the village, and the army besieged the village with bayonets and loaded rifles.

Then they set many houses on fire. The villagers were frightened and tried to put the fire out but they could not because the Japanese army shot at them and stuck them with bayonets. My house was also burned. Although my family protested against it, they tried to throw us into the fire.

In the square where the chilly wind in the early winter blew hard, men and women of all ages surrounded by the Japanese soldiers armed with guns and swords had nothing to do except look at the fire burning our houses. Pathetic screaming voices resounded around and the whole village was in flames that almost reached the sky. The people whose houses were burned down lost all of their property. They had no food, no clothes, and no houses. Under the cold winter sky the only thing they could do to survive was to sleep on farms. Thus . . . even the people who fortunately survived lost their families, houses, and property and lost their means of livelihood as well.

Until then we never had any plague patients in and around this village. It is so sure that this tragic incident was caused by the Japanese army's bacteriological warfare. Not only did they spread the plague germs but they also vivisected the villagers like animal subjects. The Japanese army did not treat us like human beings and trampled our dignity underfoot.

The scene at Chongshan described by Wang Lijun in her testimony shows a bold escalation in biological warfare tactics by Unit 731. The doctors were now taking the human vivisection procedures, pioneered behind the high walls at the Beiyinhe and Pingfan prison laboratories, and bringing them out into the open, at the sites of their outside germ warfare attacks. The place at Linshanshi mentioned by Wang Lijun was a Buddhist temple, commandeered by the Japanese doctors and technicians and transformed into a makeshift vivisection laboratory. The BW teams, composed of personnel from both Unit 731 and Unit 1644 wearing high rubber boots, white uniforms, rubber gloves, and masks, also pulled terrified and ailing Chongshan villagers into nearby fields and vivisected them there, out in the open. In doing so, they took their methods of inspection and assessment to another level.

The plague epidemic abated and the Japanese left Chongshan. Weeks later, on October 11, 1942, just as Wang Lijun said, they returned to burn more than 200 of Chongshan's houses. They torched the village as a plague-containment measure, reminiscent of the burnings in Ningbo, described by Archie Crouch in his memoir. In the case of Chongshan, the BW units may have acted to prevent the possibility of plague spreading to Japanese troops billeted nearby, or they may have simply been field testing the effectiveness of burning houses as an antiepidemic method. In any case, the destruction of the villagers' houses and property piled cruelty upon cruelty.

In June 1942, about three months before the attack on Chongshan, a BW squad from Unit 1644 came to Yiwu City to isolate plague victims, reassuring family members and neighbors that they were there to "treat" the plague victims. As would later happen at Chongshan, people still alive and in the grip of plague were forcibly taken away from their homes by the Japanese, then vivisected nearby. At Yiwu a Japanese photographer caught the Unit 1644 team in action. His photo appeared in Tokyo's *Asahi Shimbun* a short time later, together with an article explaining that the Japanese personnel in rubber contamination suits were there to help the people by organizing quarantine measures in Yiwu, thereby preventing an outbreak of plague from becoming an epidemic.

The photograph shows three Japanese men clad in protective

clothing and high boots, carrying a doorframe like a stretcher, upon which lay a Chinese man, obviously ill. The Japanese BW team members are alarming in appearance, wearing rubber capes and masks that completely cover their heads in bulblike fashion, with small nose and mouth vents, and large, oval goggles wrapped around the mask. One is instantly reminded of a science fiction movie featuring aliens from another planet.

In some of the 1942 attacks, it may never be known exactly what kinds of bacteria were disseminated. In one incident in Yushan, Jiangxi Province, Japanese troops dumped two containers of germs into a well before retreating, according to victim Zu Szu-Gyu, a woman who lost ten of her thirteen family members in the village to the BW assault. Indeed, the entire village got sick after drinking the well water. The villagers' symptoms included diarrhea, vomiting, and fever, but at the time there were no doctors on hand to make a diagnosis. The BW germs dropped into the well may have been typhoid, paratyphoid, cholera, dysentery, or any combination of those organisms. Japanese testimony confirms that all these different intestinal disease germs were used in the 1942 campaign, but in some cases it is difficult to discern in retrospect what caused a particular BW ailment.

By 1942 and 1943 Unit 731, Unit 1644, and a Unit 731 branch in Peking called Unit 1855 were carrying out large-scale BW operations specifically aimed at achieving military objectives against Chinese forces. The attacks cannot be described merely as field tests, as they were purposefully constructed attacks, designed to eliminate Chinese troops and friendly civilian populations in order to allow the Japanese army to advance in its campaign offensives. The most effective and most shocking example of this occurred in May 1942, when a joint operation of Unit 731 and

Unit 1644 dropped cholera germ bombs in the city of Baoshan, Yunnan Province. Cholera attacks appear to have created the largest recorded BW epidemic. At Baoshan and surrounding villages, this cholera epidemic is estimated to have claimed more than 200,000 lives. Its strategic objective: to contaminate the Allied supply route to China leading from Burma, through Baoshan, north to the hub city of Kunming.

The tropical region surrounding the border between southern China's Yunnan Province and Burma constituted one of Imperial Japan's strategically most important areas of battle. British, Australian, and American forces ensconced in Burma's thick rain forests fought to keep a critical Allied supply route open, running through Burma to Yunnan's provincial capital of Kunming. From Kunming, supplies of food, medicine, war materiel, and other equipment were transported north to Nationalist China's capital city of Chongqing and elsewhere. The Burma pathway and the limited supply route open by air transport from bases in India, over "the Hump," as it was called, of the Himalaya, were China's only routes of access to significant quantities of Allied material aid.

In April 1942 the Japanese military began assaulting Yunnan Province with cholera germs by airplane-dropped germ bombs, and ground BW unit contamination of local water sources. The resulting epidemics caused western Yunnan to become a disrupted region of such dangerous levels of contagion that the Chinese Nationalist Army was unable to base its troops there. This enabled the Japanese to withdraw large numbers of troops for use in other battlefronts. The use of biological warfare had successfully achieved a major strategic war objective.

Within the Japanese Southern Army, ten divisions maintained personnel trained to deploy germ weapons. In April 1942 a special BW group within the Fifty-sixth Division of the Southern Army began contaminating the water supplies of villages along the Yunnan-Burma border. The group, called Unit 113, moved with its division up the Nu River that flows along this border, dispersing bacteria along the way, then moved eastward to reach the city of Baoshan. One Unit 113 veteran, Minori Shinano, confessed: "using BW in the battlefield, my most frequent experience was during 1942 . . . when the higher command ordered my squad leader Hisatsune to bomb the water source of Loi Mwe, he was actually ordered to release bacteria into the water source there."

Near Baoshan Unit 113 linked up with two germ-warfare detachments sent from Unit 1644 in Nanking and Guangzhou (also known as Canton), whose experimental station was known as the Unit 8604, or the Nami Unit. Colonel Masuda traveled to the area with his Nanking team to supervise the cholera attacks.

In April these three units, acting in concert, dumped cholera germs into the water sources of Baoshan, sparking outbreaks within the city. On May 4, 1942, a fleet of fifty-four Japanese bomber planes attacked Baoshan with a combination of explosive bombs, ceramic-shelled germ bombs, and fire-starting incendiary bombs designed to raze whole neighborhoods of Baoshan's densely packed wooden houses. That day Baoshan was leveled: More than 78 percent of its buildings and property was destroyed, and an estimated 10,000 people were killed. The city's dazed survivors fled into the surrounding countryside.

Those who had already been infected with the cholera germs disseminated by the army BW teams in April carried the cholera with them into the hills, mountains, and nearby villages in which they found refuge. In addition to being hosts of the bacteria, the fleeing Baoshan residents brought along contaminated food, clothing, and other personal items.

Three more bombing runs against Baoshan were launched on May 5, 6, and 8. But the city was already destroyed. These attacks were somewhat puzzling in that they seemed on the surface merely to bomb Baoshan's ruins and rubble into more rubble. But the true purpose of these attacks was unique in the history of conventional aerial bombardment: the explosive shells were dropped in order to further the epidemic-creating goals of the bacterial bombs. The Japanese had the intention of driving out the city's remaining population that had been huddling in the wreckage that had been their houses, hospitals, and schools, and in so doing spread more cholera to outlying areas, further fueling the refugee-carried cholera epidemics with a flood of more refugees, desperately clinging to their contaminated belongings.

Axis Japan had added its own twist to the slaughter of whole civilian populations by mass aerial bombing, a practice pioneered by the Nazis during the Spanish Civil War that is famously portrayed in Pablo Picasso's masterpiece *Guernica*. Baoshan was a city far larger than the town of Guernica in northern Spain, and at Baoshan the slaughter of innocents included biological warfare. It was an expanded Guernica with lethal germs, a scientific innovation that presently transported invisible death and misery to people dwelling far beyond the original urban target.

The tide of humanity flowing out of Baoshan soon reversed course. With the city almost empty, impoverished rural people left their farms and villages to venture into the ruined city, to collect items that the city folk had left behind. Upon returning to their homes, they too unwittingly became carriers and spread the cholera into more of Yunnan.

One such person, Ai Shan, lived on a farm near the village of Jin Ji. Shan went into Baoshan after the bombing and left with a roll of attractive cloth. He brought it back home to stitch together some clothes for his family. Within days of his return, Shan came down with cholera, suffering severe bouts of vomiting and diarrhea. He died and communicated the cholera to his family members. Such stories are typical of May 1942 in Yunnan Province.

The germ bombs dropped by planes on Baoshan were of the ceramic-walled variety designed and manufactured by Unit 731, which dubbed them the Yagi type bomb. Unit 731 personnel referred to this bomb as the "maggots bomb" because it shattered upon impact, breaking up into small ceramic fragments and splattering a gelatinous bacterial emulsion filled with living flies. The insects flew away from the impact site and then landed on people, animals, food, latrines, water sources, utensils, and other places. Flying from point to point, along the way they deposited the deadly laboratory-cultured cholera bacteria. Once a person became infected, that individual could then transmit the contagion to another person through infected body fluids. Dogs and other animals also carried the bacteria to humans in this way.

One of the Yagi bacterial bombs dropped on Baoshan cracked open when it hit the ground, but did not completely shatter. Lin Yuyue, a retired elementary school teacher at You Wang village, in Yunnan's Shi Dian County, observed this bomb lying on the ground. Lin matched it to a picture of the Yagi type bomb, presented to him in 1999 by the Japanese Biological Warfare Crimes Investigation Committee, a Chinese group of researchers piecing together a history of the cholera attack. Lin and three other witnesses recalled the germ bomb as being about twenty centimeters in diameter and one meter in length. According to their interviewers, the four men described seeing a "yellowish waxy substance" with "many live flies struggling to fly away." Another witness, Huang Zhengkang, saw a cracked Yagi bomb in another location. Huang's aunt, sister, and younger cousin died in the cholera epidemic.

Up to this point in all the recorded medical history of the area, even going back to ancient records, there had been no known cholera epidemics. But by June, less than a month after the maggot bombs were dropped, the disease had spread to 66 counties out of the total 118 counties in Yunnan Province. The official municipal record of Baoshan, "The History of Baoshan City," reports the cholera situation in and around Baoshan as it developed in May: "Starting approximately May 12, 1942, cholera spread quickly along the highway in the countryside; it was especially serious in Ban Chieao and Jin Ji . . . townships and villages . . . the retreating soldiers, garrison soldiers, and refugees also were infected in large numbers. There was largely no medicine to treat the majority of them. Many dead bodies were left in roadside ditches for a long time without anyone to cover or burn them. Our official record shows more than 60,000 dead."

The epidemic did not begin to subside until July, by which time it had decimated the population of scores of villages. In the village of Jin Ji, 300 out of a total population of 900 were killed by cholera. When the first recorded cases of the epidemic occurred in Ji Jin village, the mother of one afflicted family, Zhang Xiyuan, said that their food must have been poisoned. The members of her family began having the acute diarrhea and vomiting symptoms of cholera all at the same time, a highly unusual outbreak that nobody in Jin Ji was able to identify. At Hai Tang village the cholera wiped out approximately half the population of 600 people. The same occurred at Xi Zhuang village, whose unfortunate residents lost about 200 of their 400 neighbors and kin to the rapidly spreading microbes of Unit 731. The cholera scourge produced mortality rates of 25 percent to 50 percent per village for a numbingly long list of villages. Chinese historian Li Jiamao noted two typical cases: "Xia Guan, i.e. Dali had suffered about 2,500 deaths, Yong Ping county suffered about 1,500 deaths."

James Yin, a member of the Chinese group of researchers who in 1999 traveled to Yunnan to investigate Japan's biologicial warfare, noted, "At 2,000 deaths average per county we'd have an estimate of about 128,000 from 64 counties other than Baoshan and Shi Dian counties. . . . According to eyewitnesses on the highway from Baoshan to Kunming, in Yong Ping, Yangbi, and Dali counties, bodies found near the bus stations in May 1942 were as many as 'more than 10' in Yong Ping, and 'more than 30' in Dali on the road side. Dali is about 125 miles from Baoshan. We can now conclude that the total numbers of deaths in Yunnan Province due to Japanese cholera might have exceeded 210,000."

The Chinese group interviewed eighty-one-year-old Feng Desen in 1999. "Under the heel of the cholera epidemic in 1942, all around Baoshan County many families lost relatives, crying all the days," he said. "In all the counties some children cried out for fear; some cried out with pain or vexation still three months later." He Dexiang, a seventy-six-year-old man in 1999, whose father and uncle were killed in the epidemic, said, "How I wish I could cry bitter tears. . . . I carried my daughter, running away from the village, but she died as I held her after making a last-ditch struggle."

Sixty-three-year-old Zuo Yongquan described his childhood experience: "My parents and whole family died in the cholera epidemic or were killed by bombing in May 1942. There was only me left. At that time, I was just six years old. So I begged for alms all day."

In August 1943 the Japanese attacked western Shandong Province with cholera germs. The aim was to strategically weaken areas of communist military strength and popular support by killing off that base of support with lethal and fast-spreading cholera epidemics. Although Kuomintang forces in 1937 had driven them to a remote base area in northern China at Yanan, the Chinese communists, led by Mao Zedong, Zhou Enlai, and Red Army General Zhu De, had been growing in fighting strength and number since the Second Sino-Japanese War and were able to mobilize large sections of the population of North China, Central China, and southern Manchuria into fighting the Japanese army. By 1945 the communists had accounted for more than 80 percent of Japanese combat casualties in China.

The scheme of Japan's cholera BW campaign in Shandong is reminiscent of the tactics used in the cholera microbial bombing that had devastated the people of Yunnan Province four months earlier.

As in Yunnan, the army's combination of bacterial dissemination and conventional military assaults on civilians created masses of infected carrier refugees, a sickened population on the move whose human contagion would then spread among the population of outlying areas, and serve to decimate an entire region that the Japanese had targeted for their military and political control. And as had occurred in the Yunnan cholera epidemic, the resulting fatalities were massive: in Shandong and its neighboring provinces of Hebei and Henan they numbered approximately 200,000 people. A former sergeant in the Fifty-ninth Division of the Twelfth Army, Nagade Tomoyoshi, recounted in 1954 that Dr. Kiyoshi Hayakawa, a close associate of Ishii in Unit 731 and a cholera expert, arrived in Shandong in March 1943, for his appointment as the chief of the Military Surgeon Detachment of the Twelfth Army, the position in which he would direct cholera BW attacks. Interestingly, Hayakawa had earlier attended graduate school in microbiology in the United States, for six months in 1939, at the University of Michigan in Ann Arbor. Upon his Shandong appointment, Hayakawa began supervising the training of some 200 non-commissioned officers in the Fifty-ninth Division in the dissemination techniques of cholera biological warfare. He also ordered preventative cholera vaccine shots for the division and the rest of the Twelfth Army. This made the Japanese immune to the deadly disease they would soon employ.

Hayakawa trained the Fifty-ninth Division officers with the help of medical personnel from the Unit 731 affiliated BW detachment stationed in Beijing, a city not far from Shandong Province. This detachment was called Unit 1855, and it had a branch subunit in the Shandong town of Jinan. The Jinan subunit had its own human experiment prison, similar to those at Pingfan and Changchun, and lab facilities for breeding large quantities of bubonic plague, cholera, and typhoid bacteria.

Beginning on August 20, 1943, the Japanese Twelfth Army, then occupying part of Shandong Province, dispatched soldiers to drop cholera bacteria into the water supplies of certain towns and villages, or to leave cholera-tainted food bundles lying around outdoors, containing such edibles as fruit or rice cakes, tempting items for the hungry and war-torn Chinese population to eat and to bring back to their homes to share with others.

The cholera-targeted communities were located to the west of the Wei River, in flat, low-lying territory vulnerable to flooding. Soon, cholera outbreaks took hold and the people residing in these lowland counties began dying in large numbers.

Troops of the Fifty-ninth Division then blew up three embankments that had been damming the Wei River, causing a massive flood that forced thousands of residents in the cholera-stricken, and now water-ravaged, lowland communities to flee for higher ground, abandoning their flooded homes and carrying with them many personal items that harbored the lethal cholera bacteria.

Soon the highland areas to which the refugees had fled began experiencing their own cholera cases and an epidemic swept twelve counties in the west of Shandong along with nine counties in Hebei and two counties in Henan, two provinces adjacent to Shandong. This region was not yet occupied by Japan, and the Twelfth Army waited and observed as the cholera epidemic they had started began to decimate the higher ground villages, then moved in for the kill with a series of three infantry offensives, striking in three successful advances into the region progressing from mid-September through late October.

With this campaign, the Japanese managed to temporarily push back communist resistance forces. But despite the hundreds of thousands of civilians killed by the cholera BW of 1943, the communist guerrillas in western Shandong regrouped and continued to engage Japan's occupation troops and win popular support until the end of the war.

The final days of the bio-war units are notable for the scientists' last malicious and gratuitous actions against the Manchurian population. In the second week of August 1945 the Soviet army poured across the border with massive infantry divisions, 5,500 tanks and almost 3,900 combat planes, as the USSR kept its agreement with the United States to attack Japan in Manchuria and along the Pacific coast. It seems that those BW contingency plans for contaminating livestock and crops in the event of a Japanese territorial withdrawal were prescient, because the vaunted Kwantung Army quickly collapsed into full retreat. Unit 100 began frantically evacuating all its personnel and dynamiting its buildings to rubble, trying to destroy all evidence of their activities. Chinese civilian laborers who had worked at the unit were rounded up and administered lethal cyanide injections. The experiment prisoners were also killed in this way. A few Chinese workers escaped execution after being ordered by the Japanese to help push a truck out of a muddy quagmire after they had loaded equipment onto it. After the truck got loose, the workers simply hid in the mud, remaining overlooked by the frantically busy Japanese personnel. They escaped when the coast was clear and survived to tell their insider accounts of the Changchun complex.

But the last officers to leave Unit 100 wreaked havoc upon the Chinese even after Japan had unconditionally surrendered to the Allies on August 15. The following week, on August 20, they opened the stables and let loose sixty horses after feeding them glanders-infected oats. Six Unit 100 men drove the horses from the camp environs onto six roads radiating out in different directions, into the nearby villages and farms. On that day other Unit 100 personnel set free thousands of bubonic plague–infected rats from their enclosures in the camp. The rodents swarmed across a twenty-mile area surrounding Unit 100 and spread plague to the local human population. As a consequence, the people in and around the city of Changchun experienced plague epidemics in 1946 and for years thereafter.

Germs, of course, know no surrender terms. Even in the post-war era, a sinister aspect of biological warfare was made manifest: the ability of artificially spread disease to go on infecting the people of northeastern China (the former Manchuria) and Zhejiang, Jiangxi, and Hunan provinces indefinitely. Laboratory-cultivated organisms are released into a region, and if conditions are right, they enter into a natural cycle of microbial breeding such as in the plague bacterium-flea-rodent host cycle that afflicted the people living in and around Changchun. Once seeded, the germs may persist in reproducing themselves for generations.

The continuing presence of Unit 731 cultured and disseminated bacteria is a dangerous legacy of Japan's biological warfare program. Even today, some mice and rats in the rodent populations in parts of northeastern China and east-central Zhejiang Province test positive for bloodstream antibodies to plague bacillus originally dispersed by Units 731 and 1644.

It is currently thought that the total number of persons in China who died as a result of Japan's bio-war program—that is, who were killed from infections caused by germ warfare and in death-camp experimentation—reaches a minimum cumulative figure of about 580,000. At the December 2002 International Symposium on the Crimes of Bacteriological Warfare, held in China in the city of Changde (site of the November 1941 aerial plague flea spraying attack), this number was explained by conference organizers to be a summation based upon the accounting of subtotals for the approximately 210,000 people killed by cholera BW in Yunnan Province, the 200,000 people dead by BW in Shandong Province in 1943; the estimated 20,000 civilians and prisoners of war who died in assorted medical experiments while held captive in army field hospitals and at the BW research death camps of Pingfan, Changchun, Nanking, Peking, Canton, and elsewhere; and at least 150,000 people believed to have died in various germ warfare outbreaks in many other instances from 1937 to 1945, and in recurrent outbreaks of illness that continued after the war, in various Chinese provinces, cities, and villages.

In just one urban locality, the Zhejiang Province city of Quzhou and its suburbs, more than 50,000 civilians died from bubonic plague and cholera that had been spread by Japanese BW squads in 1942. This is the recent finding of a research team led by Dr. Qiu Ming Xuan, who presented their conclusions at the Changde International Symposium. Outbreaks of plague and cholera continued to erupt in the Quzhou area each year from 1942 through 1948.

Another such study has been done in the plague-hit districts of Hunan Province. Beginning in the mid-1990s, and working steadily over the course of seven years up to the present day, more than 100 researchers have conducted interviews in Changde and 486 nearby villages with the families and neighbors of plague epidemic victims. The interviewers are fielded by a local investigation committee that filed a legal brief with the Tokyo District Court in support of the plaintiffs for the 1997–2002 germ warfare lawsuit. This document presented their tabulated interview results: It states a total figure of 7,643 confirmed deaths from plague BW in Changde and surrounding farming villages. The Changde committee noted that its research was still ongoing and turning up new cases (as are similar, ongoing investigations in other BW-attacked places in China), and also that the number of 7,643 was one derived from only the most conservative accounting method used in the study, and was thus probably an undercount and incomplete. A more realistic total, they say, would be about 10,400 fatalities from the epidemic.

The huge mortality figures appear with numbing frequency for the many BW-hit areas ranging across the enormous, geographically diverse nation of China. These amounts, moreover, continue to expand as new in-depth investigations are initiated. They fill statistical tables with dry and abstracted numerical sets that belie the incredible pain and misery visited upon so very many innocent men, women, and children: 4,500 dead from plague in the county of Nongan, near Harbin, in 1942; 165 plague fatalities in 1941 at Longquan, and 309 killed at Meiwu that year, both towns in Zhejiang Province; 3,000 killed by a cholera attack launched in July 1942 in Wenzhou, Zhejiang Province; 100 killed by typhoid in Xinxiang, Henan Province; 25,089 died in 1947 from a post-war plague epidemic in the district of Tonglian, Inner Mongolia, that had reemerged after being initiated during the war by Unit 731; and on and on.

The mass killings through man-made epidemics constituted acts of genocide against the Chinese people, and the war goal of the BW network was to help secure victory by selective and strategic human extermination.

Wang Xuan noted in a statement she made in 1997 for the germ warfare victims' lawsuit, "Japanese BW war criminals were not tried for their mass production of BW by human experimentation and large-scale use of BW against the Chinese, most of them civilians. They had been granted immunity for their war atrocities against humanity, arranged through secret dealings between governments.

"Our case," she said, "is just the tip of an iceberg."

EIGHT

WHAT AMERICA KNEW

IN THE FATEFUL FIRST TWO WEEKS OF AUGUST 1945, THE LONG catastrophic drama of World War II reached its short, shocking final act as the United States dropped atomic bombs on Hiroshima and Nagasaki, and Soviet forces quickly flushed out the Kwantung Army, liberating Manchuria and Korea from their Japanese occupations to the cheers of tens of millions of long-suffering people. On August 15, the citizens of Japan were astonished to hear over their radios the first-ever public broadcast of the sacred voice of Emperor Hirohito, their living god, as he announced the nation's surrender to the Allies.

At the Pentagon, plans were being hastily drawn up and enacted to airdrop men and supplies into POW camps where Allied prisoners were being held as soon the Japanese laid down their arms, and transport home the former captives, virtually all of whom had suffered brutal treatment by camp guards and officials. One of these plans is especially interesting: it indicates that although the U.S. military did strongly suspect that Japan was using germ warfare or conducting horrific human experiments, the U.S. government made no public statement during the war that American prisoners of war were being used as human guinea pigs. Moreover, the secret operation appears to have specifically targeted Ishii's central facilities in Manchuria as the place into which to send commandos to seize both the assumed POW experiment subjects, and the data obtained from the experimentation upon them.

Code-named "Operation Flamingo," this mission had been planned by the Office of Strategic Services (OSS) intelligence agency to liberate American POWs in Manchuria. An OSS document containing orders for the operation was found at the U.S National Archives in 1994. The document, dated August 13, 1945, specified that an OSS team was to fly into the Harbin area and rescue American and Allied prisoners "on a moment's notice on V-J Day." The team was instructed "to immediately contact all Allied POW camps" in the area, to "notify headquarters of the number, condition, etc. of the prisoners in the concentration camps," and "to render any medical assistance necessary and feasible." They were also ordered to advise the "Senior American Officer" among the POWs on the need to arm the "physically able POWs" to defend themselves.

What is especially noteworthy about these instructions is the fact that there were no Allied POW camps in or near Harbin. The nearest one was "Camp Mukden" (called the "Hoten" camp by the Japanese), where American, British, Dutch, and New Zealand POWs were held, located more than 300 miles to the south of Harbin, near the Manchurian city of Mukden. The formation of an OSS squad to enter Harbin therefore suggests that U.S. officials suspected American prisoners were being held in a human experiment camp, since U.S. intelligence did know that some bio-war experimentation was going on in Harbin and nearby (it remains unclear whether they knew of the location and description of Pingfan), and there is no indication elsewhere, in another context, that they believed a POW camp to exist there.

It seems that something other than faulty information inspired the plan to immediately contact the presumed POWs in the Harbin vicinity, and this may have been the belief that some

Americans had been taken there to be experimented upon.

The mission orientation toward obtaining experiment and BW information may also be reflected in the team's orders to "secure immediately all Japanese documents and dossiers, and other information useful to the United States government."

As it turned out, the Harbin OSS mission was never launched, because by the time V-J Day came, on August 15, 1945, the Soviet military had already invaded and occupied Manchuria, gaining control of Harbin, and of the remains of the destroyed Pingfan complex. They also reached the city of Mukden and liberated the Allied prisoners being held at the nearby Mukden POW camp, who numbered more than 1,000 men.

It was at Camp Mukden where, according to both Unit 731 veterans and the ex-POWs of Mukden, experiments were performed upon Americans. In 1949, at the Khabarovsk trial, Major Tomio Karasawa testified that a Pingfan researcher named "Minato" told him in a Mukden hospital that he had been sent to Mukden by Unit 731 to "study immunity among American war prisoners," and that he was traveling to "camps where Allied war prisoners were kept to study the immunity of Anglo-Saxons to infectious diseases." The prosecutor also noted that in 1943 Minato had tested "the properties of the blood and immunity to contagious diseases of the American soldiers."

More than three decades after Khabarovsk, at two U.S. House of Representatives Veterans' Affairs Subcommittee meetings, the American former POWs of Camp Mukden told their stories of abuse and experimentation at the hands of their captors. At these hearings, one held in 1982 and the other in 1986, veterans described constant hunger and malnutrition from the time of their arrival at the camp in November 1942 to their liberation in August 1945 (in general, conditions at other POW camps of the Japanese across Asia were even worse than those at Mukden, and one-third of American POWs died in captivity). Most of the Americans sent to the Manchurian camp had been captured in the Philippines, and many had been on the notorious Bataan Death March, where they suffered beatings, exhaustion, and dehydration.

At the 1982 session, Oklahoman Warren W. "Pappy" Whelchel described camp medical exams in which groups of prisoners were carefully segregated, given a series of unknown injections, and sprayed in the face with droplets of an unknown substance, while detailed medical notes were taken and filed by doctors. In 1986, ex-POW Frank James recalled his work at a camp building in the spring of 1943 assisting in the burial preparation of the many Americans who had died at the camp during the winter, where he witnessed the organs and body parts of those soldiers carefully removed, labeled with each prisoner's ID number, and put into special containers. Gregory Rodriquez told of the episodic, chronic illness that he had suffered for decades since being interned at Mukden, whose origin he associated with the placing of an infected feather under his nose by the Japanese. His son, Gregory Rodriquez, Jr., produced documents from the National Archives for review by the House Subcommittee members, which provided evidence of Japanese experiments at Mukden and of a postwar U.S. cover-up on the matter.

In the postwar years, Rodriquez senior attempted to have his mysterious, sporadically flaring ailment of fever, pain, and fatigue diagnosed correctly, making a number of fruitless visits to medical clinics. Finally, a doctor confirmed that he was suffering from recurrent typhoid, a strikingly large number of that bacterial strain having been found in his blood. This disease had been the subject of research by Unit 731 and its branch detachments.

In a 1995 interview with the author, the elder Rodriquez noted that he knew of two other Mukden POWs who had feathers put under their nose by Japanese medical personnel, and he also recalled the puzzlement of the Mukden POWs upon opening their Red Cross packages and finding numerous feathers of varying colors placed among the items of food inside. Rodriquez and the other prisoners were sure that it was their Japanese captors who had placed them in the boxes, but they had no idea why, although in the case of the yellow feathers, they considered it might be the Japanese way of calling them cowards. "We thought maybe they were trying to tell us we were yellow," said Rodriquez. As it is well documented that the Japanese used lab-infected feathers as BW devices, the possibility cannot be discounted that these feathers were a means to deliver bacteria to the men, and that their varying colors were code for the type of germs placed on each one.

In 1985, a Japanese Unit 731 veteran recalled his work with a group led by Dr. "Minato" (the first name was left unstated, as it also is unstated in the published Khabarovsk trial transcript) in performing tests on American Mukden POWs involving dysentery bacteria, a specialty of Minato. This veteran, Tsuneji Shimada, said that blood tests were taken from the POWs, and that they were given liquids to drink that had been infected with pathogenic bacteria. Those prisoners who died were then subjected to autopsies to assess the internal effects of the bacterial strains with which they had been secretly dosed. Shimada's recollections corroborate the Khabarovsk statement of Major Karasawa regarding Minato's activity at Camp Mukden. The 1986 congressional testimony of Frank James also independently complements the 1949 Karasawa testimony regarding Unit 731 studies of "the immunity of Anglo-Saxons," in that James described the singling out of certain POWs for exams by a visiting Japanese team of medical personnel who then questioned them as to their ethnic background, demanding specifics: "It had to be Scotch, French, English, or whatever," said James. This was the same outside medical team who had earlier directed James in the removal of organ specimens from the bodies of U.S. prisoners (most of whom appear to have died from severe dysentery).

Frank James suffered chronic health problems after the war, including lung and skin disorders that may have resulted from his exposure to experimental BW pathogens.

Dysentery, the disease that figured so prominently in the illnesses of American Mukden POWs and the studies of Minato's Unit 731 research group, also appears to have been deliberately disseminated among the ailing American prisoners interned at the Shinagawa POW hospital, in Tokyo. The Japanese displayed a notable interest in the effects of dysentery upon Americans at both Shinagawa in Japan, and Mukden, in Manchuria. On September 2, 1945, the *New York Times*, just below its banner headlines proclaiming the news of Japan's official surrender signing ceremony with General Douglas MacArthur, carried a front-page article about Shinagawa by well-known reporter Robert Trumbull: "Enemy Tortured Dying Americans with Sadist Medical 'Experiments'." This dispatch from Japan describes the experiments of a physician, Captain Hisikichi Tokoda, in which virulent strains of the malaria organism were injected into Americans suffering from beri-beri, and tuberculosis patients were injected with strange concoctions of acid mixed with dextrose, ether, or blood plasma. The objective was to develop medicinal treatments, using the Americans as expendable human guinea pigs. Other Japanese physicians at the hospital cruelly forced experimental solutions upon infirm prisoners that "caused the patients unspeakable pain and often death," wrote Trumbull. An American doctor working at the camp, who had been captured in the Philippines, Dr. Robert Gottlieb from New York City, is quoted: "Latrines were mere holes in the ground lined with concrete.... The Japs took the excrement, which was full of amoebic dysentery germs, and sprayed it throughout the camp."

Gottlieb and another American POW physician who worked at the Shinagawa laboratory, Harold Keschner, said that the infected bile of POWs with amoebic dysentery was intravenously injected into tuberculosis-patient prisoners, an act that raises the possibility that the POWs were being sprayed with the dysentery amoebas in order to farm those who contracted the organism for experimental drugs derived from their still-living organs.

There were murderous experiments on Allied POWs elsewhere. On the Chinese island of Hainan, Australian and Dutch prisoners in a Japanese camp were fed a diet carefully constructed to be devoid of certain vitamins, including rice that had been polished to obliterate its vitamin content. The Japanese physician in charge of their feeding was conducting a malnutrition test. The emaciated prisoners were forced to surreptitiously catch and eat rodents to obtain enough nutrition to survive. Australian, New Zealand, and American prisoners at Rabaul on the island of New Britain off the coast of New Guinea were used in malnutrition and malaria experiments. Some died due to injections of malaria-infected human blood. The Japanese physician leading these tests was Captain Enosuke Hirano of the Rabaul "Water Purification Unit" branch detachment of Unit 731.

In May 1945, on the southern Japanese home island of Kyushu, eight American airmen from a downed B-29 "Superfortress" bomber, who had been captured on Kyushu, were killed in experiments at a hospital in the city of Fukuoka. The experiments were conducted by faculty physicians and medical students of the medical department of Kyushu University. No direct connection between the perpetrators of these experiments and Unit 731 has yet surfaced, but the vivisections they conducted were similar to those that had become common practice of the Japanese across China and Manchuria.

Various surgical experiments were performed on the fliers, including excisions of the stomach and heart, a study to see how well one could survive the partial removal of the liver, and the extraction of a portion of the brain to test an epilepsy treatment technique. The first prisoner handed over to the Kyushu University doctors, Teddy Ponczka, was used in two experiments: in the first, one of his lungs was removed. In the second, he was injected intravenously with seawater, to see if it would work as a substitute for the saline solution normally used as a blood volumizer in medical treatments.

All the airmen used in the experiments died as a result, and the facts of what happened to them emerged only as the result of a postwar inquiry by the U.S. military as to their fate.

Dr. Toshio Tono had assisted in these experiments as a young man, and had held the bottle of seawater used in Ponczka's injections. In May 1995, a *Baltimore Sun* reporter interviewed him in the Fukuoka hospital where he was on staff. Dr. Tono said that the American prisoners, upon first seeing the white-coated medicos coming toward them, "didn't struggle. They never dreamed they would be dissected." He also recalled: "There was no debate among the doctors about whether to do the operation—that was what made it so strange."

So how much knowledge did the U.S. government have of Axis Japan's "Secret of Secrets," the human experiments and biological warfare, during the war? The answer in brief is: quite a lot, and that America's wariness of possible Japanese intentions in germ warfare began even before World War II, due to a strange incident that happened right in the heart of New York City.

In February 1939 a group of Japanese medical researchers made an unannounced visit to the world-renowned Rockefeller Institute for Medical Research, at East 66th Street and York Avenue in Manhattan. They had come all the way from Tokyo and also, unknown to the New York microbiologists who received them, from the Tokyo laboratories working with Japan's human experiments in Manchuria. From the Rockefeller Institute they requested stocks of yellow fever virus, a mosquito-borne pathogen that can cause deadly epidemics in human populations. The institute turned down their request, whereupon they tried to bribe a technician into slipping them the virus.

These events sparked a State Department investigation into the matter. The State Department's report was sent to the U.S. Army Surgeon General, and while the report does not attempt to state any firm conclusions about the possible motives of the Japanese, it does say that their behavior seemed highly suspicious. It also notes that the pathogenic agent they were seeking could conceivably be used as a biological weapon.

The matter was kept confidential, and the U.S. government lodged neither an inquiry nor a protest with any Japanese embassy or consulate. It is possible that with a war raging in Asia between China and the Japanese invaders, and another one looming in Europe, into which the United States believed it would soon be drawn, the U.S. government did not want to challenge the Japanese over such an esoteric matter.

Following the attack on Pearl Harbor the United States had a more immediate reason to pay attention to reports emerging from China of germ warfare attacks by the Japanese occupiers of Manchuria. Their own soldiers might be the next targets. The Chinese government's release in April 1942 of the Chen Report, the scientific exposé of Japan's aerial plague, had caused much alarm among American intelligence officials.

This report, made public in April 1942, was the product of a Chinese epidemiological team headed by Dr. Wen-Kwei Chen, and specialists of the Chinese Red Cross released a documentary account of Japan's germ warfare, complete with laboratory results, concluding that Japanese planes had released bubonic plague–carrying fleas over the city of Changde in Central China's Hunan Province, in November of 1941. The Chen Report explicated history's first detailed scientific investigation of biological warfare attacks. It covered not only the Changde incident, but also earlier germ warfare attacks in 1940, against the civilian populations of Quzho, Jinhua, and Ningbo.

Also in April 1942, the Kuomintang government held a press conference in Nationalist China's wartime capital city of Chongqing, to present the evidence of Japanese BW to a gathering of international reporters. Dr. Peter Z. King, the director-general of the National Health Administration in China, delivered a speech at this conference accusing Imperial Japan of creating bubonic plague epidemics through the use of biological warfare, and circulated a document containing the Chen Report on the historical details and scientific analysis of the methods used by Japanese forces to spark epidemics.

The Chen Report was translated into several foreign languages, including English, and delivered to ten foreign embassies in the Chinese wartime capital city of Chongqing. It was also excerpted in the internationally read journal *Epidemic Prevention Weekly*, in an article coauthored by Dr. King and an American, Dr. Robert Pollitzer, who worked with the National Health Administration as a foreign expert in epidemic prevention.

Dr. Pollitzer led emergency plague-containment efforts in the city of Quzhou, following a recurrence of plague in March 1941, a flareup of the previous autumn's plague epidemic caused by the Unit 731 plane that on October 4, 1940, had sprayed a mixture of wheat, millet, and infected fleas.

Surprisingly, the Chen Report, the article of King and Pollitzer, and other public accusations that Japan was waging germ warfare failed to reach any significant level of public awareness in the Allied or neutral nations of the world during World War II, despite their obvious anti-Japanese propaganda value at this time when China was one of the key Allied nations, along with the United States, Britain, and the Soviet Union, in fighting the Axis Powers. The Chen Report's investigations are meticulous and compelling. For example, concerning the October 1940 incident in Quzhuo, it reads:

> On October 4, 1940, a Japanese plane visited Quzhou, Zhejiang province. After circling the city it scattered rice and wheat mixed with fleas over the western district of the city. There were many eyewitnesses among whom was a man named Hsu, who collected some grain and dead fleas from the street outside of his own house. He sent them to the local air raid precautionary corps for transmission to the provincial hygiene laboratory. The laboratory examination result was that "there were no pathogenic organisms found by bacteriological culture methods." However, on November 12, 38 days after the Japanese plane's visit, bubonic plague appeared in the same area where the grain and fleas were found in abundance. The epidemic in Quzhou lasted 24 days. Resulting in 21 deaths.
>
> Available records show bubonic plague had never occurred in Quzhou before. After careful investigation it was believed that the strange visit of the enemy plane was the cause of the epidemic and the transmitting agent was rat fleas, presumably infected with plague and definitely dropped by the enemy plane. As plague is primarily a disease of rodents, the grain was probably used to attract the rats and expose them to the infected fleas mixed therein. It was regrettable that the fleas collected were not properly examined. Owing to deficient laboratory facilities, an animal inoculation test was not performed.

In retrospect, it appears that despite those inferior lab facilities, the Chinese investigators did an admirable medical detective job in assessing the Japanese methods. Postwar testimony by Japanese scientists and the flight crews of the disease-disseminating planes confirms that the purpose of dropping grain was indeed to attract local rodents, which would then act as host carriers of the fleas to bring the infection to people.

But the report's findings, based on eyewitness accounts and scientific study, elicited no official comment from the governments of the United States and other Allied nations. The media of foreign countries also failed to react, and few news outlets carried reports of the Chongqing announcement, despite the sensational nature of its germ warfare charges. In the United States only the *Rocky Mountain Medical Journal*, a regional medical periodical published in Wyoming, carried a substantial article about the Chen Report and the known casualties of Japan's plague assaults.

Yet inside the American government and military, officials did quietly take note of the Chen Report allegations. And as U.S. forces advanced across the islands of the Pacific, capturing Japanese POWs, the military would get a much clearer picture of the extent of the Japanese BW program. Many soldiers in the Kwantung Army were transferred from Manchuria to the Pacific islands. Some who became POWs of the United States provided information on bio-war detachments with which they had been associated. By 1945, U.S. military intelligence understood that major BW research was being conducted in Tokyo, and that Shiro Ishii had founded the program and set up its headquarters in Harbin. Captured documents also gave key pieces of information on Japanese bio-weapons and the methods used to disperse them. In 1944 a lieutenant captured on the island of Peleliu revealed to his U.S. interrogators that he had once been attached to a bio-war research facility in the Manchurian capital city of Changchun and had served as a lab assistant in the production of glanders bacteria. Two other Japanese POWs described in detail the biological warfare production of diseases at the Unit 1644 facility in Nanking. One of them also hinted of the macabre human experiments being conducted there. A prisoner captured on May 12,

1944, reported that he had once held a civilian job in the bacteriology department of Chuzan University at Canton. This man explicitly named Shiro Ishii as a major figure in Japanese bio-war research. The report on this prisoner also includes schematic diagrams, evidently provided by him, for several types of Japanese bacterial bombs.

A mimeographed army manual titled "NI Diversionary Tactics," discovered among the belongings of a dead Japanese lieutenant on the island of Morotai on September 24, 1944, proved to be of great significance. It advised, "Great results can be obtained by contaminating their food and drink in kitchen by bacterial strategy." The fact that suggestions for bacteriological sabotage would be printed in a manual given to low-ranking officers indicated that germ warfare was a common strategy among Japanese troops. The widespread use of bacterial contamination by Japanese soldiers would be confirmed decades later in the confessional recollections of army doctor Ken Yuasa and others.

A document captured on the Philippine island of Luzon in March 1945 outlined the BW assault tactics to be used in a scheme to contaminate an island with cholera in the event of a Japanese retreat from the Philippines. There is no known evidence that this cholera dissemination was carried out by the Japanese when they did withdraw from the Philippines in the spring of 1945, but the revealing document lays out a well-developed variety of techniques to start epidemic in its "Methods of Attack" section, suggesting that the Japanese had learned from a great deal of BW experience. These techniques include "Spraying bacterial solutions by airplane," "Spraying powdered bacteria," "Dropping ampules containing bacteria," "Dropping infected insects, animals, animal tissues," "Firing shells and bullets containing pathogenic organisms," and "Spreading bacteria by agents."

The Japanese military drew up various plans to use biological warfare against American troops in the Pacific theater. It appears that neither the United States nor its Allies had information on any of these planned operations. One scheme finalized in March 1942 called for BW units to release plague-infected fleas on American and Philippine troops defending Bataan. However, the battle ended in victory for Japan at the beginning of April, and the plague attack, which would have unleashed a thousand kilograms of fleas in ten separate BW assaults, had to be called off.

In 1942, Japan's top strategists, the chiefs-of-staff generals, devised plans to wage BW in U.S. and Allied-held territories including Dutch Harbor, Alaska; Calcutta, India; and parts of Australia, but it appears that those plans were never put into effect.

In June and July of 1944, U.S. and Japanese forces battled for control of Saipan Island in the Northern Marianas chain. The United States won and promptly built an airbase on Saipan to launch bombing raids against the Japanese Home Islands. Anticipating the American attack, Japan dispatched a ship carrying biological warfare troops to Saipan in April 1944. This BW contingent was on Saipan when the U.S. began its invasion, but the Japanese defenders were so quickly and effectively demolished that they were unable to launch any germ attacks. Some of the BW team members had earlier left Saipan for the island of Truk, another highly strategic location, but their ship was sunk en route by an American submarine, sending most of those aboard and their containers of lethal microbes to the ocean depths.

Perhaps the wildest germ warfare scheme against the United States was a planned BW attack against the American mainland dubbed with the delicate code name "Cherry Blossoms at Night." This operation entailed a bubonic plague attack on the city of San Diego, California, in which one of Japan's unique plane-carrying, long-range diesel submarines would stealthily approach America's West Coast and release a small airplane with fold-out wings (the Japanese navy had a minimum of five such subs). The plane would then fly over San Diego and scatter plague-infected fleas in much the same way that Unit 731 had done over Chinese cities.

At the same time, a squadron of men taught in germ warfare sabotage would ride a small launch boat from the sub to the California shore and secretly disseminate bacteria of cholera and plague at selected targets.

The "Cherry Blossoms" plan was approved by the chiefs of staff in March 1945, and Ishii began meeting with Unit 731–trained soldiers in his Pingfan Administration Building office to sternly inform them that they had been chosen to participate in a raid on the continental United States, a BW assignment which could only be considered a suicide mission from which they had no hope of returning home. However, the plan was canceled in its final preparation stages by the head of the chiefs of staff, General Yoshijiro Umezu, who had previously overseen the activities of the Unit 731 and Unit 100 BW network in his former post as the top general of the Kwantung Army. Umezu understood the obvious fact that the desperate attack could serve no practical military purpose, and would only result in strengthening the fury and resolve of the United States to utterly defeat the nation that would stoop to such evil and universally condemned measures.

The persistent U.S. Army intelligence reports filtering in from China and the Pacific islands impressed upon the American Joint Chiefs of Staff that Japan was likely engaging in biological warfare on a large scale. On August 15, 1944, they issued an urgent memorandum ordering that soldiers in the Pacific theater be "impressed with the importance of capturing and securing any medical documents and supplies" and to "report immediately" all "evidence of enemy use of bacteriological warfare, no matter to what extent."

In December 1944 U.S. officials learned that three months prior, in the jungles of Burma where American troops were fighting, Burmese resistance forces had discovered a few ampules, twenty cubic centimeters in volume, each containing a suspension of cholera bacteria. They had been dropped from Japanese planes. Other reports stated that the Customs House in occupied Rangoon, where Unit 731 had dispatched a Water Purification Unit, was being used by Japan as a makeshift prison for gruesome human medical experiments.

That December the U.S. military was jolted into high vigilance against biological warfare by the sudden appearance of a possible Japanese germ warfare threat on American soil. The menace came in the curious form of hydrogen-filled balloons: Beginning in November 1944, more than 9,000 of them were sent aloft from Japan's main island of Honshu to ride the jet stream winds over the Pacific Ocean and eventually drift down over the United States and Canada. They were thirty-three feet (ten meters) in diameter, and composed of a paper made from mulberry bush. Suspended from each balloon's equator was attached a ring of taut cords, bearing gondolalike carriages that contained incendiary bombs. An array of altimeters and gears on each balloon alternately dropped sandbags to raise each balloon, or released hydrogen to lower it, to keep it at the right altitude for catching the westward jet stream, which could push the balloons along toward North America at speeds of up to sixty miles per hour. As a consequence, the journey from Japan to North America took no more than three days.

The balloon weapons had been conceived and designed by Japan's Ninth Army Research Technical Division, the same division that tested poisons on Unit 1644 prisoners at Nanking. They were manufactured at secret factories in an assembly line process that employed hundreds of Japanese civilians. Many of these people were teenage girls, whose small, nimble fingers made them desirable for the work of pasting together the balloon paper patches. The Japanese military High Command had multiple goals in mind for the balloon bombs: to create forest fires on the U.S. mainland that would divert men and resources from the war effort; to kill significant numbers of civilians and cause panic, sapping American morale; and to serve as weapons of revenge for the April 1942 Doolittle raid on Tokyo. The High Command hoped that when Japan's public read the articles and saw pictures of the fires and destruction in America, they would be cheered and encouraged by the havoc wreaked in the United States.

The balloons flew over Mexico and up the length of California, Oregon, Washington, and Canada, all the way up across the northwest to Alaska and the Aleutian Islands. They flew east into the Southwest, over the Great Plains, and beyond. While U.S. fighter planes shot down some of them, far more often they fell, across Hawaii, Texas, Utah, Wyoming, Montana, Iowa, the Dakotas, Alberta, Manitoba, and as far east as Michigan and the St. Lawrence River. Scraps of the mulberry balloon paper were found lying in the streets of Los Angeles. One balloon landed in the woods of southern Oregon, where a minister and his family on a fishing trip discovered the mysterious object and tried to drag it away toward a picnic area so that they could examine it more closely. It exploded, killing his wife and five children. They were the only confirmed balloon bomb casualties.

On March 10, 1945, a balloon bomb happened to randomly drift down over Washington state and blast the electrical lines running between the towns of Granite and Benton City. This caused a temporary power failure at a nearby top-secret military installation, located in Hanford. It was a research unit of the Manhattan Project, and the power loss caused an interruption in the processing of plutonium destined for use in the atomic bomb that the United States dropped four months later on Nagasaki.

Because the U.S. military strictly censored media reports of any balloon observations or incidents, Americans and Canadians were kept in the dark about their existence. Finally, in May 1945 the War Department and navy issued a warning to the public, revealing the Japanese balloon bomb invasion. In the June 4, 1945, edition of *Newsweek* magazine, a small article appeared about this announcement and the numerous balloon sightings. *Newsweek* noted that the announcement urged people not to touch "unfamiliar objects found in remote places." The article describes the balloons as carrying "either high explosive demolition bombs or incendiaries."

In Japan, propagandistic newspaper articles appeared in 1945, falsely claiming that the balloons had killed 10,000 Americans, and that both vast forest fires and mass panic were raging. In reality, about 230 balloons were recovered and destroyed by police and military teams, and the vast majority of those launched from Japan did not detonate. Most of those that did descend landed harmlessly in the ocean or in remote, uninhabited areas where they failed to cause any known problems.

The Japanese military launched the last of the balloon bombs in April 1945, having realized they were a disappointment. To U.S. military investigators, however, the transoceanic parade held fearsome potential. What would keep the Japanese from employing hydrogen-filled balloons to deliver germ warfare and disease outbreaks to American populations and crops? A scientist at the army's two-year-old biological warfare research facility at Camp Detrick, Maryland, named Lieutenant Colonel Murray Sanders, was sent to examine a number of balloons found intact, along with their cargo.

Sanders had the scientific background needed to analyze BW data. He was a physician and microbiologist and had been a lecturer and assistant professor at Columbia University before enlisting in 1943 in the program at Camp Detrick (whose name changed to Fort Detrick in February 1956). Entering the army team with the rank of major, he directed research units in a plethora of disciplines, including human physiology, bacteriology, virology, and pharmacology. In just two years of duty, Sanders had developed a storied reputation in the field of biological weapons. The first major problem he had to deal with involved a continual vexation for Camp Detrick: the accidental contamination of building floors where organisms were bred, cultured, and tested on animals for their lethality. The subsequent infection of scientists and laboratory technicians sometimes resulted in deaths. On one such occasion in 1943, ten researchers laboring in the same building came down with brucellosis, a bacterial disease of cattle and man that is called undulant fever when it manifests in humans.

One of those men afflicted was Gifford Bryce Pinchot, the blueblood son of the former governor of Pennsylvania, and Sanders's former student at Columbia University College of Physicians and Surgeons. Sanders and other Detrick physicians fought an intense, around-the-clock struggle to cure the governor's ailing son with a combination of what were then the cutting-edge antibiotic drugs of penicillin and streptomycin. While others who became infected in the building died of the disease, succumbing to the effects of its persistent high fever, Pinchot recovered.

Shortly afterward, Sanders was coincidentally scheduled to have dinner with Gifford Pinchot Sr., along with U.S. Supreme Court justices Hugo Black and Theodore White. During the meal, Sanders revealed the details of the brucellosis outbreak he had just worked to contain, explaining to Governor Pinchot for the first time what had happened to his son. Sanders not only startled his powerful dining companions, he also broke the vow he had sworn to uphold regarding the confidentiality of the research that went on at Camp Detrick. At the time, absolute secrecy surrounded the U.S. military's germ warfare research, on a level comparable to that of the Manhattan Project. The following day, Sanders's superior officer, the major general in charge of the Army's Chemical Corps, phoned him to say that he needed to "shut up," and that he was now under house arrest.

But a grateful Pinchot Sr. went to meet the Secretary of War, Henry Stimson, and after two days Sanders was not only freed, he was immediately promoted to the rank of lieutenant colonel. Proper doses of antibiotics and a well-connected patient had worked wonders for the health of Dr. Sanders's career.

In 1944 high-ranking Camp Detrick personnel received word from military intelligence that the Japanese were believed to be waging germ warfare against the population in Manchuria. Bubonic plague and anthrax were cited as two specific diseases employed. The scientific director of Camp Detrick, Dr. Oram C. Woolpert, arranged a meeting with Sanders to relate the briefings on Japan. "We think they've killed a lot of people, Murray," Woolpert told him. "We think that they've been poisoning wells and reservoirs."

Then came news of the balloon bomb invasion. In December 1944 Sanders received a phone call requesting that he investigate a suspicious balloon that had been found in Butte, Montana. That balloon and another one recovered from the beach in San Diego were shipped to Washington, D.C., where Sanders and other scientific experts inspected them in the presence of military officials. It was obvious to the investigators that the balloons were of Japanese origin, and Sanders's task as the Camp Detrick specialist was to assess the likelihood that the balloons, if they were fitted to carry germs, could function as effective initiators of disease outbreaks.

In a 1985 interview for British television, Sanders recalled that the assembled military and scientific personnel gathered in a circle around the retrieved balloons, looking them over, and that the report he presented to them on the balloons' BW potential "scared them stiff." He pinpointed the Japanese B encephalitis virus as a particular balloon-delivered pathogen threat, because it was mosquito-borne and usually fatal. "Mosquitoes were the best vectors—and we had plenty of those in the States—and our population had no defenses against B encephalitis. We had no experience of the disease in this country. . . . And four out of five people who contracted it would have died, in my view."

Sanders also remembered that he cited anthrax as another particularly dangerous organism with respect to the balloons, because he knew that the Japanese had already "used it in China," and that the anthrax bacterium "is a tough bug. It's sturdy. It's cheap to produce. . . . They could have splattered the west and southwest of Canada and the United States . . . contaminated the pastures . . . killed all the cows, sheep, horses, pigs, deer—plus a considerable amount of human beings. The hysteria would have been terrible. One of the strengths of BW as a weapon is that you can't see it, but it kills."

In January 1945 Sanders met in Ottawa with a Canadian military attaché to examine a transparent box that had been discovered in one of the balloons. He then flew to Hawaii to inspect a balloon there. Soon he was back on the U.S. mainland, traveling aboard a B-19 Army Air Corps plane flying low along the Pacific Coast, eyeing the trees and ground below for any fallen balloons on which he could conduct on-site inspections for germs or chemical poisons.

As it turned out, no traces of any biological or chemical agents were found on any of the balloon parts that Sanders examined, nor were any balloon-related disease outbreaks reported.

Unbeknownst to U.S. military investigators, however, the Japanese *were* using balloons to spread disease against the Soviet Union. Yoshikuma Ogura, a former intelligence agent who worked on germ warfare in sabotage missions—"I used to carry back bacteria from Unit 731, inject them into pigs and other domestic animals, and release the animals into Soviet territory"—said that specially trained teams sent balloons over the border from Manchuria into the Soviet Union carrying infectious organisms.

It was exactly what Murray Sanders said he had feared.

In 1994 the elderly Ogura remembered: "There were also what we called 'Q' operations. We would fill balloons with nitrogen and suspend containers of bacteria below them. They would be released to drift over Soviet territory to disperse bacteria. We never found out what effects this tactic had."

But Ogura's brief description of the germ-carrying balloon operations begs some basic questions. How were the bacteria disseminated from the suspended containers? Was there a timing device attached to the container or remote-control equipment? What types of bacteria were used and how was it expected that the microbes could survive the descent to earth and land in spots deemed suitable to create outbreaks? If these considerations were not addressed by the balloon deployers, the balloon method of germ delivery would seem to be an extremely impractical BW method. Unfortunately, Ogura did not elaborate on the balloon "Q operations" in his 1994 statement, and to this day little is known publicly about the design or mechanics of these bacteriological balloon weapons. There is no public record of the Soviets finding the germ balloons or suspecting their deployment by the Japanese.

In contrast, the tactic of using pigs and other animal vectors, as described by Ogura, ensures that the BW pathogens have a living host that humans might take into a farm or home, and that they might directly infect people or other animals. This would seem to be a better, more reliable method. The concerns voiced by Sanders to the top brass, that Japanese B encephalitis and anthrax germs could be effectively delivered by the balloons they were finding, make little sense from a scientific standpoint. The Japanese B encephalitis virus would need to be seeded within a native mosquito population to create an epidemic in a larger incubator than anything a balloon could carry. Sanders said that a liter of Japanese B encephalitis, freeze-dried in powder form, "would have put America at Ishii's mercy." But freeze-dried virus powder would stand virtually no chance of getting into the bodies of American mosquitoes once it arrived via balloon, and mosquito-to-human transmission is the only way a human case of the B encephalitis could occur and spread to others. A man of Sanders's qualifications and experience would have known this.

Similarly, a load of anthrax bacteria would almost certainly remain in or near its receptacle, wherever it happened to land. And although anthrax in its hardened spore form is in some respects "sturdy" and "tough," as Sanders said, the bacteria are killed by prolonged exposure to sunlight and air and generally ineffective at infecting people through the air except at close range. Therefore someone would have to find the downed balloon and handle the anthrax load in order to get the disease—which would be unlikely and at most would infect just that person. These facts were confirmed in both the BW research results at Camp Detrick and in Ishii's gruesome human experiments.

Given these inherent weaknesses in BW transmission by balloon, of which Sanders must have been aware, one might wonder why he would express such exaggerated concern to senior officials over the balloons' supposed germ warfare potential. Sanders's insistence that the many recovered balloons be scoured for BW microbes may reflect not so much fear as urgent curiosity—curiosity about what the enemy had achieved in the advancement of germ cultivation.

Sanders's disingenuous playing up of the destructive capacity of germs may also have stemmed from his aspirations and those of other Camp Detrick principals to increase their prestige as the experts on this terrible threat, and to boost the funding allocated to U.S. Army BW units.

*　　*　　*

Meeting at military bases in San Francisco and Omaha, Sanders and four officials from Washington, D.C., held talks in March 1945 with commanders of both the army and the navy who were responsible for the defense of the United States mainland. The main topic of discussion was the Japanese balloon invasion, but Sanders and the others laid other revelations regarding Japan's biological warfare operations on the military chiefs, including the existence of a "bacillus bomb" described by POWs and in enemy documents captured on the island of Kwajalein in the Southwest Pacific (which referred to the bomb as the "Special Bomb Mark 7, Experimental Type 13, 1 Kg"). They reviewed the 1942 reports and announcements by the Nationalist Chinese government regarding the plague attacks at Changde and in Zhejiang Province. They incorrectly told the army and navy commanders that the location of the Japanese BW program's headquarters was Nanking.

One item disclosed at these meetings would assume special importance to Lieutenant Colonel Sanders later that year; this was a State Department report on the 1939 attempt by Dr. Ryoichi Naito to procure a sample of yellow fever virus from the Rockefeller Institute. In light of the key role Naito played in the Americans' secret postwar response to Japan's BW atrocities, it is worth reviewing the details of that attempt, as disclosed in that State Department account.

The report includes a description of frightening coercion and attempted bribery, which occurred on a rainy New York City morning in February 1939, as a young laboratory technician at the Rockefeller Institute for Medical Research steered his car into the parking area on East 68th Street. His name is given only as Glasounoff; he was at work that Sunday as he was every Sunday, to tend to his primate research duties feeding the laboratory animals and monitoring the body temperatures of disease-infected monkeys. While he walked from his parked car to the building entrance, a stranger approached him, a man he later described as a middle-aged Japanese man. The stranger did not offer his name but said he had something that would be of great interest to the technician, a vital fact that he would share only if Glasounoff were to agree to rendezvous again, at 1 P.M. that afternoon at an inconspicuous site around the corner, near the East River.

At one o'clock, Glasounoff drove to the meeting place. A different Japanese man was there to greet him. Well dressed in a hat, blue suit, and chestnut coat, he was fortyish, with a square mustache in the style of Adolf Hitler or Emperor Hirohito.

He got into Glasounoff's car. He would not disclose his identity but stated that he was working with a distinguished scientist, also unnamed, who was doing important research in Glasounoff's field. This research was being blocked by the lack of a key material, he explained—a certain virus culture unavailable in Japan. The virus he needed was yellow fever, the highly virulent *Asibi* strain of yellow fever, to be exact.

The viral culture was kept locked up in a refrigeration unit at the Rockefeller Institute and handled with caution. The stranger wanted Glasounoff's assistance; as a technician, he might have access to the culture vials. Glasounoff politely refused, telling him he should go through the proper channels and make a request to Dr. Wilbur Sawyer, the Rockefeller Institute director.

The Japanese man replied that such a request would be futile because Sawyer was doing competitive studies in the same area and did not want a Japanese lab to gain an edge. Glasounoff said that he wanted no part of this end-run around his superiors. The Japanese man then offered a bribe of $1,000 cash, an enormous sum in those Depression-era days. Glasounoff refused. Seemingly desperate, the stranger upped it to $3,000.

If the culture was locked in the cooler and could not be accessed, the Japanese man pleaded, couldn't Glasounoff simply draw blood from an infected monkey and deliver the sample to the stranger, waiting here outside? Glasounoff said no. When he moved his arm toward the back of the car, the stranger, perhaps thinking he might be reaching for a weapon, clutched Glasounoff and commanded him to be still. Then he grabbed Glasounoff's car keys, begging for a sample of the deadly virus even as he held the stolen keys. When it became clear that Glasounoff would not reconsider, the stranger jumped out of the car, slammed the door, and made a fast getaway in his own Buick sedan. Glasounoff sped back to work to report the encounter to his bosses at the institute.

The unsuccessful brute force of Glasounoff's harriers from the Epidemic Prevention and Water Purification Corps had been preceded three days earlier by a more conventionally styled visit to the Rockefeller Institute by Dr. Naito. At this time Naito presented a letter of introduction from the Japanese military attaché's office in Washington. The letter identified him as an assistant professor at the Tokyo Army Medical College and stated that he was seeking a sample of unattenuated *Asibi* yellow fever virus for the development of vaccines. Naito was granted an interview with institute director Sawyer. Politely, Sawyer refused Naito's request, basing his refusal on a League of Nations public health protocol that banned the importing of yellow fever virus into any country in Asia, a part of the world where the virus did not naturally exist.

Dr. Naito had arrived with an appropriate enough set of credentials: He was an English-speaking hematologist who had attended graduate school at the University of Pennsylvania in Philadelphia, several years earlier. His letter said that the request for the yellow fever virus had come from the director of a world-renowned infectious disease research institute, the Densenbyo Kenkyu-jo. This institute was a branch of Tokyo Imperial University, a preeminent school that could reasonably be called the Harvard of Japan.

Not mentioned in the letter, of course, was the fact that Naito was at the time also working for his friend Colonel Shiro Ishii, in military-affiliated research at the Tokyo Army Medical College that would take his expertise in hematology and apply it in the commission of unspeakable atrocities, including the planning and execution of germ warfare against civilians, the pumping of horse blood into Chinese prisoners, and the dissection of bacteria-infected prisoners while they were still alive, without anesthesia.

Even after the unsuccessful meeting with Sawyer, Naito returned to the Rockefeller Institute to pester lab workers entering and leaving the building, trying to get information on the institute's stocks of yellow fever at its research station in Brazil. Several scientists reported that Naito mentioned that he had recently returned from Berlin. There, he said, he had studied at the Robert Koch Institute for over a year.

This salient bit of information, included in the State Department report on Naito's visit to the Rockefeller Institute, must have come to the attention of State Department officials and analysts at the Military Intelligence Service of the War Department, usually referred to simply as G-2. A 1940 report on the Naito incident by G-2 stated unequivocally that Japan was attempting to "obtain virulent strains of the yellow fever virus for the purpose of bacteria warfare." Given this assertion, it seems likely that Dr. Naito's ties to the top biologists of Nazi Germany assumed some importance in the minds of American national security officials.

A few months after the March 1945 meetings in which he reviewed the Rockefeller Insititute incident, Lieutenant Colonel Sanders was ordered by General Douglas MacArthur to come to Manila to meet with him, the G-2 chief General Charles Willoughby, and the head of the Scientific Intelligence Surgery and former president of the Massachusetts Institute of Technology, Dr. Karl T. Compton. When Sanders arrived in the Philippines that summer, the atomic bombs had not yet been dropped on Hiroshima and Nagasaki, but MacArthur was already drawing up plans for the U.S. occupation of Japan. MacArthur told Sanders that he had been selected to conduct an on-the-ground assessment of the kinds of BW attacks the Japanese might be launching on U.S. troops as they invaded the main island of Honshu, and that he would be sent to join the American amphibious landings on that first day of battle; a dangerous mission, to say the least, as the Home Island–defending Japanese were expected to put up a ferocious resistance, as they had when the U.S. invaded the Japanese island of Okinawa and the Americans suffered more than 12,000 casualties in battle.

The abrupt end to the war in August resulted in a change of orders for Sanders. Now he was given the peacetime task of assessing what Axis Japan had managed to accomplish in the area of germ warfare, and to identify and interview the top scientists involved. In particular, he was to locate the one called Shiro Ishii, whom G-2 understood to be the mastermind of the program, but otherwise knew little about. Sanders conferred with Compton and Willoughby on what information U.S. intelligence had collectively assembled on Japanese BW, and in September he boarded a ship bound for Japan, together with other experts in various fields—a select group chosen by MacArthur. The men were to help supervise the first phase of the United States military occupation of Japan and to conduct postwar intelligence gathering. One can imagine that Sanders embarked on this ocean voyage with mixed feelings of curiosity and trepidation. He could only guess vaguely at what he might find, but he knew at least that the Japanese doctors had done some terrible things, and he would soon be face-to-face with them and their terrible deeds.

NINE

THE SECRET DEAL

When Sanders's vessel, the USS *Sturgiss*, cruised into the harbor at Yokohama, he immediately found himself relieved of one problem: how to locate the scientists for whom he was searching. Among the first sights that Sanders laid his eyes on was a Unit 731 germ warfare expert rushing toward him on the dock, with a photograph of Sanders in hand and a friendly greeting.

Somehow the veterans of Unit 731 were tipped off to Lieutenant Colonel Sanders's arrival. They sent this expert, a high-ranking Pingfan doctor and member of Ishii's inner circle, to head off Sanders at the pier where the *Sturgiss* had docked and try to arrange a group deal for immunity from war crimes prosecution in exchange for the results of their experiments. This doctor spoke English fairly well—he mentioned that he had studied in America at the University of Pennsylvania. He was none other than Ryoichi Naito. Sanders, in a 1985 interview, recalled that when he "docked in Yokohama, there was Dr. Naito. He came straight toward me. He . . . said that he was my interpreter." This time around, the Ishii Unit's Dr. Naito was to have a great deal more success in his dealings with the Americans.

Sanders invited Naito to a series of one-on-one meetings at his Tokyo office, an almost collegial setting. As the American point man in ferreting out information of Japan's wartime BW activities, Sanders tried to get details on the specific people and places involved, but Naito, whom Sanders recalled as "a very humble and shy person," always evaded giving any direct answers, all the while suggesting that he and a coterie of fellow BW scientists had a secret cache of valuable knowledge, which they would parcel out to the Americans—in return for complete immunity from war crimes prosecution.

Each night after his meeting with Sanders, Naito consulted with various Unit 731 senior staff members to decide what information should be given to or concealed from the Americans, and to resolve how best to steer his discussions and negotiations. Sanders eventually grew impatient with Naito's failure to provide specific content and threatened to bring Soviet interrogators in to explore the BW matter jointly with him. At the mere mention of a Soviet probe, Naito quickly ended his evasive behavior and compliantly produced a detailed chart, in English, of the Japanese bio-war hierarchy. Sanders recalled that "the Japanese exhibited a deadly fear of the Communists and they didn't want them messing around," hence the turnaround in the negotiating game.

Naito's chart included the names of medical institutes and military detachments that had produced germs and animals for BW purposes and their administrative departments. It refers to Ishii's unit as the Boeki-Kyusuibu (Water Purification Unit) of the Kwantung Army, and that was the only place in the chart where a Japanese phrase was used. Together with this chain-of-command illustration, Sanders was given an English language manuscript, which affirmed that the Japanese had been actively researching biological weapons as a potential means of warfare.

However, the text denies that Japan ever used biological warfare, and contains no mention of human experimentation. It implies that germs had never been used on human beings, and advances misinformation and protective lies couched in the form of partial admissions. For example, Naito's manuscript states: "It is true, I dare say, that the Jap. Army had some organization not only for defensive BW, but for active offensive," and goes on to claim, falsely, "General Head Quarter has had no attempt to begin active BW attack to his enemy, before the enemy begin any illegal warfare. As none of the fighting nation (enemy) began such an attack, Japanese Head Quarter had no chance, no reason to use BW."

Still, Sanders was excited. He now had it in writing that the Japanese had been at least involved in the research of "offensive" germ warfare, and Naito's chart of the BW chain-of-command listed the Emperor ("Tenno-Heika") at the top, downward through a hierarchy that included the General Staff, the Bureau of Medical Affairs, and the Kwantung Army, as well as the China Expeditionary Force operating in Central China, and the South Army fighting in southern China, Indochina, and the Pacific theater. Harbin, Peking, Nanking, Canton, and Singapore are cited as locations of offensive BW research work.

Naito's manuscript also revealed the timeline of succession for the chiefs of the "organization [at] Harbin," where the "main part of research work concerning BW was done." Harbin is obviously a reference to the Pingfan BW headquarters, but nowhere in the text is the name Pingfan mentioned. Naito identified Colonel Shiro Ishii as being in charge from 1936 to 1941, Major General Masaji Kitano commanding in 1942 and 1943, then Lieutenant General Shiro Ishii back as the head of the network in 1944 and 1945. The dates were incorrect. Ishii did not resume his command position until March 1945.

Sanders went directly to General MacArthur, who as the Supreme Commander for the Allied Powers was the man principally responsible for Japan's postwar reconstruction. Sanders showed MacArthur the documents that Naito had given him. At the bottom of the final page of Naito's manuscript, Sanders had written in longhand: "I asked Dr. Naito whether prisoners were used as experimental 'guinea pigs.' He 'vows' that this has not been the case." Sanders's use of quotation marks around the word "vows" would seem to indicate either of two possibilities. One, that Sanders was expressing skepticism about Naito's claim of innocence, or two, that Sanders wished to stress to MacArthur that Naito was denying the use of human experiment victims in a way that was strong and emphatic.

MacArthur examined the documents that Naito had given Sanders and decided to grant the Unit 731 veterans' wish. Complete immunity from prosecution and concealment from public disclosure would be granted to BW confessed criminals, in exchange for the documentation of the results of their experiments and germ warfare field operations.

Sanders returned to Naito with news of MacArthur's offer, and the deal was struck. In subsequent meetings, U.S. military interviewers received a flood of information, including many autopsy reports of Chinese and Russian vivisection victims, and thousands of slide samples of human tissues and germ warfare pathogens. "The data came in waves," Sanders recounted. "We could hardly keep up with it."

The information handed over by the Japanese scientists was archived and scrutinized by American BW scientists in the U.S. Army Chemical Corps, both in Japan and at Camp Detrick. Lieutenant General Shiro Ishii remained in hiding in Tokyo until February 1946, when, feeling that MacArthur's immunity offer made it safe for him to surface, he attempted to contact Sanders's office. However, even the U.S. Army could not overlook the fact that Ishii had been the founder and architect of Unit 731 and Japan's BW program, and he was immediately placed under house arrest. Two researchers from Camp Detrick, Lieutenant Colonel Arvo Thompson and Dr. Norbert H. Fell, were sent to interview Ishii at his home.

On January 9, 1947, the Soviets made a formal request of General MacArthur to be allowed to question Ishii and two other top Unit 731 scientists, Colonel Kiyoshi Ota (who had led Unit 731's plague bombing of Changde in November 1941) and Colonel Hitoshi Kikuchi, both of whom had been implicated in germ warfare attacks by Unit 731 officers that the Soviets had already captured and interrogated. MacArthur cabled the Joint Chiefs of Staff in Washington to ask whether the Soviets should be permitted to do so. MacArthur noted in the February 7, 1947, message that the Soviets based their request on the knowledge "that experiments authorized and conducted by above [Ishii, Kikuchi, and Ota] . . . resulted in the deaths of 2000 Chinese and Manchurians."

By this time, decision makers at the highest levels of the Pentagon were already moving to secure for the United States military the exclusive possession of Japanese BW and human experiment information. On January 24, 1947, just thirteen days prior to receiving word from General MacArthur of the Soviet appeal to begin questioning Ishii, Kikuchi, and Ota, the Joint Chiefs of Staff had sent a missive to MacArthur ordering that the appalling revelations made by BW scientists to American interviewers be kept secret both from the public and from the governments of other nations; and not only the Soviet Union but even U.S. allies as well. Referring to the Unit 731 network, this directive stated: "[A]ll intelligence information that may be detrimental to the security of the country or possibly detrimental to the friendly relation between the U.S. and other friendly countries must be held confidential, the release of which must have prior approval from the Joint Chiefs of Staff and if necessary with the consent of the State-War-Navy-Coordinating Committee (SWNCC)." The SWNCC was a combined military–State Department group, headquartered in Washington, D.C., which supervised Japan occupation policy.

On March 21, the Joint Chiefs issued their reply to MacArthur's February 7 cable concerning the Soviets. They told him to accede to the Soviets' request and allow them the interviews, but to this permission they attached the stipulation that Ishii, Kikuchi, and Ota were to be instructed by Americans before their meetings with the Soviets not to divulge any important information on BW, nor discuss their experiences with American interviewers.

To these limitations, MacArthur's headquarters added a delaying tactic, as the U.S. occupation authorities did not allow the Soviet interviews to take place until the middle of May 1947, stonewalling and rebuffing numerous Soviet pleas to immediately convene the meetings. They then insisted on placing American officers in the same room with the Soviet officers as they were asking questions.

In a 1982 interview with the *Japan Times*, Ishii's eldest daughter, Harumi, then fifty-seven years old, remembered the Soviet examination of her father at their house: "One day I was told by the Americans that Russian officers were to visit my father. And they warned me not to betray any hint of the friendliness we had shown the American officers accompanying the Soviets even if we recognized anyone. . . . The Soviet officers visited our home only twice. One was a female soldier who was apparently a stenographer. During their interviews with my father, American officers were present at all times. . . . I presume further requests by the Russians to interview my father were rejected by the Americans."

Harumi also recalled the extensive interviews with Ishii by the scientists from Camp Detrick. She remembered that Colonel Arvo Thompson "said he had come as an emissary for President Truman. He literally begged my father for top-secret data on the germ weapons. At the same time, he emphasized that the data must not fall into the hands of the Russians." She also noted: "I was told that the first thing General MacArthur, supreme commander for the Allied powers, did upon arriving at the Atsugi airfield was to inquire about my father: 'Where is Lt. General Ishii?'"

Ishii told Harumi that he had been able to verify his belief that Japan was ahead of other countries in research on biological warfare by the deferential manner with which the Americans treated him: "by the sort of respect he received from the U.S. experts who asked him technical questions during lengthy interviews," she said.

As the months of interviews went on, the atmosphere of professional respect loosened to become cozy and even festive at times. Ishii's wife, Kyoko, served the American visitors meals, thoughtfully preparing for them both Japanese dishes—sukiyaki, for instance—and the sort of Western fare they had enjoyed back home. The head of G-2, Major General Willoughby, attended a dinner party at the Ishii family's residence in the Shinjuku district of Tokyo, near where Ishii formerly had his biological warfare labs at the site of the Tokyo Army Medical College.

Ishii's second interviewer, Norbert Fell, a Ph.D. in microbiology who headed the "Planning Pilot–Engineering Section" at Camp Detrick, had conducted numerous interviews with other top Japanese BW scientists prior to his first meeting with Ishii on May 8, 1947. These included Ishii's close friend Tomosada Masuda, Kitano, Naito, and Wakamatsu. Fell received a sixty-page compilation report on biological warfare assembled by nineteen Japanese veteran BW scientists, a two-hundred-page report on crop destruction experiments, a piece focusing on bubonic plague experimentation co-authored by ten human experiment experts, and approximately eight thousand slides and photomicrographs that had been spirited out of Unit 731 and its affiliated units in the rush back to Japan before the Soviet takeover, along with some six hundred pages of similarly rescued secret articles on human experiments, germ warfare, and chemical warfare.

In the initial three-day round of meetings with Fell, Ishii declared that he and his colleagues could give the Americans much more of their precious information, but only if he and all others involved in the Japanese military's biological warfare and human experiments were first provided the security of "documentary immunity" from prosecution. Documentary immunity meant giving the guilty parties extra insurance in the form of a written promise. It would enable one of them to point to that document, verifying the immunity deal, in the event that at some point in the future the United States reneged on its promise and failed to shield them from war crimes prosecution.

To this immunity request, Ishii added a job query, and a note of support to America's nascent Cold War fight against communism. Fell reported to G-2 that Ishii told him, in what appears to be a carefully worded short speech: "If you will give me documentary immunity for myself, superiors, and subordinates, I can get all the information for you. I would like to be hired by the U.S. as a biological warfare expert. In the preparation for the war with Russia, I can give you the advantage of my 20 years research and experience."

Fell had already verbally promised immunity to the Japanese bio-war scientists. That was how he had obtained the voluminous outpouring of data from them, along with the first admissions of human vivisection experiments. But Ishii's proposal of a documentary immunity deal now offered the United States the full set of keys to the secret kingdom.

Fell communicated the results of his meetings with Ishii to General MacArthur. He also sent a report to the Pentagon's top official in chemical and biological warfare research, General Alden Waitt, which relayed that Ishii had told him, "My experience would be a useful advantage to the United States in the event of a war with the Soviet Union."

In a May 6, 1947, radio message to the SWNCC in Washington, General MacArthur communicated the request for documentary immunity and urged the policymakers to give Ishii and his associates what they wanted. Said MacArthur: "Additional data, possibly including some statements from Ishii, probably can be obtained by informing Japanese involved that information will be retained in intelligence channels and will not be employed as 'war crimes' evidence . . . complete story to include plans and theories of Ishii and superiors, probably can be obtained by documentary immunity to Ishii and associate."

In his plea, MacArthur even went so far as to cite the living human dissections performed at Pingfan as a particular bonus for America: "Request for exemption [from prosecution] of Unit 731 members. Information about vivisection useful," he advised Washington.

On the matter of documentary immunity, the SWNCC did not issue a response to MacArthur anytime soon. At this time the Tokyo War Crimes Trial was well under way, and it is likely that they were monitoring the proceedings to see what if any revelations of germ warfare or human experiments might surface in court, in full view of the public eye. Instead, they sent two more Camp Detrick experts to Japan, bacteriologists Dr. Edwin V. Hill and Dr. Joseph Victor, to further assess the Japanese BW information that had been provided to Fell, and to conduct more interviews with the top scientists of Unit 731, Unit 100, Unit 1644, and the other bio-war detachments.

In Washington, the SWNCC formulated a policy of protecting Ishii and other BW criminals from prosecution while collecting information on those war crimes that other nations, among them the Soviet Union, and perhaps China, Great Britain, and Australia, as well, would have preferred to publicly prosecute. The SWNCC sent a communiqué in June 1947 to Alva Carpenter, an investigator in MacArthur's Legal Section, asking him to gather "what evidence is now in possession of the U.S. authorities against Ishii or any member of the group for whom he has now requested immunity."

In his response, Carpenter stated that there were "allegations" of Japanese BW and experiments against Chinese people, but that they were "unconfirmed" and based on anonymous notes and hearsay. He indicated that should any other nation bring up these charges, the U.S. military officials could point to a lack of solid evidence that experiments and BW had in fact occurred, and thus defend their decision not to seek prosecution, while covertly collecting for themselves the valuable scientific data to be gleaned from the records of the mass atrocities. Specifically, Carpenter stated: "Legal Section interrogations of the numerous persons concerned with the BW project in China do not reveal sufficient evidence to support war crimes charges. The alleged victims are of unknown identity. Unconfirmed allegations are to the effect that criminals, farmers, women and children were used for BW experimental purposes."

Carpenter's office also cited the possible use of the American military's own people, captured U.S. soldiers, as experiment victims while held as POWs by the Japanese. Legal Section stated that Unit 731 may have performed "experimentation on captured Americans in Mukden and that, simultaneously, research along similar lines was conducted in Tokyo and Kyoto." These allegations were said to have come from sources in the Japanese Communist Party that had been spying on Ishii and his cohorts.

In late 1945 the International Prosecution Section, the body that carried out the Tokyo war crimes trials, began independent of the U.S. military interviewers to investigate the allegations of Japanese germ warfare. The IPS interviewers collected information that Japanese aircraft had disseminated plague-carrying fleas over various places in China in 1940. The IPS investigators soon corroborated the findings of the report made by Dr. Wen-Kwei Chen in 1942. IPS investigators also attained testimony from a

BW criminal then in custody of the Soviets, Major Tomio Karasawa, that Japanese had field-tested typhoid, cholera, and
bubonic plague at the cities of Ningbo and Hangzhou in 1940.
Karasawa had worked in the labs which mass produced the germs
used in these BW attacks. He said that Ishii and all of Unit 731
were under direct orders from the Tokyo General Staff, Japan's
leading generals, to carry out and expand biological warfare testing. He also stated that numerous Manchurian prisoners taken by
the secret police had been killed in grotesque human experiments
to improve the virulence of anthrax and plague bacteria strains,
cultured in their living blood as part of the BW weapons development process.

In Shanghai, on April 17, 1946, a Japanese BW veteran and
defector named Osamu Hataba gave an affidavit for IPS describing
biological warfare he had been involved in, which was carried out
by Unit 1644. The affidavit was delivered to IPS investigator
David Nelson Sutton, an assistant prosecutor for the United States.
The document was titled "Affidavit of Osamu Hataba, on Bacterial
Warfare carried out by Ei 1644 Force in China, 1943." Hataba
stated that the unit "was active in disease application duties at the
front by airplane. The corps had certainly more than two specially
assigned airplanes . . . I know that the above-described inhuman
acts were carried out under the euphemism of 'Holy War,' and I am
one of those that deserted from the corps. Furthermore, in the scientific section they were also carrying out research on poisons."
Hataba, disgusted with Japan's germ warfare and human experiments, had defected from Ishii's Nanking force to the Nationalist
Chinese side during the war (he was one of thousands of Japanese
soldiers to defect during the war, either to Nationalist or Communist Chinese-governed areas).

Another conscience-stricken veteran of Unit 1644, Hasane
Hari, volunteered to write an affidavit that he titled the "Certifi-

cate of Crimes of the Japanese Army." Submitted to the IPS on April 29, 1946, it stated: "the epidemic prevention unit outwardly maintained the health of soldiers as its mission, but actually manufactured germs of cholera, typhoid, bubonic plague, [and] dysentery to be used to attack Chinese soldiers and civilians." Hari's confession also exposed the Nanking unit's collaboration with Ishii in disseminating lethal bacteria in rivers, reservoirs, and wells, and in giving three thousand Chinese POWs dumplings that had been contaminated with typhoid and paratyphoid germs. The dumplings were presented to the POWs as a holiday special treat, and the men were then released early to go back home and spread the diseases to their families and communities.

The IPS attorneys had amassed a collection of solid evidence linking Japanese forces to BW and human experiments. Said Dr. Chen, "an American judge . . . came personally to [Chongqing] to call on me and ask me to give him the Report on the Plague Epidemic at [Changde]. I was also asked to sign a copy of that report [which I did] . . ."

Despite this, they informed General MacArthur's office in December 1946 that IPS would not call for any Japanese military or civilian medical personnel to be prosecuted or called as witnesses to such activities. At the Tokyo war crimes trial, neither Karasawa's, nor Hataba's written testimonies was introduced, or even indexed as relevant documentary material.

More amazing still is the failure of the American IPS attorneys to bring up the issue of the already publicized Zhejiang and Changde plague attacks at the Tokyo war crimes trial. An American physician, Dr. Robert Pollitzer, had been among those looking into the Zhejiang Province aerial plague attacks and had concluded that a germ weapons assault had definitely occurred. On top of this, there had been the February 1939 incident in which Naito's team had badgered the Rockefeller Institute staff for a secure culture of dangerous yellow fever virus. As we know, the State Department had been alerted to this almost immediately after the event.

Exactly why this decision was reached by IPS remains undocumented; however, it is worth noting that the IPS chief prosecutor, Joseph Keenan, consulted closely with General MacArthur throughout the IPS proceedings and evidence-collecting phase. Pressure from MacArthur and the War Department to suppress BW details from the Tokyo trials may have been exerted.

Nevertheless, a brief mention of human experiments at Nanking did emerge at a hearing of the Tokyo war crimes trial, in the form of three short sentences uttered by David Sutton on November 17, 1946.

Sutton had previously headed IPS investigations into the infamous Rape of Nanking atrocities, and he was reading into the court record a document prepared by an attorney of the District Court of Nanking—a heavily censored, edited, and diluted version of Hataba's explicit confessions of conducting Nazi-like medical experiments and bacteriological warfare massacres. Even such a tiny fragment as a three-sentence statement was enough to cause a flurry of anxiety at the Tokyo proceedings and bring them to a sudden halt.

Sutton read, in a passage that was subtitled, "Particulars Regarding Other Atrocities": "The enemy's Tama detachment [another name for Unit 1644] carried off their civilian captives to the medical laboratory, where the reactions to poisonous serums [were] tested. This detachment was one of the most secret organizations. The number of persons slaughtered by this detachment cannot be ascertained."

According to courtroom reporter Arnold Brackman (later to

gain fame as the author of *The Last Emperor*), Sutton continued to read through the next part of the text, which had nothing to do with biological warfare, as if what he had just said were routine and unremarkable. The chief judge, the Australian Sir William Webb, interrupted him.

"Are you going to give us any further evidence of these alleged laboratory tests for reactions to poisonous serums?" Webb asked him pointedly. "That is something entirely new, we haven't heard that before. Are you going to leave it at that?"

Sutton replied, "We do not at this time anticipate introducing evidence on the subject." He continued reading, but was interrupted again, this time by Alfred Brooks, a defense lawyer for two Japanese generals. Brooks worried that it would be risky for such a serious charge to emerge in the court proceeding, even if only in this brief fashion, and he objected to Sutton's mentioning it at all. He implied that the "poisonous serums" might really be just regular inoculations in a kindly public health program the Japanese were providing for the Chinese. Brooks said, "We would like to inquire of the prosecution if this does not consist of a series of vaccines of these people."

Another defense counsel, Michael Levin, attempted to take advantage of the shocking nature of the allegation by trying to spin it as a ridiculous and slanderous charge. It was simply too inhumane to be true.

"I believe the defense ought to have some protection against the use of a document of this character," he told Judge Webb.

Levin's effort was successful. Judge Webb immediately concurred, saying: "The evidence I take you to be objecting to is that referring to tests on Chinese apparently with poisonous materials. Subject to what my colleagues think, that appears to me to be a mere assertion unsupported by any evidence."

Levin then nodded, and added for good measure that prosecutors should uphold ethical standards and be more discreet about raising such disturbing issues as lethal human experimentation or "matters of this kind." When Levin had finished, Webb again stated that he approved of the defense objection and pronounced the court's rejection of anything brought up as evidence that was unsupported.

From this point on, nothing at all relating to Japanese biological warfare, chemical warfare, or human experiments was brought up at the Tokyo trials, which had been billed by the international press as the "Nuremberg Trial of the East." The prosecution continued to sit on the crucial incriminating Hataba and Karasawa statements, and none of the judges of the international tribunal attempted to probe further into such matters.

There was, however, one war crimes tribunal held in Japan that did indict Japanese doctors for conducting lethal human experiments. This was a 1948 trial held at Yokohama for the physician-professors and medical students of Kyushu University who performed vivisection experiments on the eight U.S. fliers who had been captured after parachuting from their shot-down B-29 bomber. It was one of the many trials of the "Class B" and "Class C" Japanese war criminals held by Allied nations at Yokohama, Singapore, Manila, Rabaul, Hong Kong, and elsewhere in the Asia-Pacific region that had come under Japanese control. These trials received much less media attention than that afforded the IMFTE Tokyo trial of the high-ranking "Class A" defendants.

At this little-known trial, an accusation of cannibalism was also made: it was stated in the court indictment that following the vivisections, the prisoners' inner organs "were cooked for a gourmet dinner served in the dining room of the medical faculty of Kyushu University." Cannibalism of war prisoners had become a frequent phenomenon among hungry and desperate Japanese troops in the Pacific cut off from supply lines, and there were also recorded instances of the ritualistic cannibal consumption of the organs of U.S. aerial combatants, especially the liver, which was thought to be a source of the fliers' spiritual energy. When the details of the case are examined, the Kyushu medical faculty's "gourmet dinner" of their experiment victims appears to have had aspects of such ritualism.

On August 27, 1948, the U.S. military court conducting this trial delivered its sentences: two of the Kyushu University professors involved were ordered to be executed by hanging. Others of the accused got prison terms ranging from fifteen to twenty-five years. The two doctors sentenced to be hanged never did go to the gallows: one committed suicide and the other later had his sentence commuted to life imprisonment.

The postwar U.S. Army investigation into the fate of the missing B-29 airmen had been organized by General MacArthur's SCAP headquarters, and the trial at Yokohama had been set up by SCAP's Legal Section. By this time, SCAP personnel, along with many other American government and military officials in occupied Japan, knew the details of Japan's massive wartime human experiment network, and the commonplace army field vivisections of the Chinese. Yet no mention of these thousands of similar lethal experiments was brought up by attorneys at the Kyushu trial. The striking omission of the Unit 731 tests in the Kyushu courtroom duplicated the silence of the Tokyo War Crimes Trial, maintaining the curtain of official U.S. secrecy that had been dropped on the matter to preserve the secret arrangement that the United States made with Ishii and his many medical and scientific co-conspirators.

The only official court action inquiry into the activities of the Unit 731 criminal doctors and military officers came in the Soviet Union, in 1949, when the Soviets put twelve leading Unit 731 and Nanking Unit 1644 officials on trial in the city of Khabarovsk, a city located beside the Amur River, on the Russian border with Manchuria. The twelve had been captured in

Manchuria, when the Soviet forces swept through in August 1945 and discovered the remains of the massive Pingfan BW complex, and the Unit 731 branch units dotting the region at Harbin, Changchun, Mukden, Hailar, Mudanjiang, Songo, Linkow, Dairen, and other places. Unlike Ishii, Naito, and most of the other BW and human experiment perpetrators, these twelve had not had time to escape the Soviet invasion and flee back to the safety of Japan. Also on the stand at Khabarovsk were Japanese army personnel who had participated at lower levels in actions relating to human experimentation and germ warfare but who gave courtroom testimony as witnesses, not as the accused, and so were not subject to prosecution. A partial transcript of this first trial was published in English in 1950, and is still readily available to readers at many American libraries. The following excerpt of the courtroom examination of Major General Kiyashi Kawashima, just one example among many, shows that the public record was filled with proof in the immediate aftermath of the war of Unit 731's deeds.

> **Question:** Will you tell us about the expeditions to China?
>
> **Answer:** I shall first speak of the period when I myself was serving with Detachment 731. In this period, there was one instance in 1941 and another in 1942 when Detachment 731 expeditions employed lethal germs as a weapon against Chinese troops in Central China.
>
> **Question:** Continue your testimony.
>
> **Answer:** The first instance, as I have said, was in the summer of 1941. One day, Colonel Ota, Chief of the 2nd Division, told me that he was going to Central China and said good-bye to me. Some time after his return he told me that plague fleas had been dropped from aircraft on the Chinese in the area of the city of Changde, near Lake Tung Ting Hu, in Central China.

This in effect, was a bacteriological attack, which was the term he used . . .

After this, Colonel Ota made a report to Chief of Detachment 731 Ishii, at which I was present, to the effect that the Detachment 731 expedition had dropped plague fleas from an aeroplane in the Changde area, and that an outbreak of plague epidemic had resulted, a number of persons being stricken with the disease, but how many, I do not know . . .

Question: How many members of Detachment 731 took part in this expedition?

Answer: About 40 or 50.

Question: What technique was used to contaminate localities with plague during the 1941 expedition?

Answer: Dropping fleas from aircraft at a high altitude.

Question: Was this done by dropping bacteria bombs or by spraying the fleas from aircraft?

Answer: By spraying.

At the conclusion of the Khabarovsk trial, in which all twelve of the accused were found guilty and sentenced to labor camp terms varying from two to twenty-five years, the Soviet newspaper *Izvestia* charged that chief prosecutor Joseph Keenan "closed his eyes when, in September 1946, the Soviet prosecution at the Tokyo trial delivered to him, as the main American prosecutor, the evidence of the leading officials of this detachment."

Izvestia further asserted, "This evidence exposed the Japanese militarists in preparation of bacteriological warfare and in bestial experiments performed on living beings." In late December 1949, when the Soviet media announced the guilty verdicts of the just-completed Khabarovsk trial, *Izvestia* ran an article calling for Ishii to be apprehended and tried by the U.S. occupation forces in Japan as the ringleader of the secret Japanese program.

In response, General MacArthur's office in Tokyo denounced

both the Khabarovsk trial and *Izvestia's* charges of Japanese biological warfare and a U.S. cover-up as false communist propaganda.

Perhaps that explains why the Western media at the time took
no notice of the Soviet denunciations. But more than three decades
later, in October 1981, the *Bulletin of the Atomic Scientists* published a
long, well-researched piece by John W. Powell detailing Unit 731
experiments and germ warfare open-air tests on civilian populations. Powell graphically described Ishii's experiments—he
described how dozens of prisoners were tied to stakes in a large
field and were bombarded with shrapnel from anthrax bombs
dynamited at close range, to test their effectiveness. He described
the laboratory infection of Chinese female prisoners with syphilis
to study the disease; he described Naito's horse blood–to–humans
experiments and the killing of prisoners through radiation, their
livers having been exposed to lengthy X-rays. He described the
wide array of deadly diseases used as biological weapons by Japan:
plague, cholera, smallpox, typhus, and typhoid. Powell's article
received wide publicity in the United States and was reported by
wire news services. It also led to a 1982 *60 Minutes* segment on
Unit 731, for which Powell was briefly interviewed.

Printed with Powell's piece in the *Bulletin*, there appeared a
statement by B.V.A. Roling, the last surviving judge from the
Tokyo trials, who represented the Netherlands on the international tribunal. He commented that Powell's exposé was the first
he had heard of Unit 731 and the Japanese BW, and he expressed
a strong sense of revulsion, betrayal, and justice denied.

"As one of the judges in the International Military Tribunal
for the Far East, it is a bitter experience for me to be informed
now that centrally ordered Japanese war criminality of the most
disgusting kind was kept secret from the Court by the U.S. government," Roling wrote.

In a later interview, he added that the United States ought to be "ashamed because of the fact they withheld information from the Court with respect to the biological experiments of the Japanese in Manchuria on Chinese and American prisoners of war."

In Washington at the time of the Tokyo trials, knowledge of the mass atrocities was relayed all the way to the top, while the official silence of the prosecution's legal cover-up continued. IPS evidentiary documents detailing Unit 731 BW and human experiments were stamped to be read by the "Commander-In-Chief" of the U.S. forces and sent in 1947 to President Harry Truman. By then the Tokyo trials already had been under way for seven months. However, no record has surfaced on what Truman thought of the documents he read. He certainly never commented publicly on the matter.

As the Tokyo War Crimes Trial was drawing to a close in March 1948, and it became clear that no more evidence would be accepted in court, the SWNCC at last fulfilled the dearest wish of Ishii and associates, granting them complete documentary immunity.

On March 13, 1948, the War Department cabled its instructions back to MacArthur's Legal Section headquarters in Tokyo: "Permission granted" to immunize in documentary form all Japanese BW and medical atrocity suspects from prosecution. "Information retained from Ishii and associates," they messaged, "may be retained in intelligence channels."

The "Secret of Secrets" of imperial Japan had become America's big secret.

The SWNCC was not without a sense of concern that their actions might someday return to haunt them in the form of public exposure, but it is apparent from the archival records that they displayed no moral reservations whatsoever about what they were doing. Remarked one of the SWNCC decision makers,

Colonel R. M. Cheseldine, in a secret SWNCC subcommittee meeting held in Tokyo:

"This government may at a later date be seriously embarrassed [but we] strongly believe that this information, particularly that which will finally be obtained from the Japanese with respect to the effect of BW on humans, is of such importance . . . that the risk of subsequent embarrassment should be taken."

Scuttling morality and justice for naked technological advantage would in fact give the United States an edge in the Cold War world that was looming on the horizon. As Camp Detrick's Dr. Edwin Hill put it in a December 1947 letter to Alden Waitt, "Evidence gathered in this investigation has greatly supplemented and amplified previous aspects of this field. It represents data which has been obtained by Japanese scientists at the expenditure of many millions of dollars and years of work. . . . Such information could not be obtained in our own laboratories because of scruples attached to human experimentation. These data were secured with a total outlay of Y250,000 [about $700] to date, a mere pittance by comparison with the actual cost of the studies. . . . It is hoped that individuals who voluntarily contributed this information will be spared embarrassment because of it and that every effort will be made to prevent this information from falling into other hands."

TEN

WHAT THE
DEAL BOUGHT

IN THE HISTORY OF JAPAN'S BIOLOGICAL WARFARE OPERATION, the final indignity may be the fate of many of the BW and human experiment leaders after they fled back to Japan in 1945, leaving the Pingfan complex a shell of dynamited ruins and rubble. Not only did they escape war crimes proceedings and public scrutiny by virtue of their cooperation with the U.S. occupation authorities, they also became prominent public health officials and respected academic figures in Japanese university and government circles. A few became quite wealthy as executives of pharmaceutical companies.

This was not surprising, perhaps, given that many of them were top or up-and-coming figures in their scientific fields before and during the war, so the postwar period saw the unhindered continuation of their career paths. Even the twelve doctors and military officers on trial at Khabarovsk were repatriated to Japan in 1956, a year of post-Stalin "liberalization" in the Soviet Union, though one of the Khabarovsk twelve, the army physician Major Tomio Karasawa, committed suicide in 1956 shortly after being granted the freedom to go home.

Why those judged guilty of such horrendous crimes should be treated so leniently—the longest sentence any served was seven years—remains something of a mystery. It has been suggested that the Soviet government, mindful of the American immunity-for-data deal with Ishii, Kitano, and the other Unit 731 principals, thought it necessary to exchange clemency for information and advice in the field of biological warfare research. In the Cold War years the American bio-war researchers, having obtained the knowledge of the most important Japanese BW experts and having much greater funding and resources than the Soviets, enjoyed a significant advantage over the Russians.

Shiro Ishii, the man who started it all, retired to his home in Chiba Prefecture, a short distance from Tokyo, from 1945 until his death in 1959 from throat cancer. He lived to be sixty-seven. The army allowed him to keep his lieutenant general pension, and he received those funds to supplement a bank account already richly endowed with family wealth. Friends and former colleagues in the military and scientific community often came to Ishii's house for visits, while shunning any visible public contact with him. Ishii stayed free, but he had to lie low because he was infamous enough to draw attention, were he to resurface and get a job. It is likely that both the Soviets and the Japan Communist Party were monitoring his activities, and he must have been aware of them as well.

In 1985 Murray Sanders said that he had heard from a friend who was a high-ranking officer employed at Fort Detrick, Maryland, that in the 1950s, Ishii had actually secretly traveled to the United States to lecture at Fort Detrick on how to best conduct germ warfare, drawing from his unparalleled experience in the arena. Sanders left the military in 1946, landing a university teaching position in Florida where he was no longer formally attached to the Detrick labs, so his statement on this must be taken as hearsay. Still, given the fact that the United States employed German scientists with Nazi SS backgrounds after the war in domestic military research labs, there is a disturbing plausibility to the idea that Ishii, the world's leading biological warfare expert, would be brought in to advise the burgeoning U.S. bio-war program. Ishii had, after all, already obtained protection from a council comprised of both State Department officials and the Pentagon's Joint Chiefs of Staff generals. And it is a matter of record that the Pentagon did, in the late 1940s, hire two Nazi doctors to lecture and conduct research at the Air Force School of Medicine in Texas. Both these men, Dr. Kurt Blome and Major General Walter Schreiber, had conducted death camp experiments in which prisoners were killed by plague, typhus, and tuberculosis infection, according to evidence presented at the Nuremberg trial.

In 1982 Ishii's eldest daughter, Harumi, denied that her father had ever lectured in the United States. She also denied a Reuters wire report of 1951 that Ishii, Kitano, Wakamatsu, and other Japanese BW veterans traveled by freighter to South Korea that year, for the purpose of advising the U.S. military in the use of biological warfare against North Koreans and Chinese in the Korean War. In that conflict, the governments of the Democratic People's Republic of Korea, China, and the Soviet Union made public declarations in 1951 and 1952 that the Pentagon was employing germ warfare on a large scale and through a wide variety of methods. The Chinese announced that emergency sanitation and quarantine measures were being enacted in Communist-held territory to stem the spread of such diseases as bubonic plague, smallpox, and anthrax that were disseminated from U.S. military planes. They showed footage and photographs of metallic U.S. shells, similar in appearance to the U.S. leaflet-releasing bombs, which, witnesses claimed, snapped their hinges upon hitting the ground and released a swarming cargo of insects.

The film shows numerous small spiders streaming out of one

such bomb, onto a snowbank, in the middle of winter. Chinese and North Korean investigators likewise reported finding dense black clusters of fleas huddling together in the snow. Both events are impossible unless the cold-shunning creatures had been bred indoors, out of their normal seasonal life cycle, and artificially dropped out in the chilly environment by man. An international scientific investigating team, headed by an esteemed British bio-chemist, Cambridge University professor, and scholar of Chinese history Joseph Needham, was invited by the Communists to come to Korea, do research, and issue a report on the BW claims. Needham agreed that the sudden appearances of insects and spi-ders, of species not normally known to the region, in winter, and in association with the dropping of strange containers and objects by U.S. military planes (an oddity reported by many Korean vil-lagers and urban residents) constituted strong evidence of bio-warfare. In the 700-page scientific report issued by his Independent Scientific Commission (ISC), Needham wrote, "Such a witch's sabbath was certainly not called together by any natural means."

Laboratory tests that were performed on fleas discovered in such odd circumstances, or fleas dropped from airplanes, posi-tively showed the presence of bubonic plague bacteria. In one dramatic instance of a plague rodent aerial drop, the entire village of Kan-Nan in Northeast China awoke on the morning of April 5, 1952, to discover a large number of dead and dying voles lit-tering their rooftops, courtyards, and even in their homes and beds. The voles (similar in appearance to mice) appeared quite sick. The Kan-Nan villagers gathered all the voles together and burned them, except for one live and ailing vole, which they gave to Chinese scientists. The Chinese reported to the ISC that this vole tested positive for plague. Moreover, the people of Kan-Nan and the Chinese Air Observer Corps had noted a low-flying American F-82 night-fighter plane soaring overhead at about

11:30 P.M. the night before the vole discovery. The ISC report noted that the village was located in an area of China that had been experiencing overflights by U.S. warplanes on a near daily basis, and might have become a prime target for experimental disease contamination by the Americans.

In the autumn of 1952 Needham and the dozen other highly respected (and politically left-leaning) ISC scientists from Sweden, Italy, Brazil, France, and the Soviet Union issued a unanimous statement of support for the BW accusations against the United States, after completing a lengthy investigation. The Soviet member of the team had served as a court biomedical consultant at the Khabarovsk trial. In the course of the investigations, the ISC team met with captured American fliers who had confessed publicly and in great detail about their planes' scattering of germ bombs across North Korea. Their confessions appeared to be given without undue duress, threat, or coercion on the part of their captors, and the men appeared to be in adequate health. The team also interviewed many ordinary Korean citizens in the course of traveling across North Korea, and near the ongoing battles of the shifting Korean North-South frontlines. They also visited areas in northeastern China (the former Manchuria). Here, the Chinese reported other BW attacks in addition to the Kan-Nan plague voles incident. In some cases, U.S. military jets, usually F-86 fighters, had flown over from across the Korean border and dropped masses of fowl feathers tainted with anthrax. Chinese residents in the area had contracted and died from the extremely rare disease of respiratory anthrax after coming in contact with the feathers, and the ISC presented these anthrax cases as further convincing evidence that a U.S. bio-war campaign was underway.

Interestingly, Joseph Needham had been in Chongqing for the 1942 press conference announcing the aerial plague attack at Changde by a Japanese plane. At that time, Needham had sent a message to British military officials in London stating his belief that Changde had indeed been the victim of a germ warfare attack by Japan. His opinion was received skeptically by leading British BW researchers back home. Ten years later Needham found himself in Korea, observing the U.S. military engaging in modes of germ warfare that were reminiscent of Japanese techniques. He noted the findings of porcelain shells fragmented on the ground that were said to have released plague fleas and flies that tested positive for cholera bacteria. Such delivery systems, along with anthrax-containing feathers, were identical to methods confirmed to have been used by the Japanese against China, as was revealed in testimony at the Khabarovsk trial.

In the ISC report Needham and fellow commission members cite by name Shiro Ishii as being a prominent biological warfare perpetrator who was alive and well in Japan, and "unfortunately himself not in the dock" at Khabarovsk, having escaped prosecution as a war criminal. The report further speculates that Ishii may have been working with the U.S. Army to conduct BW operations. The report notes Shiro Ishii's possible involvement in Korean War germ warfare: "Whether occupation authorities in Japan had fostered [Ishii's] activities and whether the American Far East Command was engaged in making use of methods essentially Japanese were questions which could hardly be absent from the minds of members of the Commission."

The germ warfare allegations were brought to the attention of the United Nations Security Council by the Soviet Union, whose representatives wanted the UN to officially condemn the United States for using BW, and to demand that it ratify the Geneva Convention of 1925. (At the time of the Security Council furor in 1952 the United States and Japan remained the last major countries not to ratify the biological weapon–banning treaty—Japan finally ratified it in 1970, the United States did so in 1975.) U.S. officials strongly and indignantly denied all allegations that it was committing biological warfare, and were supported in that denial by the United Kingdom and the nations of Western Europe. The charges were roundly dismissed in the Western media, and the majority of the American public scoffed at the idea that their military would commit germ warfare, finding it too outrageous to be anything other than a propaganda attempt by the Soviets, Soviet-allied nations, and their left-wing sympathizers.

In 1956 journalist John W. Powell, who helped bring the long-suppressed facts of the Unit 731 experiments to light in the early 1980s with his *Bulletin of the Atomic Scientists* piece, was charged, along with his wife, Sylvia Powell, and his editorial assistant Julian Schuman, with thirteen counts of sedition. Their alleged crime? Reporting from Shanghai, during the Korean War, that the allegations of U.S. biological warfare attacks were true. Powell's 1952 article in the English language *China Monthly Review* stated: "the American invaders, by a systematic spreading of smallpox, cholera and plague germs over North Korea have shocked and horrified the entire world. Since VJ Day Japanese war criminals turned into 'experts' have been working for the Americans in developing bacteriological warfare."

When Powell returned home to San Francisco in January 1953, he found himself the target of FBI Director J. Edgar Hoover's fury, and at Hoover's urging the McCarthy-era Justice Department brought Powell before congressional committees ferreting out "un-American activities" like publicly supporting the Korean War BW accusations.

But after formal grand jury charges were brought against the Powells and Schuman on April 25, 1956, the government's case against them soon began to sputter. After their defense lawyers began subpoenaeing the State Department, CIA, and other agencies for documents they thought would show that the United States had in fact used biological weapons, the prosecution came under pressure from the Department of Defense to back off the case altogether. In 1961 the trial was dropped, along with all investigations, on an order from President John F. Kennedy.

In Western Europe, newspapers and magazines ran vivid articles laden with photos of the alleged U.S. germ bombs and their insect cargos. In France, *Ce Soir*, a pro-communist journal, ran a cover story titled "La Guerre Bacteriologique en Corée et en Chine"—"The Bacteriological War in Korea and China"—with a close-up photograph of flies that were said to have been coated with deadly bacteria and dropped on Koreans. The alleged releases of anthrax and cholera-smeared flies were some of the accusations against the U.S. military, a BW method reminiscent of the cholera Yagi type fly-releasing bombs that had been dropped by the Japanese over Yunnan Province and killed more than 200,000. *L'Humanité*, the newspaper of the French Communist Party, ran numerous articles on the "monstrous" U.S. bio-war attacks, and featured denunciatory statements against the American germ warfare from Chinese Premier Chou En Lai and Nobel Prize–winning physicist Frédéric Joliot-Curie.

To this day the Korean War BW allegations against the Pentagon remain a controversial and little known episode in the history of the Cold War. Scientists and historians in Russia, China, and North Korea continue to maintain that the charges are true, and U.S. military historians continue to deny them. Yet an increasing number of journalists and documentary makers in Germany, South Korea, and Japan are even now producing investigative reports that support the charges and include interviews with Koreans who were allegedly witnesses to American BW attacks.

While the United States, following its immunity deal with Ishii and company in the 1940s, continued to throw a veil of Cold War secrecy over the Unit 731 story into the 1950s and beyond, the principal figures of Pingfan and the other experimental death camps were able to move around openly in postwar Japanese society. Their postwar careers read like a litany of enviable professional achievements.

Dr. Tachiomaru Ishikawa, once a pathologist at Pingfan who shared thousands of Unit 731 slides and specimens with Camp Detrick researchers after the war, became president of the prestigious Kanazawa University Medical School in the 1970s. Dr. Toru Ogawa, who worked at the Nanking 1644 unit developing strains of paratyphoid and typhoid germs to use in the unit's BW attacks, obtained a research position at Nagoya Prefecture Medical University. Dr. Kanau Tabei, who had forced one Pingfan prisoner to suffer the explosion of bacteria-tainted buckshot and others to drink typhoid-laced milk, was invited to join the faculty of elite Kyoto University (the former "Kyoto Imperial University") as a professor of bacteriology. Dr. Hisato Yoshimura, the leader of Unit 731's frostbite experiments, became the president of the Japan Meterological Society in 1973, and led research expeditions into Antarctica in the 1960s and 1970s, where he conducted scientific studies, using voluntary human subjects, on the effects of extreme cold on human physiology, some of which were published in peer-reviewed medical journals. He also became a corporate consultant to a Japanese packaged frozen-fish food company. Like Tabei, Yoshimura also held a professorial position at Kyoto University, in the medical college.

A number of Unit 731 and Unit 100 veterans also rose through the ranks of the major Japanese public health organization, the Japan National Institutes of Health. Major General Yujiro Wakamatsu, the former leader of the Unit 100 laboratory death camp and BW bacteria mill at Changchun, conducted JNIH research into streptococcus bacteria infections of young children in Japan. One is struck by the fact that at Unit 100, Wakamatsu and his teams specialized in diseases that might cross over from horses to infect humans, and that virulent streptococcus infections in horses are a frequent problem for stablehands. The strep bacterial infection is called "strangles" when it manifests in horses. One wonders how Wakamatsu's wartime human-and-horse experiments informed him in his postwar NIH human research.

The Midori Juchi ("Green Cross"), a Japanese pharmaceutical company with more than $1 billion in assets and offices worldwide, including in New York City and Los Angeles, was founded and directed shortly after the war by three of the principal Unit 731 organizers of germ warfare and horrific human biomedical experiments, the physicians Hideo Futaki, Masaji Kitano, and Ryoichi Naito. The company was formed in 1947 by the trio under the name of Japan Blood Plasma Company, and secured an early lucrative contract with the U.S. Army in 1950, supplying blood to American medical units in Korea. In 1982, the year of Naito's death, the Green Cross created the Ryoichi Naito Foundation for Medical Research in honor of the blood expert Naito, who had continued on as the chief executive of the company until he died. To this day the Osaka-based Naito foundation dispenses millions of dollars in funds for applied research in blood products and cellular proteins that might be of profit to the company. The corporation's focus on blood research is striking, given the gruesome animal-to-human blood experiments Naito conducted on his victims in the chambers of Unit 731.

The past came back to haunt the principals of the Green Cross in the late 1980s and 1990s, when it was revealed that the company had sold HIV-tainted blood products that transmitted AIDS to hemophiliac people in Japan, the United States, and South Korea. The Green Cross had processed and sold unheated blood and blood-derived compounds, apparently ignoring AIDS-screening sterilization procedures that had been put in place by the government.

The AIDS victims of that screening failure, numbering more

than 2,000 in Japan and the United States, sued the company in Japanese civil courts, and in the process of discovery the Unit 731 pasts of some of the company officials came to light.

The blood scandal dragged on for several years in Japan; eventually the company was forced to pay millions in damages and three company executives were sent to prison. However, the scandal received only limited coverage in the Western media, which, unlike the Japanese media, nearly always failed to discuss the matter of Unit 731 veterans involved, or to include relevant background details on what Unit 731 did and the history of Japanese germ warfare and human experimentation.

In 1998 the Green Cross changed its name to Midori Pharmerica, then in 1999 to the Welfide Corporation, and in October 2001 it merged with the pharmaceutical branch of the Mitsubishi Corporation. The adverse publicity from the AIDS–Unit 731 scandal had forced a drastic curtailment of its operations and even made necessary the hiding of its very identity from the public. Still, the Green Cross lives on even now as a distinct corporate entity within the enormous Mitsubishi conglomerate, one of the zaibatsu corporations.

On August 30, 2002, the Tokyo District Court delivered its verdict in the lawsuit led by Wang Xuan and 180 Chinese plaintiffs, initially filed in 1997 on behalf of themselves and 2,100 people the plaintiffs' legal team had confirmed as being killed by Japanese germ warfare in various localities across China.

The court's decision was expected, but it was still shocking. The judges ruled that Japan would neither formally apologize nor give any compensation to the plaintiffs. The judges based their ruling on the court's reading of agreements made between Japan and China in 1972, when the two nations restored diplomatic relations. The 1972 Japan-China Joint Communique and China-Japan Treaty of Peace and Friendship stated that China would give up its claims for compensation from Japan involving wartime-related damages; therefore, the Tokyo judges wrote, the victims of Japanese wartime germ warfare could not be awarded. These 1972 accords have been cited by Japanese judges in lawsuits for damages from various other war crimes. They have used them as the basis for refusing damage awards to former slave laborers, "comfort women" sex slaves, and former prisoners of war of Imperial Japan.

The verdict announcement was paradoxical in that the judges agreed that the Chinese plaintiffs' accusations were true, and that Japan had in fact committed the heinous acts of germ warfare. It was the first such formal admission of biological warfare crimes from a Japanese court.

The 180 Chinese victims vow to press on with the case. On May 20, 2003, they filed an appeal to the Tokyo High Court. Their attorneys have stated: "We, as the defense team, with the plaintiffs and support groups, are determined to fight in court until we win a trial."

Their appeal continues.

ENDNOTES

CHAPTER ONE: A DOCTOR'S VISION

1 **It began in Kyoto in 1927** Kei'ichi Tsuneishi and Tomizo Asano, "The Bereaved Family" in *The Bacteriological Unit and the Suicide of Two Physicians* (Tokyo: Shincho-Sha, 1982).

2 **Titled the "Protocol for the Prohibition . . ."** Robert Harris and Jeremy Paxman, *A Higher Form of Killing* (New York: Hill and Wang, 1982), p. 45.

3 **Ishii pleaded with them to begin researching** Sheldon Harris, *Factories of Death: Japanese Biological Warfare, 1932–45, and the American Cover-Up* (London: Routledge, 1994), p. 18.

4 **Furthermore, a remarkably high level of concern** Yuki Tanaka, *Hidden Horrors: Japanese War Crimes in World War II* (Boulder, Colo.: Westview Press, 1996), pp. 72–74; Hal Gold, *Unit 731 Testimony* (Tokyo: Yenbooks, 1996), pp. 17–21.

5 **He was born on June 25, 1892, to a wealthy family** Peter Williams and David Wallace, *Unit 731: Japan's Secret Biological Warfare in World War II* (New York: Free Press, 1989), p. 5.

6 **Professor Ren Kimura, Ishii's Ph.D. adviser** Kei'ichi Tsuneichi and Tomizo Asano, "The Ishii Bacteriological Warfare Unit" in *The Bacteriological Unit and the Suicide of Two Physicians* (Tokyo: Shincho-Sha, 1982).

8 **Former army major general Chiso Matsumura** Kei'ichi Tsuneishi, chap. 1 in *The Germ Warfare Unit That Disappeared: Kwantung Army's 731st Unit* (Tokyo: Kai-mei-sha Publishers, 1981).

9 **Throughout his life Ishii proved himself prone** Sheldon Harris, *Factories of Death*, p. 33.

9 **When he returned to civilian life and Kyoto Imperial University in 1924** Williams and Wallace, *Unit 731*, pp. 5–6.

10 **The paper was coauthored with a childhood friend** Sheldon Harris, *Factories of Death*, pp. 18–19.

11 These were younger, more hawkish, and more adventurous Saburo Ianega, "The Beginning: Aggression in China," chap. 4 in *The Pacific War 1931–1945* (New York: Pantheon Books, 1978), *passim*.

12 "Our power will naturally have to extend . . ." Ibid., p. 75.

12 "Biological warfare must possess distinct possibilities . . ." Harris, *Factories of Death*, p. 19.

13 General Nagata is also known as one of the collaborators Ianega, *Pacific War 1931–1945*, pp. 59–61.

14 The other patron who became instrumental in Ishii's success was Colonel Chikahiko Koizumi Williams and Wallace, *Unit 731*, pp. 8–9.

17 Ishii's Tokyo research facilities expanded quickly Tanaka, *Hidden Horrors*, p. 136.

17 "There are two types of bacteriological warfare research . . ." Harris, *Factories of Death*, p. 21.

18 Lieutenant Colonel Ishiwara, one of the main plotters of the September 18 Mukden Incident, had written Ianega, *Pacific War 1931–1945*, p. 12.

19 With the Mukden Incident in 1931, Japanese army divisions Rana Mitter, *The Manchurian Myth* (Berkeley and Los Angeles: University of California Press, 2000), *passim*.

CHAPTER TWO: FORTRESS OF FEAR

21 a 1935 census estimated its population Harris, *Factories of Death*, p. 6.

21 the South Manchurian Railway maintained five lines Mitter, *The Manchurian Myth*, p. 42.

22 provided Major Ishii with the generous sum of 200,000 yen Williams and Wallace, *Unit 731*, p. 15.

22 Harbin was inhabited by 240,000 Han Chinese Ibid., p. 14.

22 The army had established Ishii's station in an abandoned sake distillery Harris, *Factories of Death*, p. 25.

24 The Kwantung Army officer charged with overseeing Ishii Saburo Endo, *The Fifteen Years War Between Japan and I* (Tokyo: Niccho Sorin, 1974), p. 162.

25 The central edifice in the camp, called the Zhong Ma Fortress Gold, *Unit 731 Testimony*, pp. 34–35.

26 "When construction started . . ." Ibid., p. 35.

26 Within a year of breaking ground at Beiyinhe Harris, *Factories of Death*, pp. 35–36.

29 "Ishii told me that he had experimented on cholera and plague . . ." "Statement of Major Karasawa Tomio," Record Group 331, Doc. 9306, National Archives, p. 10.

30 In 1933 he invited Lieutenant General Saburo Endo to inspect James Yin, *The Rape of Biological Warfare* (San Francisco: Northpole Light, 2001), p. 7; Harris, *Factories of Death*, pp. 27–28.

34 A year later the popular movie *The Island of Lost Souls* John Baxter, *Science Fiction in the Cinema*, (New York: Paperback Library, 1970), pp. 46–47.

35 That night, a prisoner named Li Gold, *Unit 731 Testimony*, pp. 37–38.

36 One of those men who made it out safely Interview with Han Xiao, Changde, People's Republic of China, December 8, 2002.

CHAPTER THREE: THE END OF HUMANITY
37 By the middle of 1935 the Beiyinhe complex Interview with Han Xiao, Changde, People's Republic of China, December 8, 2002.

37 An order by Emperor Hirohito himself *Materials on the Trial of Former Servicemen of the Japanese Army Charged with Manufacturing and Employing Bacteriological Weapons* (Moscow: Foreign Languages Publishing House, 1950), p. 104.

37 Ishii quietly contracted with a Tokyo corporation Harris, *Factories of Death*, p. 47.

38 Yue Zhen Fu, who worked as a coolie laborer Han Xiao, "Compilation of Camp Unit 731 Fascist Savage Acts" in *Unforgettable History* (Harbin, 1985).

39 One former laborer told an American *Dateline NBC*, NBC television, August 15, 1995.

39 Another Pingfan worker, Fang Zhen Yue Han Xiao, *Unforgettable History*.

39 Heroin and opium had been legalized Arnold C. Brackman, *The Other Nuremberg: The Untold Story of the Tokyo War Crimes Trial* (New York: William Morrow, 1987), pp. 190–195.

40 Divisions 1, 3, and 4 *Materials on the Trial*, pp. 9–13.

41 "formed by command of the Emperor of Japan Hirohito . . ." Ibid., p. 104.

44 "The results of the effects of infection . . ." Gold, *Unit 731 Testimony*, p. 44.

45 "As soon as the symptoms were observed . . ." Ibid.

45 Pingfan's facilities included world-class microbiology laboratories Harris, *Factories of Death*, pp. 47–48.

46 In a 1946 postwar interview with an American Doc. No. 29510, April 3, 1947, General Headquarters, Supreme Commander for the Allied Powers, Military Intelligence Section, General Staff, Allied Translator and Interpreter Section, National Archives.

47 In 1989 construction workers Articles by Kawazuki Kawamura; Shinjuku Ward assembly member; and Torii Yasushi, Secretary General of Research Group on Shinjuku

Human Bones Issue, in *Hidden Holocaust in World War II by the Japanese Army* (Tokyo: Kei-ichiro Ichinose, 1998), pp. 81–84.

47 These were Ishii's family members Williams and Wallace, *Unit 731*, p. 31.

47 The prison blocks were in a three-story edifice *Materials on the Trial*, pp. 117, 250–51.

49 From the Japanese official line Ibid.

49 Technician Yoshio Shinozuka, who participated in several Statement of Yoshio Shinozuka, "Unit 731: A Killing Factory," in *Hidden Holocaust in World War II*, pp. 13–14.

51 In 1997 the technician Yoshio Shinozuka Ibid., p. 14.

51 Whenever the victim died before a live dissection Harris, *Factories of Death*, p. 63.

52 a baby who had died of smallpox *Unit 731 Is Alive*, KBS television documentary, 1997 (English language dubbing and subtitles. Produced by W.H. Lee.), South Korean television.

52 One Unit 731 veteran Nicholas Kristof, "Japan Confronts a Gruesome Wartime Atrocity," *New York Times*, March 17, 1995, p. A17.

53 "Someone asked me whether I had seen any women . . ." Gold, *Unit 731 Testimony*, "Civilian Employee of Unit 731 in Tokyo" statement, p. 218.

54 Nishino has underscored the particular abuse Article by Rumiko Nishino in *Hidden Holocaust in World War II*, p. 90.

54 In December 1994 Nishino delivered a disturbing Ibid., p. 159.

54 "She had several fingers missing . . ." Ibid., pp. 165–66.

54 One Russian woman was pregnant *Materials on the Trial*, p. 117.

55 "At first we infected women with syphilis . . ." Gold, *Unit 731 Testimony*, pp. 163–64.

56 Unit 731 researcher Dr. Kanau Tabei Harris, *Factories of Death*, p. 65 (citing the U.S. military report). An account of Tabei's experiment was also given at the 1949 Khabarovsk war crimes trial by the witness Furuichi: See *Materials on the Trial*, pp. 16, 355–56, 432.

58 This kind of biological friendly fire "Japanese Preparations for Bacteriological Warfare in China," POW interrogation report, HQ, USAF, China Theater, Office of the AC of S, G-2, December 12, 1944, Group 319, National Archives.

58 The case of Colonel Takeo Tachibana *Materials on the Trial*, pp. 362–65.

59 Colonel Tadashi Tamura, chief of the personnel division Ibid., pp. 153–54.

60 The sinister-looking dark Dodge vans Russell Working and Bonna Chernyakova, "The Martyrs of Harbin: the 20th Century's Forgotten Villains," *Moscow Times*, April 27, 2001.

61 Miou Yutaka was a former member Gold, *Unit 731 Testimony*, p. 31.

61 "My father, who ran a photography studio . . ." From "Suo Pei" group court witness testimonies, in "Just Compensation to the Chinese War Victims" publication of the Society to Support the Demands of Chinese War Victims, 1999, Tokyo, Japan.

62 under the general heading of "SPIES (saboteurs)" Gold, *Unit 731 Testimony*, pp. 165–67.

63 the category of "Ideological Criminals . . ." Ibid. See also p. 363.

63 Unit 731 veteran Ishibashi Williams and Wallace, *Unit 731*, p. 36.

CHAPTER FOUR: SCIENCE SET FREE

65 He mastered the skills of flying and personally piloted *Materials on the Trial*, pp. 287–88; Harris, *Factories of Death*, p. 58.

65 the Anda open-air proving grounds Ibid., pp. 17, 371.

66 "Ishii was like a god to us, and we thought . . ." *Dateline NBC*, NBC television, August 15, 1995.

66 "Ishii, the unit leader, was an exalted . . ." Gold, *Unit 731 Testimony*, p. 179.

67 noted that the strain of plague seemed to be stronger Wang Xuan, personal communication.

68 and is the disease that in March 1945 killed Anne Frank Irma Menkel, "I Saw Anne Frank Die: By Holocaust Survivor Irma Menkel," *Newsweek*, July 21, 1997.

68 into two types of scientific activity: defensive research and offensive research Harris, *Factories of Death*, p. 59.

69 In a Pingfan cholera vaccine-development experiment Xiao, "Compilation of Camp Unit 731 Fascist Savage Acts."

70 while both primates, have distinct physiological markers *Unit 731 Is Alive*, KBS television documentary, 1997 (English-language dubbing), South Korean television.

70 One case written by Dr. Masaji Kitano and Dr. Shiro Kasahara Williams and Wallace, *Unit 731*, pp. 38–40. See also Shiro Ishii's journal article, "Studies on Song-go fever," *Japan Army Medical Journal* 355 (1942), pp. 1755–58. This article and two by Kitano and Kasahara are cited as reference literature in a 1981 article in the American medical journal *Infectious Immunology*—without an explanation that the subjects were not monkeys but actually human death camp prisoners. That article is "Korean Hemorrhagic Fever Virus" by the South Korean team of Lee et al., *Infectious Immunology* 31 (1981), 337. (Thanks to Greg Rodriquez, Jr., for the article.)

71 Prisoners would be given tainted tools, utensils, and cloth Harris, *Factories of Death*, p. 62.

72 Lethal anthrax sweets were also Ibid., p. 77.

72 in rows of specially designed ovens Ibid., p. 60.

72 Kiyoshi Kawashima, the former chief of Division 4 *Materials on the Trial*, pp. 253–54.

73 In 1994 a Unit 731 veteran described a scene Gold, *Unit 731 Testimony*, p. 181.

74 One such shell, called the HA bomb Report of Scientific Intelligence Survey in Japan, November 1, 1945, Record Group 165, National Archives.

74 Another type of steel bomb was called the Uji Ibid., Harris, *Factories of Death*, pp. 60–61.

74 On the assembly lines, clay and water *Materials on the Trial*, pp. 374–75.

76 Unit 731's "Mother and Daughters" bomb system Doc. No. 29510, April 3, 1947, General Headquarters, Supreme Commander for the Allied Powers, Military Intelligence Section, General Staff, Allied Translator and Interpreter Section, National Archives; Harris, *Factories of Death*, pp. 60–61.

77 The massive toll on innocent human lives Yin, *Rape of Biological Warfare*, passim.

77 The number of people killed at Pingfan *Materials on the Trial*, p. 257.

78 experiments conducted by Unit 731 that make the mind reel Accounts of these experiments can be found in the 1997 KBS documentary *Unit 731 Is Alive*, and in the landmark article by John W. Powell, "Japan's Biological Weapons: 1930–1945," *Bulletin of the Atomic Scientists*, October 1981.

79 "Professional people, too, like to play," Gold, *Unit 731 Testimony*, p. 57.

80 Yoshimura's frostbite experiments on the inmates *Materials on the Trial*, p. 289.

81 The optimum temperature of the water Kristof, "Japan Confronts a Gruesome Wartime Atrocity" *New York Times*, March 17, 1995, p. A17.

81 Equally cruel were the experiments Williams and Wallace, *Unit 731:Japan's Secret Biological Warfare in World War II*, p. 49.

81 Former medical orderly Naokato Ishibashi described Ibid., pp. 47–48.

83 seventy-three-year-old former military bio-war training leader Toshimi Mizobuchi told *Dateline NBC*, August 6, 1995, NBC television.

83 "He had performed vivisections on six living women," Gold, *Unit 731 Testimony*, p. 162.

CHAPTER FIVE: WORLDS COLLIDE

86 one military admonition against well poisoning Roman proverb quotation appears on p. 18 of Jeanne McDermott, *The Killing Winds* (New York: Arbor House, 1987). Citation of well-poisoning through the use of animal carrion by the Romans and other ancient nations in *The Problem of Chemical and Biological Warfare, Volume I*, Stockholm International Peace Research Institute (SIPRI) (Almqvist & Wiksell, Stockhom, 1971), pp. 214–15.

88 In 1346 an army of Crimean Tartars besieged Ibid., *The Problem of Chemical and Biological Warfare, Volume I*, p. 215.

89 The instigator was Sir Jeffrey Amherst Ibid.

92 George Washington warned his troops not to enter Boston Gladys Thum and Marcella Thum, *Persuasion and Propaganda in War and Peace* (Evanston, Ill.: McDougal, Little and Co., 1974), pp. 39–40.

92 brewer named Louis Pasteur observed Major Arthur H. Bryan and Charles Bryan, *Principles and Practice of Bacteriology* (New York: Barnes and Noble, 1940), p. 7.

93 German physician Robert Koch Ibid., p. 8.

94 Japanese bacteriologist Hideo Noguchi isolated pure cultures Ibid., pp. 9–10.

94 a number of Japanese military advances Marius B. Jansen, *The Making of Modern Japan* (Cambridge, Mass. and London: Harvard University Press, 2000), pp. 439–42.9

95 Among them was Mark Twain "Battle Hymn of the Republic Brought Down to Date" in *Mark Twain on the Damned Human Race*, edited by Janet Smith (New York: Hill and Wang, 1962).

96 killed as war continued on into the 1920s Leon Wolff, *Little Brown Brother: How the United States Purchased and Pacified the Philippine Islands at the Century's Turn* (Garden City, N.Y.: Doubleday, 1961), passim.

96 its harsh suppression of the Korean peninsula Ianega, *Pacific War 1931–1945*, pp. 156–58.

97 in 1853, when a surprise gunboat flotilla Jansen, *Making of Modern Japan*, pp. 275–78.

98 This arrangement, known as the Tokugawa Shogunate Ibid., chap. 4, "Status Groups," passim.

101 without violating the tenets of international law Tanaka, *Hidden Horrors*, p. 194.

102 More than two dozen POW camps were established, Ibid., pp. 72–73, 194, 211.

102 "described in exciting detail how our brave and loyal soldiers . . ." Ianega, *Pacific War 1931–1945*, pp. 6–7.

103 a "people's rights" movement vigorously fought, Ibid., pp. 13–16.

103 "Kimishin tamau koto nakare" Ibid., p. 16. This poem's title appears in several different translation forms in the English language versions.

105 the Western Front of World War I, at Ypres, Belgium SIPRI, *The Problem of Chemical and Biological Warfare, Volume I*, pp. 29–31.

106 A year later, Haber actually won a Nobel Prize Harris and Paxman, *A Higher Form of Killing*, pp. 10–11.

107 This treaty sought to establish many rules for the conduct of war Ibid., p. 5.

107 the first accounts of the Ypres battle published *Times of London*, April 26, 1915.

110 noted that cultures of the glanders bacterium SIPRI, *Problem of Chemical and Biological Warfare, Volume I*, pp. 216–17.

CHAPTER SIX: THE GATHERING STORM
114 Prime Minister Fumimaro Konoe and the Foreign Ministry Ianega, *Pacific War 1931–1945*, p. 38.

115 a network of satellite sub-unit bases Yin, "The Route to Crimes" in *Rape of Biological Warfare*, passim.

116 Unit 100 covered an area of twenty square kilometers and included Yin, *Rape of Biological Warfare*, p. 10.

117 there was a major famine in Henan Province Jean Chesneaux, Marianna Bastid, and Marie-Claire Bergere, *China: From the 1911 Revolution to Liberation*, vol. 2 (New York: Pantheon, 1977), p. 275.

117 Buildings on the Unit 100 grounds contained *Materials on the Trial*, pp. 312–31.

118 Two thick sets of Unit 100 victim autopsy reports "Report of A" and "Report of G" details from Harris, *Factories of Death*, p. 94; except for the "micro-level" details on anthrax, found in Yin, *Rape of Biological Warfare*, p. 37.

120 Chinese peasants out in the fields planting Harris, *Factories of Death*, p. 86.

120 Kazuo Mitomo, who assisted in the mass production *Materials on the Trial*, pp. 322–25.

121 The events leading up to the December 1937 Rape of Nanking Chesneaux, Bastid, and Bergere, *China*, pp. 260–62.

122 The hospital, a landmark in the city because Gold, *Unit 731 Testimony*, p. 150; Harris, *Factories of Death*, p. 105.

123 he appointed his friend from childhood, Tomosada Masuda, Harris, pp. 103–05.

124 One former army private assigned Harris, *Factories of Death*, p. 108. Harris's information here on the structure and events of the Nanking Unit is in turn taken from an English translation of Tsuneishi and Asano's *Bacteriological Unit and the Suicide of Two Physicians*, which is largely based on anecdotes from veterans who were attached to the unit, or people associated with those veterans.

124 The facility could create, at peak output *Materials on the Trial*, pp. 308–09.

124 Gasoline cans functioned as the breeding Ibid.

125 This unit, the Ninth Army Technology Research Institute Harris, *Factories of Death*, p. 109.

126 A former Unit 1644 researcher Gold, *Unit 731 Testimony*, pp. 151–52.

129 more than forty BW team members who worked on the Nomonhan attack Ibid., pp. 75–76.

129 "The Japanese army had just started to attack . . ." Statement of Yoshio Shinozuka, "Unit 731: A Killing Factory," p. 11.

130 confirmed that their group was ordered to dump typhoid germs Gold, *Unit 731 Testimony*, pp. 64–65.

131 The official commendation that went along with the award Harris, *Factories of Death*, p. 76.

132 loaded a heavily guarded train with fifty kilograms of cholera bacteria *Materials on the Trial*, p. 269.

133 "a special group was left behind . . ." Ibid., p. 270.

133 "I saw a documentary film showing the Detachment 731 . . ." Ibid., pp. 287–88.

134 Archie R. Crouch, a missionary from California From Archie R. Crouch's unpublished manuscript "Biological Warfare in China: One Family's Encounter," 1998, pp. 27, 44–48, 50–51.

138 "I am the sole surviving member of a family . . ." Hu Xian Zhong, "A Grief-ridden Charge Against Unit 731 of the Imperial Japanese Army for Germ Warfare in Ningbo" in *Hidden Holocaust in World War II*, pp. 135–38.

141 An entry by Captain Imoto for July 5, 1940, refers Ibid.; Wang Xuan, personal communication, Imoto Diary entries reprinted.

143 In November the Quzhuo plague spread SIPRI, *Problem of Chemical and Biological Warfare, Volume IV*, pp. 342–44.

144 In Zhejiang Province, at least thirteen towns suffered epidemics Yin, *Rape of Biological Warfare*, p. 64.

144 Ishii then urged the health authorities in Changchun Xiao, "Compilation of Camp Unit 731 Fascist Savage Acts."

145 In July 1994 a former Unit 731 hygiene specialist Gold, *Unit 731 Testimony*, pp. 183–84.

CHAPTER SEVEN: EPIDEMIC
148 "The order," said one major general, "made special mention . . ." *Materials on the Trial*, pp. 112–13, 326.

149 commander-in-chief of the Kwantung Army, ordered Unit 100 Ibid., pp. 326–27.

149 biological weapons be deployed against the Russian cities Ibid., pp. 134–35.

149 Pingfan shipped to the Mudanjiang Unit six large boilers Ibid., pp. 336–42.

149 Unit 100 sent an expedition to the Tryokhrecheye area Ibid., pp. 315–16, 320.

150 Unit 100 had produced 200 kilograms of anthrax microbes Ibid., p. 329.

150 The report that came back to Wakamatsu, painstakingly illustrated Ibid., pp. 316–17.

150 Water Purification Units, operating under the cover Williams and Wallace, *Unit 731*, p. 73.

151 "It was practice for army doctors for winning a war," Gold, *Unit 731 Testimony*, pp. 209–11.

153 The general ordered Ishii to assemble a group of 150 to 300 men *Materials on the Trial*, p. 136.

153 Ishii and Masuda carefully planned and organized Harris, *Factories of Death*, p. 111.

153 Its objective "was to exterminate China's armed forces . . ." *Materials on the Trial*, p. 387.

154 But the planes ran low on fuel William Craig, *The Fall of Japan* (New York: Dell, 1967), pp. 225–26; Yin, *Rape of Biological Warfare*, p. 158.

155 Beginning in May 1942, the Japanese Eleventh Army Yin, *Rape of Biological Warfare*, pp. 158–63.

155 Major General Kiyoshi Kawashima recalled *Materials on the Trial*, pp. 261–62.

156 his section of Pingfan, Division 4 of Unit 731, Ibid., pp. 24–25.

156 Japanese planes also dispersed anthrax germs by scattering feathers Williams and Wallace, *Unit 731*, p. 106; Wang Xuan, personal communication.

158 Another target on the strategic Zhe Gan Railway line Yin, *Rape of Biological Warfare*, p. 167.

159 Another Chongshan plaintiff, Wang Lijun, described *Hidden Holocaust in World War II*, pp. 142–44.

162 they returned to burn more than 200 of Chongshan's houses Yin, *Rape of Biological Warfare*, p. 89.

162 At Yiwu a Japanese photographer caught The June 1942 *Asahi* newspaper clipping appears in James Yin's *Hidden Holocaust in World War II*, p. 227.

163 before retreating, according to victim Zu Szu-Gyu Ibid., p. 177.

163 dropped into the well may have been typhoid, paratyphoid, cholera Ibid., p. 168.

163 Unit 731 and Unit 1644 dropped cholera germ bombs in the city of Baoshan Details and quotes from survivors of the Yunnan BW epidemic from Yin, *Rape of Biological Warfare*, pp. 126–57; and interview with James Yin, New York City, September 18, 2001.

172 Unit 100 began frantically evacuating all its personnel Harris, *Factories of Death,* pp. 99–100.

173 test positive for bloodstream antibodies to plague bacillus *Hidden Holocaust in World War II,* p. 151.

175 "Our case," she said, "is just the tip of an iceberg" Ibid., p. 49.

CHAPTER EIGHT: WHAT AMERICA KNEW
183 In February 1939 a group of Japanese medical researchers Williams and Wallace, *Unit 731,* pp. 91–93.

187 In the United States only the *Rocky Mountain Medical Journal* Harris, *Factories of Death,* p. 164.

187 In 1944 a lieutenant captured on the island of Peleliu "A Preliminary Report of Interrogation of P/W Kobayashi, Kenzo. Captured 18 October 1944 Peleliu," Record Group 112, Entry 295A, Box 8, 33, No. 1, National Archives.

188 the Bacteriology Department of Chuzan University at Canton Gold, *Unit 731 Testimony,* p. 102.

188 It advised, "Great results can be obtained by contaminating . . ." Harris, *Factories of Death,* p. 167.

191 Burmese resistance forces had discovered Williams and Wallace, *Unit 731,* pp. 111–12.

193 a small article appeared about this announcement "Balloon Mystery," *Newsweek,* June 4, 1945.

193 Sanders had the scientific background needed Williams and Wallace, *Unit 731,* pp. 121–27.

196 Yoshikuma Ogura, a former intelligence agent who worked Gold, *Unit 731 Testimony,* pp. 236–38.

199 Meeting at military bases in San Francisco and Omaha Ibid., pp. 126–27.

199 The report includes a description of frightening coercion "Japanese Attempts to Secure Virulent Strains of Yellow Fever Virus," G-2 to Office of the Surgeon General, February 3 1941, Record Group 112, National Archives.

202 A 1940 report on the Naito incident by G-2 Williams and Wallace, *Unit 731,* pp. 92–93.

202 Sanders was ordered by General Douglas MacArthur to come to Manila Ibid., p. 130.

CHAPTER NINE: THE SECRET DEAL

202 Among the first sights that Sanders laid his eyes on Williams and Wallace, *Unit 731*, p. 131. The interview with Murray Sanders was originally conducted by Williams and Wallace for their television documentary *Unit 731—Did the Emperor Know?*, which aired August 13, 1985, on the British ITV network.

204 When he "docked in Yokohama, there was Dr. Naito . . ." Gold, *Unit 731 Testimony*, p. 95.

204 whom Sanders recalled as "a very humble and shy person" Ibid., p. 96.

205 Naito's chart included the names of medical institutes This document, written by Naito for Sanders, appears as an appendix to Williams and Wallace, *Unit 731*.

205 MacArthur examined the documents that Naito had given Sanders Gold, *Unit 731 Testimony*, p. 97.

207 "The data came in waves," Sanders recounted Ibid.

207 Two researchers from Camp Detrick Harris, *Factories of Death*, pp. 136, 192.

208 MacArthur cabled the Joint Chiefs of Staff Gold, *Unit 731 Testimony*, p. 104; Message, CINCFE to WDCSA, February 7, 1947, Number c-69947,WC 140, General Douglas MacArthur Memorial Archives and Library, Norfolk, Va.

212 asking him to gather "what evidence is now . . ." Ibid., p. 111.

213 IPS interviewers collected information that Japanese aircraft Williams and Wallace, *Unit 731*, pp. 176–77.

215 Said Dr. Chen, "an American judge . . ." SIPRI, *Problem of Chemical and Biological Warfare, Volume I*, p. 345.

216 did emerge at a hearing of the Tokyo war crimes trial Arnold C. Brackman, *The Other Nuremberg: The Untold Story of the Tokyo War Crimes Trial* (New York: William Morrow, 1987), pp. 196–97.

202 Question: Will you tell us about the expeditions to China? Khabarovsk trial excerpt from examination of Major General Kiyoshi Kawashima, *Materials on the Trial*, p. 260.

222 piece by John Powell detailing Unit 731 experiments and germ warfare John W. Powell, Jr., "Japan's Biological Weapons: 1930–1945, a Hidden Chapter in History," *Bulletin of the Atomic Scientists*, October 1981, pp. 41–45.

223 In a later interview, he added that the United States Ibid., p. 43.

223 "Information retained from Ishii and associates," they messaged Harris, *Factories of Death*, p. 218.

224 Colonel R. M. Cheseldine, in a secret meeting R. M. Cheseldine, Memorandum for the Secretary, September 26, 1947, Record Group 165, SWNCC 351, National Archives.

224 As Camp Detrick's Dr. Edwin Hill Excerpt from message appears in Harris, *Factories of Death*, p. 190.

CHAPTER TEN: WHAT THE DEAL BOUGHT
226 Shiro Ishii, the man who started it all, retired "Daughter's Eye View of Lt-Gen Ishii, Chief of Devil's Brigade," *Japan Times*, August 29, 1982, p. 12; Fuyuko Nishisato, personal communication.

226 Murray Sanders said that he had heard from McDermott, *Killing Winds*, pp. 137–38.

227 the Pentagon did, in the late 1940s, hire two Nazi doctors Linda Hunt, *Secret Agenda: The United States Government, Nazi Scientists, and Project Paperclip, 1945 to 1990* (New York: St. Martin's Press, 1991), pp. 151–55, 179–81.

227 In 1982 Ishii's eldest daughter, Harumi "Daughter's Eye View of Lt-Gen Ishii, Chief of Devil's Brigade," *Japan Times*, August 29, 1982, p. 12.

227 They showed footage and photographs of metallic U.S. shells Clips of this footage appear in *Unit 731 Is Alive*, KBS television documentary, 1997; and *Biology at War*, television documentary of the British Broadcasting Corporation, 1986.

228 Needham agreed that the sudden appearances Quotations from Dr. Joseph Needham and the International Scientific Commission on U.S. military biological warfare are from the *Report of the International Scientific Commission for the Investigation of Facts Concerning Bacterial Warfare in Korea and China* (Peking: 1952).

231 In 1956 journalist John W. Powell, who helped bring McDermott, *Killing Winds*, pp. 159–62.

233 Dr. Tachiomaru Ishikawa, once a pathologist Information on postwar activities of the BW doctors is taken from Williams and Wallace, *Unit 731*, pp. 236–39; and *Unit 731 Is Alive*, KBS television documentary, 1997.

234 The *Midori Juchi* ("Green Cross"), a Japanese pharmaceutical company Corporate brochure of Yoshitomi Pharmaceutical Industries, Ltd. (merged with the Green Cross), 1998 (English); *Unit 731 Is Alive*, KBS television documentary, 1997; "Green Cross Founder Hid Info about Unit 731: Letter," *Kyodo News International*, August 17, 1998; Iwata Itsuki, "Ex-exec: Green Cross Ignored HIV Warnings," *Daily Yomiuri*, March 4, 1996.

INDEX